D1154240

COUNTERPOINT AND SYMBOL

AN INQUIRY INTO THE RHYTHM OF MILTON'S EPIC STYLE

BY

JAMES WHALER

HASKELL HOUSE PUBLISHERS LTD.
Publishers of Scarce Scholarly Books
NEW YORK, N. Y. 10012
1971

First Published 1952

HASKELL HOUSE PUBLISHERS LTD.
Publishers of Scarce Scholarly Books
280 LAFAYETTE STREET
NEW YORK, N. Y. 10012

Library of Congress Catalog Card Number: 76-117997

Standard Book Number 8383-1052-4

Printed in the United States of America

To

Charles and Isabel Osgood

PREFACE

No one can read long in Milton without wishing to understand the rhythmic organization of his epic paragraph. Yet this is a matter concerning which the prosodists have had little or nothing to say. Their main concern in *Paradise Lost* has been the individual line. When they touch the problem of the paragraph their general comments are impressionistic and unverifiable. The following chapters are a concentrated attack on this stronghold of Milton's high poetic art. Or rather a reconnaissance, in the course of which I have had to leave beaten highways for trails where no troops of auxiliary books are at hand to pitch a tent or light a campfire. Hence I need hardly apologize for omitting the ritual of a bibliography.

From time to time, however, help has come from various people and various books in ways I am happy to acknowledge at the proper places. But to one person, my friend Charles Grosvenor Osgood of Princeton University, I stand under obligation so special and so continuous that if I could find words for my gratitude I fear it might be inferred I am making him responsible for any or all of my shortcomings. He volunteered to read my early drafts. In season and out of season he took time to weigh my proposals, challenging this passage for over-compression, that for over-documentation, keeping me alert for larger issues behind and beyond immediate rhythmic phenomena.

I would anticipate, and perhaps mollify, the reader's impatience with certain things ahead. Far in advance I would ask him to follow with special care the derivation, given on pp. 97 ff., of formulas for numerical series, especially those I have called "power progressions." And I would assure him that I, too, am loath to think of any artist, unless he is an architect, cultivating mathematics so that he may apply certain formulas to get certain covert effects in a privately conceived aesthetic program. When we find a poet calculating numerical progressions and stringing them through the lines of his masterpiece, we are forced to redefine "inspiration." We realize how far away we are from those grandiose ideals of the Baroque which were once the very pulse of European culture. Then in every field of art — yes, and in ethics and metaphysics even — men were dazzled by the undying brilliance of Euclid's constellation of theorems. Men had faith that if the eternal laws of arithmetic and geometry could somehow be incorporated in a work of art, no matter what its medium, that work could be stabilized, its form made inimitable, its utterance immortal.

Was Milton deaf to such notes of the Baroque of his age? We know he pondered Euclid and Ramus with the same retentive zeal as he did the rhythmic devices of polyphonic music. When he drew up plans for *Paradise Lost* — long before his blindness — all his talents became tempered strings of that harmonious instrument we call his epic style. In the present book I submit evidence that he often touches this instrument with certain formal chords of timelessness, new if not unique in the medium of verse, chords that include configurations of symmetry rooted in the same principles as those by which Euclid has withstood centuries of change in taste and fashion. Yet, as I shall try to show, this is not his primary motive for exploiting mathematics. Nor is his primary motive a desire to parallel the supernatural features of his theme with rhythmic devices that imply mathematical formulas of permanence and infinitude. No, his ambition is to make mathematics the servant of an overall contrapuntal ideal.

But such service would be only half-hearted and mechanistic if there were not some agent to mediate between blank-verse analogues of polyphonic music and numerical progressions. This agent is symbol, numerical symbol. I offer a host of examples, taken from many parts of Milton's epic verse, to show that the root-numbers of his progressions carry traditional symbolic meanings that are consistently, often dramatically, responsive to thought, image, or situation in the immediate context.

The computing of progressions as well as of their adjustments to paragraph-length involves a good deal of blunt, tedious arithmetic. Most of this, regardless of printing-cost, should no doubt be spread before the reader. But I shrink from burdening any more of my pages with heavy lists of figures. Regrettably, many of my computed formulas must be taken on trust. I must be content to give a few stellar illustrations that demonstrate the method presumed to be Milton's. Anyone, by employing the same method, can of course check the accuracy of all the formulas.

To save space I usually abbreviate *Paradise Lost* to PL, and *Paradise Regained* to PR.

CONTENTS

CHAPTER I

THE CONTRAPUNTAL CLUE

1. *Choice of Text*

When printer Simmons complained that buyers of PL were "stumbled" "why the poem rimes not," he secured from the poet that evasive statement about "The Verse." It exaggerates the case against rhyme. What it declares about "true musical delight" contains ambiguities so tantalizing that many a reader with classical background has actually thought that Milton must have founded his verse on principles of quantitative Latin prosody. The only part clear and unchallengeable is an assertion of the obvious: that in this poem the sense is "variously drawn out from one verse into another."

Still it does tell us nearly as much as we are ever told about the mysteries of Milton's craft. But could his answer, restricted to a note, have been any better? The only fair and frank alternative would have to be a detailed treatise disclosing things he would have his reader feel rather than rationalize.

When I found I could understand little in this note except that Milton draws out the sense from one verse into another, I decided it was hopeless to understand his epic style unless I first concentrated on the "drawing-out" process itself. No investigator had ever cared to do this. I felt that I might thus be led into unexplored regions of the Miltonic paragraph. What the prosodist calls enjambement occurs with very great frequency in both PL and PR. In Edd. 1 and 2 of PL it averages close to 60 per cent, and in some paragraphs exceeds 80 per cent. In any edited text it averages at least 50 per cent. PR is less enjambed, yet the rate is higher than that of the great bulk of blank verse written before or since. When one realizes that in Shakespeare's last plays, those in which he is most fluent and experimentally relaxed, the enjambement rarely exceeds 45 per cent, one can agree that no pains must be spared to uncover significant facts about this primary surface feature. In the first place, I wanted to know: What is the relative frequency of the rhythmic lengths that run from line to line?

I had been reading Milton in Wright's edition. I confess a weakness for Wright. In his text I first read Milton. I still think that for young beginners it is preferable to any exact reprint of Ed. 1 or 2. Wright punctuates logically. He clears the original orthography of a quaint though, to the schoolboy, repellent crust of out-of-dateness. He makes Milton look contemporary, look palatable to the general reader who wonders what an epic artist of the 17th century has to offer to the 20th.

But read almost any consecutive hundred lines in Wright and then the same lines in a reprint, and you are likely to feel mysterious forces at work, rhythmic forces that seem to deflect the punctuation away from expectations of logic. The case can't be settled by appealing to older usage or absence of usage. The punctuation of Milton's prose as set down in the earliest editions gives me no such sense of irregularity and caprice. But in many a paragraph of Ed. 1 or 2 of PL we come upon knots of commas, some of which could well be omitted to enhance the flow of verse. Yet occasionally elsewhere, even in the same paragraph, may occur a curious avoidance of punctuation. In such places the poet seems oblivious of logical pause, in the grip of an indefinable rhythmic program.

Nor can this feature be dismissed as the intrusive touch of amanuensis or printer. The closer one gets to the movement of Milton's verse, the deeper grows a conviction that one is in the presence of the most painstakingly supervised writing ever set up in type, and that the supervisor — ubiquitous, insistent — is the poet himself. Again and again he must have had every page of the edition of 1667 read back to him. And by men worthy of his trust, men who deeply respected him, and did all they humanly could to fulfil a blind man's most finicky directions, whether logical or illogical.

When I faced the question of a choice of text I did not have this conviction. To play safe, I decided to employ both Wright and the Columbia reprint. Thus I obtained two sets of data, one based on a conservatively logical and one on an intermittently illogical pointing.

2. *Integral Line vs. Enjambement*

A moment's thought tells us that enjambement in any blank verse is related in an important way to the maintenance of the five-beat metric line — the norm. The higher the rate of enjambement, the fewer the lines which the ear recognizes as integral pentameters. It follows that when a poet, deliberately and on principle, and with unprecedented frequency, variously draws out the sense from one verse into another, he is liable to obscure in the listener's mind — even obliterate — that norm.

Some critics have fancied that Milton really doesn't care to keep his norm alive in the listener's consciousness. This view is untenable. Almost the first fact emerging from my investigation was that very rarely do so many consecutive run-on lines occur as to obscure the five-beat metric frame. Even in paragraphs in which 80 per cent of the lines are enjambed we are being reminded both directly and indirectly, and regularly reminded, that Milton's declared freedom never becomes licence.

He employs two general ways to preserve the norm: one direct, the other indirect. In this section I shall describe the direct way. In the next chapter I shall give in detail certain indirect ways.

The most direct way is simply to cease overlapping the lines, thus demarcating the norm by punctuated terminal pause. The proportion of such demarcated lines in Milton's epic is far less than in Shakespeare or Keats or Tennyson.

But he has another direct way, though subtler. In the midst of enjambement he may invert the first foot of a line, or may begin as well as end it with strong monosyllabic words. His epic verse abounds in lines with strong initial and terminal syllables.

I must keep reminding the reader that in my investigation I was little concerned with the individual line as such. I wanted to know the role and function it has in the whole paragraph's rhythmic mold. Only with this relationship in mind did I separate out these lines that are direct safeguards of the metric norm, designating them "integral lines."

Now when an unpunctuated integral line occurs it is necessarily part of a longer and continuous rhythmic whole, which, even in Wright's edited text, ranges from 6 to 17 beats; though continuously run-on, unpunctuated rhythmic units of more than 10 beats are not common. The very first paragraph of PL easily illustrates

Milton's characteristically high rate of enjambement as well as his unobtrusive safeguarding of the norm by recurrent integral lines. Never for more than three or four lines can the listening ear forget the blank-verse medium. Direct safeguards are the following integral lines: 3, 8, 9, 12, 13, 16, 17, 18, 21, 24, 25, 26. Of these only the last is demarcated in the most direct way with punctuation.

Less than a third of the lines of PL and less than half the lines of PR are integral. Such infrequency is in itself remarkable: one must look far to match it with any other sustained blank verse. And in PL Milton keeps such lines to an absolute minimum by what at first looks like an inexplicable omission, certainly an omission not to be found in other blank verse. Except for a noticeable sprinkling of feminine endings in Book X, he all but excludes them. Why? Wouldn't feminine endings serve well to demarcate and safeguard the metric line in the midst of steady enjambement?

The reason for such abstinence is this: a feminine ending creates a syllabic hedge against fluent overlapping. It is a streaming banneret that would demarcate the norm when Milton has other and less obtrusive means of demarcation, less perceptible because not extrametric. But why so chary of perceptible demarcation? Because, underlying all his suspensive rhetoric, is his impulse, his well-thought-out determination to move irregular rhythms above and below the ideal metric base, even as choir-voices slide freely above and below a cantus firmus. The closer we examine the rhythmic ordonnance of the Miltonic paragraph, the more certain we are that Milton's method is consciously analogous to that of contrapuntal music. Except for Book X, we can find almost anywhere in PL a run of over a hundred lines without a single noticeable feminine ending, or any feminine ending at all. Those that do occur are likely to end a punctuated line, as at II,147: "Though full of pain, this intellectual being,".

Yet feminine endings of a very real sort do actually pervade the poem, and are perceptible. Milton reserves them for midline endings of overlaps. Such an interior ending of course causes the ensuing rhythmic unit to start with a trochee. Some of the most powerful, some of the most delicate, effects are the result. Since my investigation has had to take account of all these interior trochaic beginnings and interior feminine endings, and since I may have to refer in later pages to certain descriptions involving them, I would have the reader adopt with me an easy method of representing them. Hereafter I shall indicate a feminine ending by a superscript comma: [’], and a trochaic beginning by a superscript stroke: [′]. Thus, if we let a connecting dash represent enjambement, the overlap

till one greater man
Restore us,

is represented as 3′—1’. Here three beats ending one line are joined to one beat of the line following. The aggregate overlap is a trochaic tetrameter with feminine ending: 4′’. Again,

rolling in the fiery gulf
Confounded though immortal:

is 4′—3’.

To return to the integral line,

Though full of pain, this intellectual being,

This line is slow, so slow that it is broken by a pointed interior pause. Scores of other integral lines are almost equally slow even when there is no interior punctuation.

But some integral lines are fast, and they must be differentiated. An integral line is fast when it contains an interior light-stressed foot and has no strong interior pause. At PL I, 324,

Cherub and Seraph rolling in the flood,

the pace is increased all the more by a first-foot inversion. At PL III, 565,

Innumerable as the stars of night,

two successive feet, the second and third, are light-stressed.

Call such integral lines “quick-paced.” In Milton’s paragraph movement they not only serve as safeguards of the norm but furnish an indispensable lyric touch. Though well distributed in PL, they cannot be said to be frequent: on the average not one line in ten is quick-paced. Yet it is a surface feature that helps to distinguish the blank-verse style of PL from the style of *Comus* or PR or Shakespeare or almost any blank-verse poem since Milton. Tennyson, for instance, is rife with quick-paced pentameters: it is one of the reasons why his blank-verse movement is felt to be so predominantly lyrical. Some imitators of Milton, especially in the 18th century, seem to have been wholly unaware of his relatively frugal use of quick-paced lines.

Milton is master, however, of these lyric brevities — when he wants to be. He knows their history. Marlowe riots in them: for the most part they constitute the "mighty line." The Elizabethan discovery and development of their patterns transformed blank verse from metronome to virtuosity. Shakespeare's controlled mastery was one of Milton's richest inheritances. No wonder some of Milton's quick-paced lines are among the miniature glories of his art.

Appendix I lists all the quick-paced lines of PL and PR according to their rhythmic patterns. By a system of numerals and letters one can immediately write down the rhythmic pattern of some memorable quick-paced line in Shakespeare, say, or Browning, and Appendix I will show whether it is duplicated or approximated in Milton's epic verse. I have there recorded also the relative frequency of Milton's patterns. A striking fact emerges: scarcely three times in PL do two quick-paced lines of identical pattern occur in succession.

Unlike Marlowe or Shakespeare, Milton could not expect to invent many new rhythmic line-patterns. But what every good poet does he does: he makes his pattern seem to ring true to thought, image, or situation in his fable. The result may haunt the memory forever after. For example, at PL IV, 187 the prowling wolf

Leaps o'er the fence with ease into the fold.

The initial spondee is the crouch before the spring. The constricted front vowel in "leaps" is the muscular tension at the moment of leaping. The open back-vowel in "o'er" eases that tension as the brute body attains mid-flight in its vault. The undulatory vowel-sequence, "fence" — "ease," "-to" — "fold," reinforced by nodal pauses before and after "with ease," echoes the agile arc traced by the intruder. The uncertain inversion of the light-stressed foot, "into," lands the wolf quivering with success at reaching his goal.

Again, at the end of PL II Satan has traversed Chaos and arrives at the universe of Nature, where

> at last the sacred influence
> Of light appears, and from the walls of Heaven
> *Shoots far into the bosom of dim Night*
> A glimmering dawn; (1034—37)

Here the initial spondee of the italicized line holds the pent-up power which propels that light over two interior weak-stressed feet until its progress meets with the buffer of a terminal spondee before pressing through enjambement to "a glimmering dawn." This verse so captivated Matthew Arnold that he tried to transcribe the rhythmic pattern in what is perhaps the best-shaped line of *Balder Dead* (line 289).

No particular edition is required to discern integral lines. Not so with overlaps. This truth came home to me at this point in my investigation. I renounced as basic text all editions but those printed during Milton's lifetime. Only Beeching's reprint or the Columbia reprint or, best of all, whenever accessible, Fletcher's Facsimile Edition, suited my desire — to be as near as possible to the punctuation proof-read in Simmons's London printshop.[1]

3. *Preliminary Observations on Free Overlapping*

Free overlapping enables the poet at any time to extend the iambic line to an indeterminate length. The process not only accommodates but invites every variety of rhythmic unit that has a dissyllabic base, whether iambic or trochaic, whether of masculine or feminine ending. Observe how in the very first paragraph of PL Milton plays with rival overlap-lengths as a dexterous musician with the competing rhythms of a fugue. But note how in the last three lines — all integral — he establishes his norm by reiterating it, promising to meet future risks of obliteration by similar strategic display of integral line. The rhythmic situation is a parallel to the final harmony in which all voices come together at the end of motet or madrigal.

I must not clog these pages with statistic detail. But the following brief sequence of numbers helps to show the overall balance that obtains in the relati e frequencies of overlaps of various lengths. In PL an overlap of 2 beats occurs 134 times; of 3 beats, in various iambic and trochaic forms, 517 times; of 4 beats, 1005 times; etc., forming the sequence:

2	3	4	5	6	7	8	9
134	517	1005	1036	940	755	478	217
	[113]	[281]	[370]	[275]	[210]	[91]	[70]

Numbers in brackets show the trochaic units included.

Here we see an approximation to symmetrical balance between the frequencies for overlaps shorter than 5 beats and those longer than 5 beats, the most frequent of all being overlap-5 itself. This is significant. Overlap-5 owes its relative frequency to the fact that in the midst of brisk enjambement it may be an *indirect* reminder of the metric norm. In an indirect way it helps to keep the 5-beat measure alive. Overlapping may thus, by itself, serve, paradoxically, to counteract the very risk it produces. How Milton carries the paradox still further will occupy the next chapter.

But suppose there should occur a number of successive overlap-5's: the metric frame itself might be in danger of a dislocation, i. e., of a shift by one or two beats to right or left. To make this clear have someone read aloud Gabriel's reproof (PL IV, 917-925) in the form that follows:

> But wherefore thou alone?
> Wherefore with thee came not all Hell broke loose?
> Is pain to them less pain, less to be fled?
> Or thou than they less hardy to endure?
> Courageous Chief, the first in flight from pain,
> Had'st thou alleg'd to thy deserted host
> This cause of flight, thou surely had'st not come
> Sole fugitive.

Turn now to the printed page:

> But wherefore thou alone? wherefore with thee
> Came not all Hell broke loose? is pain to them
> Less pain, less to be fled, or thou than they
> Less hardy to endure? courageous Chief,

The first in flight from pain, had'st thou alleg'd
To thy deserted host this cause of flight,
Thou surely had'st not come sole fugitive.

The listening ear cannot prefer one of these two arrangements to the other, for an intelligent reading of either passage occupies, by a stop-watch, the same time-interval. But such a passage is exceptional and very rare. Its rarity is evidence of Milton's steady determination to keep his metric frame securely in place no matter how active is the play of cross-rhythmic currents. But the feature I would emphasize is that when the rival cross-rhythm tallies with the norm in length, the listening ear is not spirited away from the norm as is the case when the cross-currents are repetitions or medleys of non-5 rhythmic lengths.

4. *Of Certain Non-pentameter Overlaps*

Certain non-pentameter overlaps can on occasion produce notable effects. In this section I shall restrict myself to the 8-beat overlap when it is trochaic, as at PL II, 73:

if the sleepy drench
Of that forgetful lake benumb not still, .

This is the Locksley Hall measure. But to Milton's ear it is, or can be, when occurring in a suitable context, the English adaptation of either of two measures of by-gone prosody: (i) the "trochaic tetrameter catalectic" of Greek tragedy, associated with taut dramatic moments, and (ii) a hymnal measure of medieval Latin, developed at a time when classical quantitative verse was being displaced by accentual. Milton could have read about it in Bede, though he probably knew hymns composed in it.

Now a rhythmic length of 8 beats is likely to break into subordinate rhythms which may or may not be set off with punctuation. In Longfellow's "Psalm of Life," a familiar example of this measure, the subordinate rhythms occupy separate lines, and the break comes midway after a feminine ending. But with Milton, as shall appear in later chapters, punctuation in certain paragraphs seems to be subject at any point to the influence of a factor entirely separate in its working from syntactic construction or rhetorical trend. We are justified in admitting as overlap-8's both continuously unpointed rhythmic lengths and pointed, provided they are each integrated by thought or syntax into an 8-beat whole.

Of each sort, pointed and unpointed, there are over a dozen instances in Milton's epic verse. Several may unmistakably be referred to association with ancient Greek tragedy, several with medieval Latin. Let us examine two cases.

(i) At PL IX, 1051 ff. Milton describes Adam and Eve's reaction to their plunge into sensuality. They wake to guilty shame, suddenly shorn of strength and virtue. The description of their plight ends thus:

silent, and in face
Confounded long they sat, as strucken mute, (1063-64)

(Almost every editor has in some way changed this punctuation.)

A tenser dramatic moment does not occur in PL. It is precisely the kind of moment that induces Aeschylus to change his metric base to "trochaic tetrameter catalectic." From among several instances in Aeschylus and Euripides, I would specially refer to the close of *Agamemnon* where the only exchange of conversation between the guilty lovers, Clytemnestra and Aegisthus, causes this measure promptly, trenchantly, and briefly to be sounded.

But could not chance account for Milton's octameter measure? Might he not have been entirely unaware of its desolate burden of tragic overtones? The answer is no. For earlier in Book IX the measure is anticipated with Sophoclean irony. At 299-300 Adam tries to still his misgivings about Eve's power of resistance. He reassures himself by uttering a wishful thought whose metric expression is prophetic of the very thing he would avert:

Thou thyself with scorn
And anger would'st resent the offer'd wrong.

(ii) As for medieval hymnal association in Milton's use of this measure, there is of course a touch of it at the very beginning of PL:

till one greater man
Restore us, and regain the blissful seat, .

But its full hymnal intention sounds at the end of PR, where it terminates the angelic anthem of Christ's victory:

on thy glorious work
Now enter, and begin to save mankind.

(Cf. lines of a hymn by Fortunatus, quoted by C. S. Baldwin: *Medieval Rhetoric and Poetic*, pp. 119-120:

Pange, lingua, gloriosi proelium certaminis,
Et super crucis tropaeo dic triumphum nobilem,
Qualiter redemptor orbis immolatus vicerit.)

5. *Last-foot Inversion of Overlaps*

Could any overlap be more alien to the metric norm than these trochaic octameters? Yes. Milton invents a species of overlap new to blank verse and wholly novel in its effect

(A) And now his heart
Distends with pride, and hard'ning in his strength
Glories: (PL I, 571-573)

(B) Now conscience wakes despair
That slumber'd, wakes the bitter memory
Of what he was, what is, and what must be
Worse; (PL IV, 23-26)

To understand what happens let us keep in mind that Milton never inverts the last foot of his metric line. Every other foot he may invert (on the average every fifth line of PL has an inverted first foot, and every fifteenth line, on the average, has one of the interior feet inverted), but he never permits, as Shakespeare occasionally does, substitution of trochee for fifth-foot iamb.

Yet he has devised a way to invert the last foot of any overlapping rhythmic unit, no matter of what length. He lets it terminate with the metric line's first foot, and this first foot he inverts. In other words, he makes the final foot of the overlap coincide with the metric line's one position where, since Tasso, inversion has most often been tolerated. In Milton's enjambed verse such tolerance becomes hospitality, because first-foot inversion can be a valuable means of demarcating the norm. But considerations other than prosodic accompany last-foot inversion of an overlap. It usually brings into sharp focus some important concept, attribute, image, or proper name, with emphatic emotional repercussions.

Observe the difference between examples (A) and (B). In (A) the overlap is 3—1, whose second segment, inverted, may be represented as 1i; the overlap is described as 3—1i.

In (B) only the accented syllable of the second segment of 2—1 is present before pause. This syllable must be regarded as a trochee whose unaccented part is stripped away and tossed to the succeeding rhythmic unit. The result for the succeeding unit is an unstressed syllabic increment known to classical verse as anacrusis. Represent the overlap thus: 2—½i.

With Milton both —1i and —½i are original as well as characteristic.[2] But with many a later poet who has tried to write blank verse in the "grand style" such overlapping becomes a mannerism, a well-rehearsed professional trick. Wordsworth is rather exceptional in his restraint, but Tennyson, as regularly as a chime-clock, sounds either —1i or —½i. In the *Idylls of the King* we may expect it at least once every 100 lines, a frequency higher than in PL, where the distribution is just irregular enough to give every occurrence the freshness of surprise.

Other Victorians have similarly flattered Milton by adopting his invention. Arnold's use may be judged excessive. Even more so Swinburne's. The frequency of —1i and —½i in both *Atalanta* and *Erectheus* is pathological. But the Brownings refuse. For instance, in the 11,000 lines of *Aurora Leigh* neither device occurs three times.

6. *Analogy of Overlaps to Rhythmic Method of Contrapuntal Music*

For anyone in the least acquainted with polyphonic music Milton's method of free overlapping compels comparison with the rhythmic management of voices in madrigal, motet, and anthem. Authoritative pronouncements on such music confirm and stimulate analogies. Very soon in my investigation I was examining collections like Torchi's of early Italian music,[3] or like Fellowes' of Elizabethan madrigals, or the scores set down in Ernest Brennecke's analysis of Milton's father's music.

"The glory of the madrigalists," says R. O. Morris (*Contrapuntal Technique of the Sixteenth Century,* Oxford, 1922, pp. 3 ff.), "is their mastery of rhythmic device.... The rhythmic accentuation of each part is free, but, independently of the actual rhythmic accents, there is an imaginary accentuation which imposes a regular alternation of strong and weak beats to which the harmony of the composition has to conform, although the melody of each voice pursues its own way untrammeled. . . . . This is the first fact to force itself on his [the student's] notice; he finds out that in order to write in the idiom of Morley he has to slough all his old preconceptions and ask himself, perhaps for the first time, what rhythm really is.... The rhythmical accentuation of each individual part is free, that is to say, the accents do not occur at strictly regular intervals, whereas the composition as a whole does conform to a fixed metrical scheme in which strong and weak accents succeed one another in a premeditated order. In the rhythm of poetry there is precisely similar duality [Lines 1-4 of PL quoted]. Here the stress of the words must be preserved, yet the metrical scheme also persists in the back of your head as a kind of pattern or standard to which every line of the poetry is referred, more or less unconsciously, for comparison. And the delight of reading good verse arises largely from this duality of apprehension. . . . [In the superposing of irregular rhythms upon regular metric] an *irregularity which never degenerates into confusion* is the rhythmic ideal to which the composer aspires. . . . But the composers were not content with the effect obtainable by contrasting the real rhythmical accent with the imaginary metrical accent. Above all *they loved to make the rhythmical accents of each part cross and clash with those of every other part.* This constant rhythmical conflict is the most vital and suggestive feature in the whole of the 16th-century technique. . . . This volume has missed its aim entirely if it has failed to make clear that counterpoint *is* rhythm, and very little else." (Italics mine)

E. H. Fellowes, discussing the madrigal as a system of "complex and overlapping rhythms," says (*The English Madrigal,* Oxford, 1925, p. 57): "Rhythm is without doubt the feature which above all characterizes and vitalizes Tudor music, and ability to recognize it and to interpret it in all its subtle and varied and sometimes elaborate forms is a quality which a madrigal singer must of necessity be able to command."

Almost the first fruit of my study was this analogy between the rhythmic method of the music Milton most loved and practiced and the rhythmic method of his epic verse as evidenced in the unprecedentedly free enjambement. Yet I never dreamt of what lay beneath the surface of many an epic paragraph. At this stage of the investigation it is enough if we keep in mind that Milton gives all his overlap rhythmic lengths — ranging, when unfractionable, from 2 beats to 17 — a proportionate opportunity to perform. We have seen by what direct means, in the midst of all this overlapping, he safeguards his norm from obliteration. And, in the case of overlap-5's, he can refer us indirectly to the basic metric number.

Let us proceed to other indirect ways of letting us hear that number, ways which Milton was the first to exploit as a systematic enlargement of blank-verse prosody.

CHAPTER II

CROSS-RHYTHMIC CONSTRUCTION

1. *T-Construction*

For much of PL and most of PR, and for almost all non-Miltonic blank verse these more direct safeguards suffice to preserve the metric base. But in many paragraphs of PL where enjambement is very active, involving at least half the lines, Milton would keep the 5-beat norm alive in the listener's consciousness by devices more indirect and subtle. Consider the lines,

> At once as far as angels ken he views
> The dismal situation waste and wild, (PL I, 59-60).

This is a rhythmic continuum of two metric lines: 5—5. At the same time it is an aggregate of subordinate though unpunctuated currents: 1—3—6, which would be heard no matter how we re-arrange the lines. In the following rearrangement,

> At once as far as angels ken
> He views the dismal situation waste
> And wild,

the 10-beat continuum becomes a double overlap: 4—5—1; yet the subordinate currents are heard quite as clearly as before.

If the listening ear can distinguish certain rhythmic aggregates as multiples of 5 beats when these aggregates tally line for line on the metric frame, it can recognize the same aggregates when they are in double or even triple overlap arrangement in cross-rhythm with the metric frame.

Consider the lines,

That to the highth of this great argument
I may assert eternal Providence,
And justify the ways of God to men.

Now shift this 15-beat aggregate into cross-rhythm:

that to the highth
Of this great argument I many assert
Eternal Providence, and justify
The ways of God to men.

The rearrangement becomes 2—5—3 + 2—3.

Again, consider the lines at PL III, 448-449,

Both all things vain, and all who in vain things
Build their fond hopes of glory or lasting fame,

lines which become when rearranged in cross-rhythm:

both all things vain,
And all who in vain things build their fond hopes
Of glory or lasting fame,

where the comma-pause after "vain" demarcates a simultaneous current of 2 beats without destroying its rhythmic participation in the overall 10-beat aggregate. Let us indicate such a case of near-enjambement by substituting a plus-sign for the dash. Thus the rearranged aggregate is: 2 + 5—3.

Designate as T any multiple of 5 in continuous cross-rhythm. Superficially the segmentation of a continuous overlap is as follows: a metric line seems to interpose between — seems to *cut* as by "tmesis" — two flanking segments that add up to 5 beats. Thus we have four possible patterns: 1—5—4, 2—5—3, 3—5—2, and 4—5—1; abbreviated: T 1, T 2, T 3, and T 4.

If we designate the general sequence a—5—b, in which a + b = 5, we perceive three variants of each of the four patterns: a'—5—b, a—5—b' and a'—5—b'.

The following are examples of simple T-construction:

T 1 and chase
Anguish and doubt and fear and sorrow and pain
From mortal or immortal minds. (PL I, 557-559)

T 2 Soon had his crew
Open'd into the hill a spacious wound
And digg'd out ribs of gold. (PL I, 688-690)

T 3 As when the potent rod
Of Amram's son in Egypt's evil day
Wav'd round the coast, (PL I, 338-340)

T 4 the careful ploughman doubting stands
Lest on the threshing-floor his hopeful sheaves
Prove chaff. (PL IV, 983-985)

T 2 and T 3 occur much oftener than T 1 and T 4.

T is often in expanded form, so that the rhythmic aggregate is a higher multiple of 5. The general formula for such expansion is a—(n × 5)—b, where a + b = 5, and n exceeds 1. Suppose a = 3 and n = 2. Designate the resultant pattern T II 3, the value of n being shown by the roman numeral. Such an expanded T occurs early in PL: at I, 41-44:

and with ambitious aim
Against the throne and monarchy of God
Rais'd impious war in heaven and battle proud
With vain attempt.

If the sum of the beats in two line-segments a and b is 5, then the group a—(n × 5)—b may be in cross-rhythm with the metric frame in such a way that enjambement (or near-enjambement consonant with rhetorical trend) produces a continuous rhythmic aggregate which may be felt as a multiple of 5, thus serving indirectly to safeguard the norm from obliteration.

2. *E-construction*

A non-pentameter overlap, say of 4 beats, may be succeeded by an overlap of 6 beats which effect with it an aggregate of 10 in cross-rhythm to the metric frame. Consonant with rhetorical trend, it may be felt as an encompassing rhythm which, in spite of subordinate currents, is of special value as a multiple of 5. For, like the rhythmic continuum of a T-construction, such a multiple can serve as a reminder, and hence a safeguard, of the norm. Call the construction E. For example, at PL IX, 766-768,

> For us alone
> Was death invented? or to us denied
> This intellectual food?

the first overlap is 2—2', the second is 3'—3. Schematized, the construction is:

$$\left\langle \begin{matrix} 2—2' \\ 3'—3 \end{matrix} \right\rangle = 2\times5$$

or, briefly defined, E 2-2'.

At PL II, 47-49,

> And rather than be less
> Car'd not to be at all; with that care lost
> Went all his fear,

the first overlap is 3—3, the second is 2—2; schematized:

$$\left\langle \begin{matrix} 3—3 \\ 2—2 \end{matrix} \right\rangle = 2\times5$$

or, briefly, E 3-3.

E's prosodic — or extraprosodic — function is to combine alien (non-pentameter) overlap-units into multiples of the norm: make units like 3, 4, 6, and 7 serve indirectly to safeguard the norm from obscuration. In simplest form E can have twelve combinations:

$$\left\langle \begin{matrix} 1—1 \\ 4—4 \end{matrix} \right\rangle, \left\langle \begin{matrix} 1—2 \\ 3—4 \end{matrix} \right\rangle, \left\langle \begin{matrix} 1—3 \\ 2—4 \end{matrix} \right\rangle, \left\langle \begin{matrix} 2—1 \\ 4—3 \end{matrix} \right\rangle, \left\langle \begin{matrix} 2—2 \\ 3—3 \end{matrix} \right\rangle, \left\langle \begin{matrix} 2—4 \\ 1—3 \end{matrix} \right\rangle,$$

$$\left\langle \begin{matrix} 3—1 \\ 4—2 \end{matrix} \right\rangle, \left\langle \begin{matrix} 3—3 \\ 2—2 \end{matrix} \right\rangle, \left\langle \begin{matrix} 3—4 \\ 1—2 \end{matrix} \right\rangle, \left\langle \begin{matrix} 4—2 \\ 3—1 \end{matrix} \right\rangle, \left\langle \begin{matrix} 4—3 \\ 2—1 \end{matrix} \right\rangle, \left\langle \begin{matrix} 4—4 \\ 1—1 \end{matrix} \right\rangle.$$

Each of these patterns has seven variants according to the presence of trochaic beginnings or feminine endings. Thus $\left\langle \begin{matrix} 2—2 \\ 3—3 \end{matrix} \right\rangle$ may be found also in the variants,

<2′ - 2 / 3—3>, <2—2 / 3—3’>, <2′ - 2 / 3—3’>, <2—2’ / 3′ - 3>, <2′ - 2’ / 3′ - 3>, <2—2’ / 3′ - 3’>,

<2′ - 2’ / 3′ - 3’>.

Several more examples of simple E-construction:

Who seeks
To lessen thee, against his purpose serves
To manifest the more thy might: (PL VI, 613-615)

<1—2 / 3—4>

I see thy fall
Determin’d, and thy hapless crew involv’d
In this perfidious fraud, (PL V, 878-880)

<2—1’ / 4′—3>

him to unthrone we then
May hope, when everlasting Fate shall yield
To fickle Chance, (PL II, 231-233)

<3—1 / 4—2>

where woods and rocks had ears
To rapture, till the savage clamor drown’d
Both harp and voice; (PL VII, 35-37)

<3—1’ / 4′—2>

Thus far these beyond
Compare of mortal prowess, yet observ’d
Their dread commander: (PL I, 587-589)

<3′—3’ / 2′—2’>

wherefore should not strength and might
There fail where virtue fails, or weakest prove
Where boldest; (PL VI, 116-118)

<4′—3 / 2—1’>

E in its simplest form, like T in simplest form, occurs scores of times. But Milton prefers elaborate variations of design. To discover and recognize them is to acknowledge rhythmic phenomena hardly available to any other art outside contrapuntal music.

(a)

E Expanded by Augmentation of Overlap

One of the overlaps in E may be expanded by a 5 coming between the segments; e.g., instead of 2—2, there may be 2—5—2.

If the second overlap remains 3—3, the rhythmic aggregate becomes 3×5. Thus the description of the prostrate angels at PL I, 301-304:

who lay entranc'd ⟋2—5—2'⟍
Thick as autumnal leaves that strow the brooks
In Vallombrosa, where th' Etrurian shades ⟍ 3'—3 ⟋
High overarch'd embower;

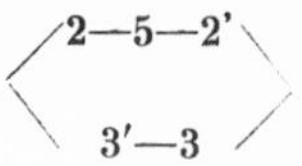

Both overlaps may be expanded. Thus at PL II, 305-309:

sage he stood ⟋2'–5—4⟍
With Atlantean shoulders fit to bear
The weight of mightiest monarchies; his look ⟍1—5—3⟋
Drew audience and attention still as night
Or summer's noontide air,

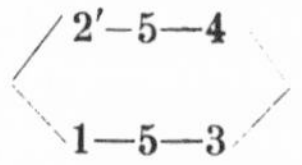

or at PL II, 957-961:

of whom to ask ⟋2—5—2⟍
Which way the nearest coast of darkness lies
Bordering on light; when straight behold the throne ⟍3—5—3⟋
Of Chaos, and his dark pavilion spread
Wide on the wasteful Deep;

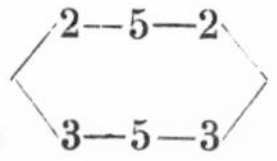

where observe that the second double-overlap has an interior pause strong enough to get a comma. But the rhetorical trend comports perfectly with the rhythmic pattern. Similar subordinate pauses are to be expected in extended aggregates.

On the surface, Milton's most characteristic blank verse is an incessant adjustment, now of syntax to prosodic device, now of prosody to syntax. Their interrelation usually seems one of harmonious reciprocity, and the punctuation often a compromise. Prosody may at times persuade syntax to ignore minor pause in the interest of continuous rhythmic design. Syntax may at times obtrude pauses that obscure cross-rhythmic construction, whether T or E. Certainly the punctuation of Edd. 1 and 2 can be no *mechanical* guide to the presence of such construction.

Before noting other modifications of E-pattern let us generalize. *If the sum of successive non-pentameter overlaps is an aggregate multiple of 5, of which the overlaps are subordinate currents of rhythm, then enjambement (or near-enjambement consonant with rhetorical trend) can produce against the metric frame a cross-rhythm which is felt to be a multiple of the norm, thus serving indirectly to safeguard it from obliteration.*

(b)

E Expanded with an Intercalated Overlap-5

At PL X, 338-341 Satan is skulking in the Garden after the Fall:

terrifi'd
He fled, not hoping to escape, but shun
The present, fearing guilty what his wrath
Might suddenly inflict;

2′—1
5'
4′—3

Here the intercalated 5 is integral: 4—1', although it has subordinate currents which receive punctuation after "escape."

At PL V, 748-753 Raphael describes the vast extent of the regions of Heaven:

the mighty regencies
Of Seraphim and Potentates and Thrones
In their triple degrees, regions to which
All thy dominion, Adam, is no more
Than what this Garden is to all the earth,
And all the sea,

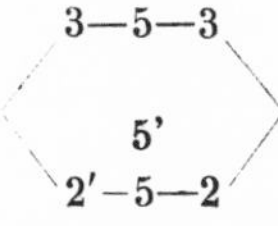

(c)

E Expanded with an Intercalated T

A fair example is at PL, I, 674-678:

Thither wing'd with speed
A numerous brigad hasten'd. As with bands
Of pioners with spade and pickaxe arm'd
Forerun the royal camp, to trench a field,
Or cast a rampart.

3′—3'
T 2′
2—2'

(d)

E Expanded with Intercalated E

An early occurrence is at PL I, 599-604:

Darken'd so, yet shone
Above them all th' Archangel: but his face
Deep scars of thunder had intrench'd, and care
Sat on his faded cheek, but under brows
Of dauntless courage, and considerate pride
Waiting revenge:

3′—3′
< 2′—4 >
1—3
2—2′
5′

E expanded in this way occurs in variant forms over 40 times in PL (in every book except the second), and twice in PR. Over 35 variant patterns appear, some of which seem curiously functional to context. Their ingenious symmetry may be regarded as inevitable elaboration of an intensely meditated method of cross-rhythmic designing. Patterns that occur more than once are:

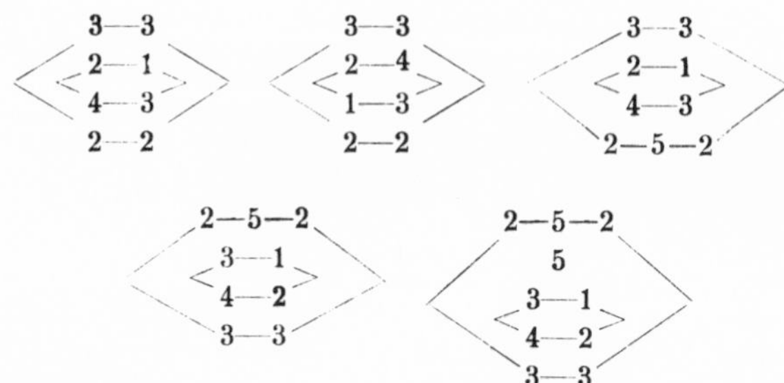

Intercalated E's are most numerous in PL VI, where there are ten in all, five of them occurring between lines 200-300 in the description of celestial warfare. Their rhythmic complexity certainly seems intended to parallel the presumed complexity of angelomachy.

(e)

E-chain

One E-construction (call it E^1) may be linked with another E-construction (call it E^2) in such a way that the second overlap in E^1 becomes the first in E^2, and the second in E^2 becomes the first in still a third E-construction (call it E^3), etc. For example, at PL V, 365-370 Adam thus addresses Raphael:

vouchsafe with us
Two only, (a) who yet by sovran gift possess
This spacious ground, (b) in yonder shady bower
To rest, (c) and what the Garden choicest bears
To sit and taste, (d) till this meridian heat
Be over, (e) and the sun more cool decline.

4—2
3—1
4—2
3—1'

From (a) to (b) is 4—2; from (b) to (c) is 3—1; from (c) to (d) is 4—2; and from (d) to (e) is 3—1'. They form an interlocking chain of three links: E^1—E^2—E^3:

E^1 4—2 / 3—1 = 10
E^2 3—1 / 4—2 = 10
E^3 4—2 / 3—1' = 10

At PL XI, 812-818 Michael says of Noah:

he of their wicked ways
Shall them admonish, and before them set
The paths of righteousness, how much more safe,
And full of peace, denouncing wrath to come
On their impenitence; and shall return
Of them derided, and of God observ'd
The one just man alive;

5'
3'—3
2—2
3—3
2—2'
3'—3

It is convenient to abbreviate a chain of this sort — one with no expanded overlap in any link, no intercalated overlap-5, and no intercalated T or E. Simply add to E as a superscript as many c's as there are links, and follow this abbreviation with the numbers of the first overlap. Thus the two foregoing examples are respectively E^{ccc} 4-2 and E^{cccc} 3′-3.

Though any succession of E-constructions may have rhythmic properties that give the effect of a chain, it is not a perfect chain if the constructions are each of different design. Thus at PL VI, 792-798 Satan's followers, grieving to see the Messiah's glory,

at the sight   2′—1'
Took envy, and aspiring to his highth,   4′—3
Stood reimbattl'd fierce, by force or fraud   2—2'
Weening to prosper, and at length prevail   3′—3'
Against God and Messiah, or to fall   2′—4
In universal ruin last, and now   1—3
To final battle drew,

where Milton keeps his successive patterns discrete, evidently feeling the context to require it.

Occasionally in PL a chain is sustained to such a length and with so little expansion or intercalation that it threatens — Milton so intends it — to dislocate the metric frame. It is an extraordinary surface response to some dramatic theme. For all its length I must cite an excerpt from the extended paragraph at PL X, 720-844. In despairing mood, Adam soliloquizes. Death, he concedes, is a just penalty for his misdeed. "O welcome hour whenever!" he cries:

why delays   2′-5—2
His hand to execute what his decree
Fix'd on this day? why do I overlive,   3 + 3
Why am I mock'd with death, and lengthen'd out   2—2
To deathless pain? How gladly would I meet   3—3'
Mortality my sentence, and be earth   2′—2
Insensible, how glad would lay me down   3—3
As in my mother's lap? There I should rest   2—2
And sleep secure; his dreadful voice no more   3—3
Would thunder in my ears, no fear of worse   T 2
To me and to my offspring would torment me
With cruel expectation. Yet one doubt   2′—2
Pursues me still, lest all I cannot die,   3 + 3
Lest that pure breath of life, the spirit of man   2—2
Which God inspir'd, cannot together perish   3'—3
With this corporeal clod;

Here the alternations of pause within successive lines are throbs of Adam's anguish, the lifting and sagging of his head shaken by cheerless hope and black despair, alternations so recurrent that the metric frame seems to shift, now forward, now backward. Nothing, surely, elsewhere in literature to surpass this functional application of a mathematically precise technique. If there is ever a blank-verse style distinguishable in its purity, it is here. One thinks of Hamlet's soliloquy on a similar theme. Shakespeare's verse, beginning with four feminine endings — a succession that never occurs in PL or PR — owes its solemn impressiveness to entirely different and conventional means, means that are no longer available to Milton, bent upon creating for epic verse a fresh method and manner.

3. *Contrapuntal Meaning of Expanded Cross-rhythmic Construction*

In simple unexpanded form of 10 or 15 beats, cross-rhythmic construction can recall the metric norm by sounding it in multiple. But to suggest that all the varied expansions of E-construction fulfil, or are meant to fulfil, this function would be dogmatic untruth, and would ignore one of Milton's central ideals as a technician. To see the situation clearly let us start with an important fact: *not one of his paragraphs ends in midline.* He builds his paragraph, conceives it in all its rhythmic surface and subsurface details as a finished contrapuntal piece. It is *sui generis.*

The ideal behind it being the rhythmic method of motet and madrigal, no wonder we perceive (i) a constant anxiety to safeguard the metric norm, and (ii) a refusal to let any E-chain, which necessarily ends in midline, end a paragraph. To do so would be to abandon the frame within which the piece is conceived.

No matter how frequent the enjambement — and it must be frequent if cross-rhythmic construction prevails — the listening ear can hear, as I suggested in the last chapter, a more or less direct demarcation of the norm every third or fourth line at most. And to perceive such demarcations we need no special reading voice, no "episcopal throat," no factitious manner of stressing or intoning at line-endings or line-beginnings. Milton takes care of all that. Read his words naturally, even as if they were prose, and you discover that syntax and word-choice have been so ordered that even if you willed it you could not misconstrue his rhythmic program, however little of that program should be at the time exactly known to you.

Since the normal metric frame is kept stabilized in our consciousness, this then is what happens on the surface when overlaps form an E-construction. Across that frame run competing rhythms, some of them metred like the norm itself. Within groups of lines their performances are simultaneous, effecting a parallel to the co-presence of competing voices (rhythms) in motet or madrigal. The reader who does not have at hand the score of some madrigal or anthem may find in Appendix III a few helpful suggestions.

Knowing Milton's lifelong passion for contrapuntal music and methods, we are safe in suggesting that one of his motives, if not his dominant motive, for enlarging blank-verse prosody to include elaborate T- and E-constructions is to secure analogues to remarkable rhythmic phenomena in Tudor music. It is the music of the elder Milton, brought to its consummation a century later in J. S. Bach, music Milton regarded as divine, and identified with the Angelic Choirs and the Music of the Spheres.

4. *Subordinate Currents of Rhythm May Be Punctuated*

An occasional surface barrier to ready perception of E or T is punctuation. Milton sometimes points subordinate currents when syntax seems not to require it, and commas may seem deliberately obstructive to overlap-continuity. In a later chapter I shall suggest the occasional presence of certain non-prosodic and non-rhetorical forces likely to cause over-punctuation. The possible presence of such forces would of course justify a degree of latitude in admitting "pausal overlaps" into cross-rhythmic construction. At the same time we must generally expect a coherent rhetoric to integrate such construction.

The blank verse of PL is a perfected instrument from the first to the last syllable. Still, as Milton progressed with his work he seems to have become freer in his use of extended cross-rhythmic constructions. With me this is a feeling more than a conviction based on statistics. In later books the links of E-chains seem to grow more tenuous, embracing longer syntactical members, which are adjusted more loosely and more covertly to rhythmic specifications. It is as if his practiced ear could now guide him with safe precision through constructions holding an unlimited number of feet. At the same time rhythmic segments seem to be somewhat more hospitable to subordinate pauses that permit but do not require commas. <2 + 5 + 5 + 2 / 3—3> may be as integral as <2—5—5—2 / 3—3>, and T II 2 (2 + 5 + 5 + 3) as integral as T II 2 (2—5—5—3). Once alive to the presence of E- and T-constructions as part of the texture of highly enjambed paragraphs, we come to realize that they are not mere mechanic functions of punctuation — either of its presence or of its absence.

Not that we do not find in the earlier books, too, constructions inspired by a large, loose, rhythmic grasp. For instance at PL I, 571-589 Milton fits into his metric frame a long inventory of legendary hosts, which appears in cross-rhythmic expansion. With text beside him, the reader may follow, line by line, the following analysis:

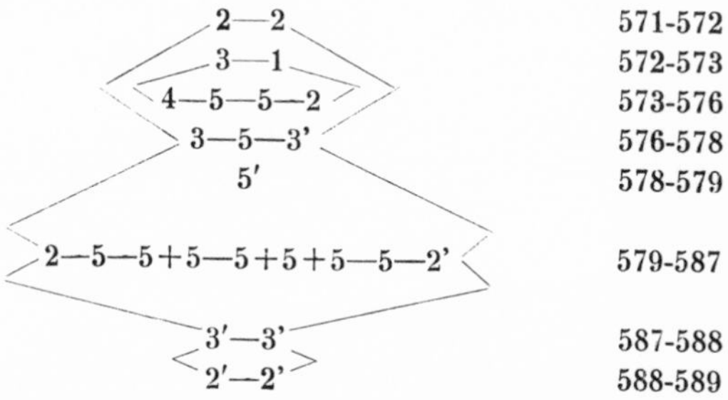

The long "overlap" at 579-587 is Milton's limit of expansion. Must we regard it as haphazard? Yes, if this were its sole occurrence. But it occurs again, of exactly the same length and for the very same purpose — to recite an inventory. At PL X, 695-706 Milton describes the winds let loose as a result of the Fall, and he casts his rhythms in the following comprehensive construction:

2—5—5—5+5—5+5—5—2' 695-703
3'-5—5+3'

5. *Responsive Features in Special Contexts*

(i)

One particular kind of metric pause often found in PL is worth describing. Usually it is an impressive dead stop at the end of a metric line in which a midline pause demarcates the last overlap of an E-construction. Once the listening ear perceives this construction, it is prepared for, it half expects, a continuation of the overlap process to get still another integration to create or to continue an E-chain.

It is as if in music a voice whose rhythm follows some recognized and expected pattern should suddenly break off in response to an impressive turn in the libretto. The voice is likely to hold the note for as many beats as the expectant ear would have heard if the voice had completed its rhythmic phrase. Indeed the composer may fill up the pause with a repetition, by another voice, of that last phrase. Analogously, some of Milton's pauses seem to invite an unheard repetition of an overlap-length to carry E-construction on into a chain.

Several examples will make the case clear.

Admittedly, here we indulge in surmise, though by no means idle fancy or special pleading. Perhaps better than surmise, for I would ask: how else can we interpret Milton's curious semicolon in the first example? It seems to be influenced by some special contrapuntal intention.

As I have done in Appendix II, I shall indicate such a pause by the letter A. It stands for Amen, since the situation first came to my notice at the end of Adam and Eve's evening prayer at PL IV, 724-735.

At PL V, 294-297 is the description of the Garden as a "wilderness of sweets" —

for Nature here	5
Wanton'd as in her prime, and play'd at will	2—2'
Her virgin fancies, pouring forth more sweet,	3'+3
Wild above rule or art; enormous bliss.	2—[2] A

Here we need only repeat "enormous bliss" [2] and we have a completed E-chain. It is impossible to read the words without pausing long enough for such a repetition.

At PL IX, 430-433 Eve, still innocent as she "works" among her plants, is described:

them she upstays	5
Gently with myrtle band, mindless the while,	< 2—1 >
Herself, though fairest unsupported flower,	< 4 + 3
From her best prop so far, and storm so nigh.	2—[1] A

The pause here is long enough to make a tragic refrain of "so nigh" — enough to complete a sequence of numbers which, as will appear in a later chapter, holds for Milton a symbolic import of calamity.

At PL IV, 167-171 Milton refers in simile to one of his favorite Scriptural stories:

though with them better pleas'd	3—5—3'
Than Asmodeus with the fishy fume,	
That drove him, though enamour'd, from the spouse	2'—2
Of Tobit's son, and with a vengeance sent	< 3—3' >
From Media post to Egypt, there fast bound.	< 2'-[2'] A

(ii)

In addition to creating cross-rhythmic parallels to rhythmic phenomena in music, cross-rhythmic construction may sometimes be so adjusted to context that every beat, even every syllable of some particular overlap may be responsive.

At PL VI, 193-195 Abdiel delivers a "noble stroke" upon the "proud crest of Satan:"

ten paces huge	< 2—2 >
He back recoil'd; the tenth on bended knee	3—3
His massy spear upstaid;	

where observe not one of the overlap-segments is augmented or diminished. It is a clean-cut 10-beat aggregate to measure off those ten paces of recoil from Abdiel's clean-cut blow.

(iii)

Now for a more elaborate illustration: the picture of Raphael as he arrives among the guardian angels that picket Paradise (PL V, 275-288). With text beside him, the reader will find the following ordonnance of rhythms:

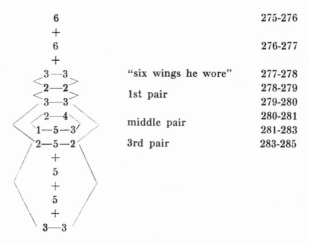

6		275-276
+		
6		276-277
+		
3—3	"six wings he wore"	277-278
2—2	1st pair	278-279
3—3		279-280
2—4	middle pair	280-281
1—5—3		281-283
2—5—2	3rd pair	283-285
+		
5		
+		
5		
+		
3—3		

Note first how the intercalated E, descriptive of the middle pair of wings, is locked in the enveloping pattern; next how Edd. 1 and 2 carefully insert comma in line 279 to demarcate a 6-unit, making evident the intended link in the chain. (Many editors drop this comma after "broad.") Here are the unit-lengths as they occur:

6 + 6 + 6 + 4 + 6 + 6 + 9 + 9 + 5 + 5 + 6

Not a single augmented or diminished variant in these eleven overlap-units; and — extraordinary for so short a passage — there are six rhythmic units of 6 beats each. Why so many 6's? The answer is supplied in the third 6-beat unit:

> six wings he wore, to shade
> His lineaments divine;

Easy enough to picture a Seraph with three pairs of wings, especially after he has just been likened to a two-winged phoenix? By no means easy! Isaiah's imagination could cope with it, but the modern mind, lamentably naturalistic, needs a stimulant. This Milton hopes to provide by iterating a rhythmic length. "When a Raphael appears," he meditates, "we *must* exalt our thought to

Isaiah's inspired 6. I will din 6 into my reader's ear: shape six rhythms of 6 beats each — and clean-cut 6's. Not a syllable more nor less than 6! No 6′ or 6' or 6″ to blur the Seraphic form or profile, still radiant with dew of Heaven."

Alas, for all this punctilious harping on 6, Milton has failed to convert his graphic illustrators. Martin, Doré, and the rest, one and all, decline to add a single plume to the familiar avian suit of two.

(iv)

At PL X, 873-895 Adam terribly reproaches Eve. The cross-rhythmic construction is as follows if we start at "But for thee . . ." (873—), ending at " . . . Mankind?" (895).

5″	873-874
5′	874-875
5'	875-876
2′—2′	876-877
3′—3	877-878
2'—2	878-879
5	879-880
3 + 3	880-881
2 + 2	881-882
3+5—3'	882-884
2—2′	884-885
3′+5+5′-3	885-888
2 + 2	888-889
3—3	889-890
2—5—1'[+rest]	890-892
+	
T II 4′	892-895

Here analysis shows rhythmic order underlying seeming disorder, broken rhythms fitting into links of a chain where, though the emotional currents disturb the flow, rhetoric conspires with cross-rhythmic construction to produce an overall rational pattern.

But this is but a part of the story of this rhythmic structure.

Some of Adam's words are loaded and barbed. He flings cruel syllables into Eve's face — thirteen syllables at a time — unlucky thirteen! According to rabbinical doctrine, Adam was created with thirteen ribs on the left side, and from the supernumerary rib Eve was made. Our "grandparents" are familiar with this lore in all its details; hence Adam's characterization of Eve at 887-888,

> as supernumerary
> To my just number found,

containing exactly 13 syllables.

Now in PL an extrametrical terminal syllable, except in the present Tenth Book, is very rare. In this particular line, however, it serves for more than a reminder of the book's dramatic quality. It is symbolic. It symbolizes Eve, the spare thirteenth rib. It actually terminates the word that terminates the line that expresses the sinister redundance. And, characteristic of the man who loves quibbles, and who has just played upon the word "sinister," such an extrametrical syllable was called, even in his day, a feminine ending!

Moreover, Milton brings it about that this redundant syllable must be pronounced, fully pronounced. Although it comes immediately before enjambement, it cannot be "thrown out," for, unlike the case of the terminal word "voluntary" at X, 61, this "-y" cannot in the least degree be absorbed by a vowel beginning the next line, because the next line starts with a consonant.

So much for the first harsh fling of missile-words. Another heartful is on the way. It arrives as soon as Adam can find the aptest words to vilify his fallen mate:

> This novelty on earth, this fair defect
> Of Nature, (891-892)

— again exactly 13 syllables. And they occur in the only overlap in all this tirade of rhythmic patterns to fail to complete an integrated E-construction.

If a syllable after "Nature" were not lacking, the rhythmic design would be a clean $<\substack{3—3\\2—5—2}>$. In very truth, the syllabic deficiency in the rhythmic facture of this twin-barbed characterization of Eve parallels and italicizes the word "defect." The overlap is the same kind of misfit in the rhythmic chain as Eve is declared to be in the chain of Nature.

Adam's first 13, by its form and prosodic position, accents the notion of superfluousness. His second 13 accents deficiency — for the reader or listener aware of the cross-rhythmic construction.

6. *Precedent in Pre-Miltonic Blank Verse*

For the moment let us try to identify ourselves with the composer as he guides his rhetoric into an E-construction. On the one hand, we may attend chiefly to overlap-lengths. To effect a simple E we need only to alternate an overlap-6 with an overlap-4, or an overlap-3 with an overlap-7. To effect a chain, we repeat the process. On the other hand, we may attend chiefly to interior pause. If successive interior pauses fall at the same place in the line (isopause), we have an overlap-5. If between its overlap-segments we admit a full metric line, we have a T-construction. In both cases we have isopause. If, as Milton tries to do generally, we avoid isopause, we may alternate pause after the 2nd foot with pause after the 3rd in consecutive lines, and we get an E:

$$<\substack{3-3 \\ 2-2}>.$$

In his simplest cross-rhythmic constructions Milton probably concerns himself with both these processes simultaneously, being quite as well aware of an interior-pause-to-interior-pause procedure as of overlap integration of alien lengths into multiples of 5. But in the case of expanded constructions involving more than three or four multiples of 5, very probably his conscious procedure is to attend to alternate pauses only. For the ear of even the most skilled contrapuntist could seldom have grasped a rhythmic aggregate of many beats more than 20. Yet, convinced that elaborate cross-rhythmic expansions may lead him to manageable complexities suggestive of complex ingenuities in the rhythms of polyphony, Milton seems to entrust their exact arithmetic to some ideally vigilant listener. What he may actually have resorted to at times was the employment of mechanical aid operable with his fingers, as in a later chapter I suggest he probably did in carrying out certain rhythmic designs and devices much more complicated than cross-rhythmic integration. Almost conclusive evidence that he computes his most expanded constructions by the pause-to-pause method is the illustration cited above: a

$$\left\langle \begin{matrix} 2—(7\times 5)—2' \\ 3'—3' \end{matrix} \right\rangle,$$

patterned, demonstrably, to be the vehicle for an extended inventory. This is the extreme of a method which in shorter aggregates can assemble alien rhythms into instantly felt multiples of 5. But in longer aggregates it can measure, by following arithmetical formula, the pattern from strong interior pause to strong interior pause.

Now there are definite manifestations of similar pause-to-pause measurement in the dialogue of the dramatists, especially in Shakespeare's latest plays. Naturally Milton had read them with an eye focused on prosodic device. In some of them he must have recognized an experimental spirit working to relax the conventions of blank verse, augmenting its expressive scope, and he must have formed clear judgments concerning the success or failure of this or that metrical practice.

Long before his final drafting of PL he knew what his desiderated epic style could and could not tolerate. Yet in this matter of expanded E-construction he was ready to go far beyond the Elizabethans in the exact calculation of beats, even syllables, between successive interior pauses.[1]

A few examples will show Shakespeare's employment of simple T and simple E, with occasional slight expansions. Speeches often begin as well as end at the same point in midline.

At *A. and C.* V.i.28-30 Agrippa says:

> And strange it is T 2
> That nature must compel us to lament
> Our most persisted deeds.

This is preceded by a speech of identical length and pattern, and is followed by an overlap-5.

At *Cor.* II.ii.52-74 the rhythmic sequence runs (analysis of loose constructions is bracketed):

5 [2'+3] + T 2 [2—5'—3] + E < 2'+4 / 1'-5—3 > + 5' +

T 2′ [2′-5—3'] + 5′ + T 2 [2—5—3] + E < 2+4' / 1″-3 > +

T 2 [2+5—3'] + T 2 [2'+5+3] + E < 2 +2' / 3′—3 > +

T 2 [2'+5—3'] + 5′.

Such patterning becomes almost as formular for dialogue as stichomythia.

E-chains occur. At *Temp.* I.ii.413-419 Miranda's spontaneous rejoinder (417-419) is in pattern to match Prospero's remark that evokes it (413-417):

5
3—3'
< >
2″–2'
< >
3″–3'
< >
2″–2
< >
3—3'

Other examples may be found at *Cym.* II.iii.27-36 and in Hermione's speech at *W. T.* III.ii.33-55.

But how different the tournure and pace of such blank verse and that of PL! Shakespeare freely uses not only feminine endings but "light" and "weak" endings. "Light" endings in Milton are very rare; "weak" endings almost non-existent. Shakespeare is indeed experimenting with E- and T-constructions for a certain purpose, but a purpose that is not Milton's. Milton wants to keep his metric frame stable in spite of any amount of enjambement, any amount of cross-rhythmic construction. But Shakespeare, influenced by John Fletcher's innovating spirit, deliberately shifts the frame forward, dislocates it from the norm with which each scene starts, and continues such dislocation to the very close of the speech. Sometimes, though but rarely, Milton's extended chain may threaten dislocation, but his paragraph always ends in correspondence with the metric line.

Milton's simple cross-rhythmic constructions in the midst of free enjambement may recall the norm in multiple. In Shakespeare there is no such need: not only is enjambement uniformly much less than in PL, but every one of Shakespeare's feminine endings demarcates his line as effectively as rhyme would do.

What Shakespeare and Fletcher strive for is a kind of ambiguity, a confusing of the ear as to where the metric frame really lies. This program is furthered by the simultaneous admission of feminine endings and weak endings, the one offering a blatant obstacle to fluid enjambement, the other tending to dissolve the boundaries of the frame altogether. The ultimate and wonderful ambition is to get a rich amalgam — an artfully metred verse that gives the illusion of spontaneity in cadenced prose: a style informal, flexible as prose, yet maintaining itself in a medium near enough to acknowledged verse to create illusions which prose seldom brooks.

The danger is intolerable mannerism, and into this Fletcher falls when he no longer has Shakespeare's restraining presence. There are plays by Fletcher in which feminine endings are so incessant that the verse is quite as end-line conscious as that of *Gorboduc.* On the other hand, there are scenes in Shirley where the blank verse is so hospitable to weak endings that it passes into amorphous prose.

But Shakespeare's intermingling of cross-rhythmic construction with light and weak endings can result in strange rhythmic effects peculiarly suited to such a play as *The Tempest,* in which at least a fifth of the lines are involved in cross-rhythmic construction, including some of the most quoted; e.g.,

We are such stuff < 2—2' >
As dreams are made on, and our little life < 3'—3 >
Is rounded with a sleep. (IV.i.156-158)

Here the only reason Shakespeare would not have rearranged the speech to read,

We are such stuff as dreams are made on, and
Our little life is rounded with a sleep.

is his determination to end as well as begin it in midline.[2]

7. *Precedent in Rhymed Verse:*

The Faithful Shepherdess

From 1600 to 1660 there was produced in England a substantial amount of sustained pentameter verse rhyming in willfully loose couplet form. John Fletcher's *Faithful Shepherdess* is an important instance. It is an experiment in rhyme, just as, for Milton, *Comus* is an experiment in blank verse. Fletcher's pentameters all rhyme in pairs except for an opening half-page of blank verse. Milton's pentameters in *Comus* (not counting the few in the lyrics) are all in blank verse except for nine couplets in dialogue at 495-512 — a curious enclave of rhyme which is pure Fletcher. Fletcher might have preferred midline speech-beginnings and speech-endings, but he would have tried for the same sort of cross-rhythmic structure as in

O my lov'd master's heir, and his next joy, 3 + 2 + 5—2
I come not here on such a trivial toy
As a stray'd ewe, or to pursue the stealth 5
Of pilfering wolf; not all the fleecy wealth 3—3
That doth enrich these downs, is worth a thought <2—2'>
To this my errand, and the care it brought. + 3'
(501-506)

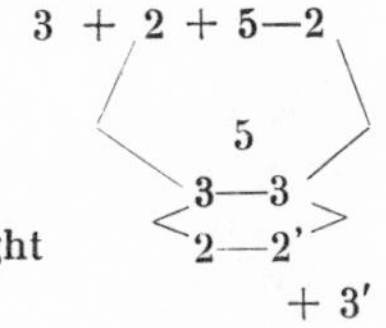

This is the nearest to an E-chain in *Comus,* save for one of the same length at 316-321. That it should come at the only patch of rhymed pentameters shows how sedulously Milton scanned Fletcher, yet how thoroughly on the whole he rejected Fletcher's uniting of cross-rhythmic construction and rhyme.

At least 20 per cent of *The Faithful Shepherdess* is involved in cross-rhythmic construction, and in this the interior pause is nearly always at the second or third foot. Frequency of enjambement, averaging at least 50 per cent, is perhaps higher than in any English play or poem written before 1608. The most sustained cross-rhythmic passage is at I.iii. 88-124, where enjambement is 75 per cent. A shorter, but typical, illustration of Fletcher's method is at V.iii. 96-104:

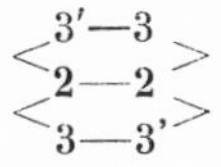

3'—3
<2—2>
<3—3'>

followed by five overlap 5's. Such consecutive overlap-5's are characteristic. For Milton Fletcher's astonishingly sustained *tour de force* of prosody was food for long thoughts on the worth and worthlessness of rhyme, the use and abuse of isopause, the opportunities to make prosodic "voices" perform contrapuntally.

In *Comus* Milton is as chary of Fletcher's free and frequent enjambement as of his insistent rhyming. The paramount prosodic concern in *Comus* (excluding the lyrics) is with the individual line. Yet the doing of this work must have suggested two important problems. Suppose enjambement to be very active, then (i) how give to cross-rhythmic constructions such variety as to make them unobtrusive yet perfect analogues to the cross-rhythmic voices of polyphony? and (ii) how make their structure, on occasion, functionally responsive to thought or action in the fable? It took some years to solve these two problems.

Frequency of enjambement in *Comus* is only 33 per cent. A succession of as many as four enjambed lines like those at 501-506 does not occur six times. Hardly 50 lines of *Comus* are involved in T- or E-construction (42 per cent of PL and 17 per cent of PR are involved). Besides the two brief chains, E occurs only twice (always E 2-2). Simple T occurs eight times (always T 2).

These occurrences are not just a fortuitous result of reading Fletcher and Shakespeare. Rather they are evidence that Milton is in sympathy with Fletcher's flair for experiment, and is already searching for means to transcend his prosody.

CHAPTER III

INTIMATIONS OF NUMERICAL SYMBOL

When certain peculiar numerical sequences about to be described first came to my notice, I thought of them as pure chance-products. But they recurred, and successive recurrences seemed consistently responsive to contextual situations. Since the response involved symbol, I did not relish the prospect of getting entangled in mystical numerology. Yet I could not deny the phenomena, and after all they seemed compatible with sound psychology.

Might they be cabalistic — a fruit of Milton's Hebrew learning? I went to see a rabbi. "No," he said, "there's nothing just like this in the Jewish Cabala, but your examples do fulfil the cabalist's ideal: of wrapping truth, at times, in symbol, so it may be guarded from all but the initiated and the worthy."

I then organized all my findings to date and sought the editorial views of three learned periodicals. At least four of their consultants acknowledged the phenomena to be not only a product of Milton's well-known interest in mathematics, perhaps pointing to the special nature of his mathematical studies, but evidence of an area in his mind and art hitherto unsuspected.

1.

A glance at Appendix II will reveal that the prevailing general pattern of E-construction is E 3-3 (or E 2-2). But the less common patterns are likely to be of greater interest in that their relative frequency seems opposed to what we should expect. In the case of two patterns this is especially true.

Let us survey the eight possible arrangements of overlap-segments in an E-pattern when the segments include each of the first four cardinal numbers.

<1-2 / 3-4> <1-3 / 2-4> <2-1 / 4-3> <2-4 / 1-3> <3-1 / 4-2> <3-4 / 1-2>

<4-2 / 3-1> <4-3 / 2-1>

Of these the first and last would seem least likely to occur with any frequency merely by chance. One can search on and on through non-Miltonic blank verse, no matter how highly enjambed, and never find either of them. After relentless search I have found two lone instances in Wordsworth's combined *Prelude* and *Excursion*. But they occur dozens of times in PL, whether in simple or expanded form. Here are some examples of E 1-2:

(a) At VII, 186-188 the Angels sing:

                                        to him
Glory and praise, whose wisdom had ordain'd
Good out of evil to create,

<1—2 / 3—4>

(b) At VII, 613-615 again the Angels sing:

                                        Who seeks
To lessen thee, against his purpose serves
To manifest the more thy might:

<1—2 / 3—4>

(c) At X, 211-215 the Son ministers to fallen man:

            then pitying how they stood
Before him naked to the air, that now
Must suffer change, disdain'd not to begin
Thenceforth the form of servant to assume,
As when he wash'd his servants' feet,

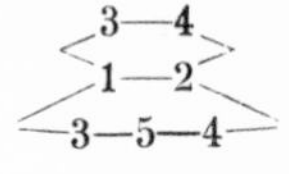

(d) At XII, 562-565 Adam confesses his faith:

                                    to walk
As in his presence, ever to observe
His providence, and on him sole depend,
Merciful over all his works,

<1—2' / 5' / 3 + 4>

(a) hymns the perfect Creator endowed with perfect wisdom; (b) hymns God's omnipotence; (c) expresses Christ's perfect humility; (d) expresses Adam's perfect faith in God's providence.

I have found no evidence to invalidate the generalization: Whenever $<^{1-2}_{3-4}>$ occurs, whether in simple, expanded, or chain form, the context is one that stresses or implies an affirmative idea of perfection, absolute completeness, order, truth, harmony, power, or some virtue.

Other examples could be cited, and some are included in Appendix II. Here I would show how sensitively responsive an ascending series can be.

At PL V, 35 ff. Satan wants Eve to see in a dream a perfect picture of Nature to match the perfection of her charms. In her version of this dream the rhythms are so arranged that the simple ascending series evolves gradually through various stages before it becomes a clear and unmistakable pattern — even as things show in a dream.

In the first stage, only the presence of a slight rhetorical pause in a T-construction makes discernible the first three terms of an ascending series, and the one heavy pause that breaks continuity in this T is deliberately softened and quickened by a mere comma instead of stronger pointing. This gives fluency to segment 4. Thus we have vaguely but indubitably outlined:

methought [1—2 >
Close at mine ear one call'd me forth to walk 3—4]
With gentle voice, I thought it thine;

The second stage is a loosely expanded E-construction:

it said, —1—2—
Why sleep'st thou Eve? now is the pleasant time, 3+5—5—4
The cool, the silent, save where silence yields
To the night-warbling bird, that now awake
Tunes sweetest his love-labor'd song;

The third stage, expressive of the full-orbed moon irradiating infinite romance, presents at last the cross-rhythmic pattern in simplest manifestation:

now reigns 1—2 <> 3—4
Full-orb'd the Moon, and with more pleasing light
Shadowy sets off the face of things;

But Satan now proceeds to declare that all this natural beauty is

in vain 1—2
If none regard:

starting another perfection-series. It is not completed, for Satan is falsifying a metaphysical point about which only yesterday Eve heard from Adam's lips:

> These then [the stars], though unbeheld at deep of night,
> Shine not in vain, . . . (IV, 674 f.)

An example of the ascending series repeated in a chain is at PL VIII, 521-529 (from "and brought . . .") where Adam acknowledges the state of bliss he enjoys in Eden. But, as in the last example, the chain breaks off abruptly in response to context.

1—5—2
3—4
1—2
3—5—5—4

whereupon a third series starts, 1—2, but it cannot progress, for Adam is now confiding to Raphael the "commotion strange" he experiences in the presence of feminine beauty that weakens his reason and vaguely threatens his male supremacy in Eden.

2.

Let us now examine cross-rhythmic series that keep a descending order.

(a) At PL II, 798-800, of the monstrous progeny of Sin and Death:

for when they list into the womb 4—3 <> 2—1'
That bred them they return, and howl and gnaw
My bowels,

(b) At PL IV, 306-308, of Eve's tresses:

but in wanton ringlets wav'd — 4'—3'
As the vine curls her tendrils, which impli'd — 2'—1'
Subjection,

(c) At PL VI, 116-118 Abdiel, in upraiding Satan:

wherefore should not strength and might — 4'—3
There fail where virtue fails, or weakest prove — 2—1'
Where boldest;

(d) At PL VI, 509-512 Satan's people dig up the constituents of gunpowder:

in a moment up they turn'd — 4'—3
Wide the celestial soil, and saw beneath — 2—5—1'
The originals of Nature in their crude
Conception;

(e) At PL VI, 629-632 the rebels are jolly over their success:

heighten'd in their thoughts beyond — 4'—3
All doubt of victory, eternal might — 2—5—1'
To match with their inventions they presum'd
So easy,

(f) At PL VIII, 76-79, of man's ignorance:

he his fabric of the heavens — 4'—3
Hath left to their disputes, perhaps to move — 2—5—1'
His laughter at their quaint opinions wide
Hereafter,

(g) At PL X, 914-918 Eve pleads in symbol:

witness Heaven — 2'—5—1'
What love sincere, and reverence in my heart
I bear thee, and unweeting have offended, — 4''+3
Unhappily deceiv'd; thy suppliant — 2—1
I beg,

(h) At PL XI, 2-7 Adam and Eve in lowiest plight repentant stood,

for from the mercy-seat above
Prevenient grace descending had remov'd
The stony from their hearts, and made new flesh
Regenerate grow instead, that sighs now breath'd
Unutterable, which the spirit of prayer
Inspired,

4—5—3
5
2—5—1

(i) At PR IV, 622-624 the hymning Angels prophesy:

yet not thy last and deadliest wound
By this repulse receiv'd, and hold'st in Hell
No triumph;

<4—3 / 2—1>

Of these nine illustrations, (a) expresses the "sorrow infinite" of Sin and Death; (b) woman's subjection to man; (c) failure of strength when virtue is lacking; (d) the "crude" elements, totally devoid of form and order; (e) ironic intimation of the rebels' doom; (f) man's ridiculous ignorance of the total universe; (g) Eve's sense of utter guilt and moral defeat; (h) Adam and Eve's complete abasement; (i) Satan's ultimate destruction.

These and other like examples warrant the generalization: Whenever <4—3 / 2—1> occurs, whether in simple, expanded, or chain form, the context is one that stresses or implies an idea of negation, imperfection, disorder, ruin, impotence, ignorance, hate, malice, abasement, or deadly sin.

Further illustrations could be cited. In Appendix II I have commented on several, especially those that occur in the analysis of the battle-scenes at VI, 193-259 and 316-341, and the transformation-scene at X, 504-584. Note particularly the reversing of series in response to context at VI, 325-328 (vs. 330-333) and at X, 504-509 (vs. 509-520).

The application of descending series to context is often less obvious than in the case of ascending. One reason for this is the difficulty of applying numerical symbol to certain concepts. Consider power. God's omnipotence, as such, calls for the ascending series, and gets it at PL VII, 613-615. But when exerted against evil, God's power becomes destruction (to the foe), destruction either in process or in prophecy. This aspect of omnipotence can account for the descending series at PL VI, 38-43, 700-708, 753-759, and 773-778.

Another concept that can have no invariable symbol is repentance. As a virtue it requires the ascending series — as Milton most elaborately gives it at the close of Book X (1089-1104). But Adam and Eve's contrition is a tearful thing. With unutterable sighs and tears watering the ground, their unfeigned sorrow may bring salvation, but can hardly count among life's joys. This prostrate couple are miserable. The perfect penitential experience is a cathartic ordeal painful in proportion to its sincerity. Hence no sooner does Milton begin Book XI than the rhythms describing the penitents are shaped to accommodate the descending series cited above (Illustration h) in symbolic preparation for the pity felt by the Son.

The creative act is positive. But the struggle of the swift stag to shake his branching antlers from underground, and of behemoth to upheave his vastness, fitly receives a negative descending series at PL VII, 469-472. Milton regards the situation empathetically. For the moment we are expected to share the act not with creator but created.

3

Are ascending and descending series of the first four cardinal numbers confined to cross-rhythmic construction? No, they occur also in straightforward, linear form: 1+2+3+4 and 4+3+2+1. And these, too, are responsive to context. Such series, however, can hardly be expected to occur as often as those in cross-rhythmic construction. For they are easier to perceive, and the evidence points to Milton's wish to keep his symbolic practices to himself. Not being tied to enjambement and integration of overlaps, linear series are more likely to seem deliberately planned. If Milton had put one on every page, the dullest ear and eye would soon detect them and relate them to context, and to his contemporaries the practice might well have seemed a weird and childish game of solitaire.

(a) At PL III, 294-297 God pronounces:

So man, as is most just, 1, 2, 3, 4 [2 + 2], 4', 4'
Shall satisfy for man, be judg'd and die,
And dying rise, and rising with him raise
His brethren, ransom'd with his own dear life.

(b) At PL V, 623-624 Milton describes the motion of the heavenly bodies:

[mazes intricate,]
Eccentric, intervolv'd, yet regular 1', 2', 3, 4
Then most, when most irregular they seem:

(c) At PL X, 492-493 Satan reports to Pandemonium that man and his world are now prey to him and his followers:

To range in, and to dwell, and over man, 1', 2', 3, 4
To rule, as over all he should have rul'd.

(It is possible that the comma after "man," as I shall suggest in later pages, is not necessarily a printer's error. Whatever its meaning, it need not disturb the integrity of this progression.)

(d) At PL X, 1060-61 Adam remembers that God once pitied him and Eve:

How much more, if we pray him, will his ear 1', 2'', 3'', 4'
Be open, and his heart to pity incline,

(a) expresses Christ's perfect atonement, (b) the perfect harmony of the Spheres, (c) Satan's delusion that he now possesses infinite power over the new world, and (d) the perfect efficacy of contrite prayer. The final term in (a) seems to be reduplicated for emphasis.

In three of the following examples the third term, as in (c) above, is broken into two subordinate currents, 2+1.

At PL II, 686-687 Satan, addressing Death, assumes heavenly power: 1, 2, 3 [2 + 1], 4.

At PL V, 372-373 Raphael tells Adam that Adam is perfectly eligible to entertain angels: 1, 2, 3', 4'.

At VI, 172-173 eternal truth animates Abdiel's indignation: 1', 2′, 3', 4′.

At VIII, 450-451 God promises Adam the perfect mate: 1', 2′, 3 [2 + 1], 4.

At IX, 1027-28 Adam's summons to sensuality seems to promise perfect joy: 1, 2, 3' [2 + 1'], 4′.

Perhaps the most extraordinary instance of an ascending linear series that the eye and ear can instantly perceive is at PL X, 515-516: 1', 2′, 3', 4′; for it is superposed on a cross-rhythmic descending series in perfect response to a spectacular context. The cross-rhythmic series, however, is *not* instantly perceived. The situation is analyzed in Appendix II.

In several passages the listening ear hears so clearly the linear ascending sequence that almost every editor has punctuated the demarcating pauses, natural pauses which are unpointed in Edd. 1 and 2. Three interesting examples are as follows.

(a) At PL I, 19-21 a strong end-line pause demarcates the fourth term of the series 1', 2′, 3', 4′, 5 (God's omniscience):

> Instruct me, for thou know'st; thou from the first
> Wast present, and with mighty wings outspread
> Dove-like sat'st brooding on the vast abyss,
> (punct. Morgan MS)

Since the Morgan MS demarcates the end of line 21, the printer may have had difficulty in following instructions.

(b) At PL VII, 364-367, of the perfect distribution of light:

> Hither, as to their fountain, other stars 1, 2', 3'', 4′, 5
> Repairing, in their golden urns draw light,
> And hence the morning planet gilds her horns.
> (punct. Wright)

(c) At PL IX, 227-228, of Eve's incomparable pre-eminence:

> Sole Eve, associate sole, to me beyond 1, 2, 3, 4
> Compare above all living creatures dear,

Here it is impossible for the ear not to demarcate 3 and 4 because the last word in 3 actually rhymes with the last word in 4.

4

Linear Descending Series

Two of the following examples serve to determine points of punctuation.

(a) At PL II, 622-624 Hell is described as including "a universe of death,"

which God by curse 4', 3, 2, 1
Created evil, for evil only good,
Where all life dies, death lives,

(b) At PL VI, 317-319 a catastrophe is imminent in the intended sword-blow of either Michael or Satan:

[Uplifted imminent] one stroke they aim'd 4', 3′, 2, 1
That might determine, and not need repeat,
As not of power, at once;

Fletcher's note in the Facsimile Ed. presents evidence that Milton seems to have intended comma after "imminent." Such a comma appears in nearly every edition since 1725.

(c) At PL IX, 495-497 Satan's manner of approaching Eve is wickedness in action:

and toward Eve 4, 3, 2, 1
Address'd his way, not with indented wave,
Prone on the ground, as since,

(d) At PL X, 572-574, of the demons' punishment:

Thus were they plagu'd 4', 3′, 2, 1
And worn with famine, long and ceaseless hiss,
Till their lost shape, permitted,

Practically every editor destroys this series by shifting comma after "famine" to after "long." See below, p. 217.

(e) At PL VI, 558 f. Satan issues orders in ironic and ambiguous words. The perfect symmetry that characterizes the rhythms of his utterance, a symmetry in contrast with the crookedness of his intentions, must be analyzed to be understood.

Only the ear perceives linear series in this passage, for they depend on the pause after "however" (563), a word which in Edd.

1 and 2 is never set off with punctuation. Probably Milton feels that it punctuates itself. But the rhythmic sequence that is brought into being by inserting a comma is so unusually apt to the passage, so hard to imagine as a product of chance, that it argues for an emendation, at least gives strong support to editors who insert the comma. Whether or not the comma is there, the pause is there, and from "That all may see . . ." to ". . . loud that all may hear" (559-567) the rhythms are thus organized:

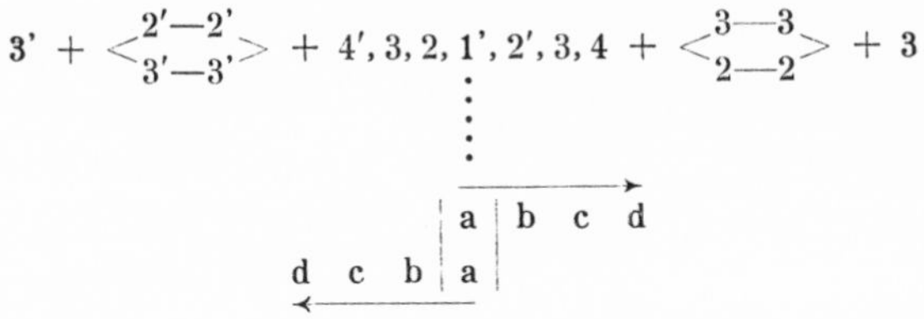

3' + <(2′—2' / 3′—3')> + 4′, 3, 2, 1', 2′, 3, 4 + <(3—3 / 2—2)> + 3

a | b c d →

← d c b | a

Satan's ambiguous words are thus paralleled by the descending-ascending linear series from "if they like . . ." (561—) to " . . our part:" (565). The entire passage is really a continuous E-chain, across which, contrapuntally, the linear symbolic sequences perform like distinct cross-rhythmic "voices." Except for the fact that elsewhere Milton does not point "however," one might explain the absence of comma after it as a concession to serve the fluency of the E-construction. The punctuation, or lack of it, would then be, as it seems often to be elsewhere, a compromise.

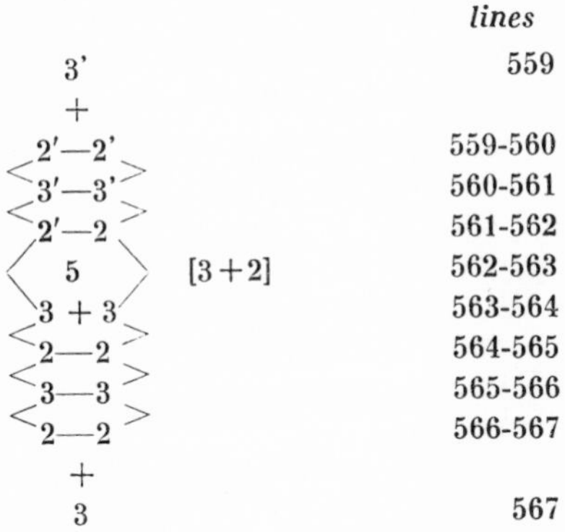

		lines
3'		559
+		
2′—2'		559-560
3′—3'		560-561
2′—2		561-562
5	[3+2]	562-563
3 + 3		563-564
2—2		564-565
3—3		565-566
2—2		566-567
+		
3		567

5

There is sound psychology and common sense behind the response of ascending series to positive, and descending series to negative concepts. Milton is not the only 17th-century writer to exploit such a response. One of George Herbert's poems in *The Temple* (1633) is relevant. In "Easter Wings" he adopts an old Greek device of arranging lines of verse in geometric shapes.

Lord, who createdst man in wealth and store, 5
Though foolishly he lost the same, 4
Decaying more and more 3
Till he became 2
Most poor; 1
With thee 1
O let me rise 2
As larks, harmoniously, 3
And sing this day Thy victories: 4
Then shall the fall further the flight in me. 5

CHAPTER IV

FURTHER INTIMATIONS OF SYMBOL

1

Before ascribing the foregoing sequences, in either cross-rhythmic or linear form, to pure chance, let us keep in mind the following facts: (i) my illustrations are not hand-picked, i.e., I have suppressed none that seem unfavorable; (ii) I have found no instances whose directional response contradicts a consistent response in the others. If these sequences are fortuitous, could anything like consistency in directional response be also fortuitous?

Arresting as these phenomena were, for some time I put them aside, unable to relate them to Milton's prosody or his paragraph-structure, and indeed very reluctant to think about them at all. I had no relish for numerical symbolism. Of course I knew Milton's admiration for Pythagoras and his familiarity with the tenets and accomplishments of the neo-Pythagoreans. I knew they had deified the number 10 as the complete and perfect number, being the sum of the first four. I recalled their notorious prayer to the "Holy Tetractys." Perhaps, I thought, these scattered sequences do owe something to the ascetic Greek thinker who reduces music to number, and propounds the high doctrine of the Music of the Spheres.

Then, even against my wish and will, I began to meet with related rhythmic phenomena equally arresting. I found 1, 2, 3, 4 multiplied by 2, and 4, 3, 2, 1 multiplied by 3, each resultant series being literally responsive to an obvious concept of duality or triplicity.

For example, at PL III, 238-241 the Son declares to the Father:

> Account me man; I for his sake will leave
> Thy bosom, and this glory next to thee
> Freely put off, and for him lastly die
> Well pleas'd, on me let Death wreck all his rage;

The series is 2, 4', 6′, 8 [4 + 4]. The multiplier 2 seems an indubitable response to the dual nature assumed by the Son: at once God and man.

At PL X, 163-168 God condemns the serpent in a passage containing intervals that accommodate the descending series 12, 9', 6″, 3′ (= 3 × [4, 3, 2, 1]).

> Which when the Lord God heard, without delay
> To judgement he proceeded on th' accus'd
> Serpent though brute, unable to transfer
> The guilt on him who made him instrument
> Of mischief, and polluted from the end
> Of his creation; justly then accurst,

The multiplier 3 parallels the triple curse of Genesis that follows at lines 175-181. But, I ventured to ask, might it carry a symbolic as well as a literal meaning? Might 3 be Milton's number for justice, and, when in retrograde series, for retributive justice? For doesn't the base-term which terminates this series contain the very word "justly"?

I was moving within a murk of mystic symbolism, and, being sceptic by nature and training, I was not comfortable. There seemed only one way to reconcile myself to what might lie ahead. I must try to identify myself with a mind of the early 17th century. I remembered the strange numerical symbolism invoked by Donne in "The Primrose." Still, I thought, however addicted to numerical symbol might be Milton's contemporaries, Milton the rationalist — no, he was too bold and independent a thinker. But boldness is relative. Was he not a pious Puritan for whom every word in the Bible was ultimate truth? And isn't the Bible a very seed-bed of numerical symbol? And then the high honor in which Milton held Dante, whose life-blood ran red with symbol.

I consulted Philo Judaeus and St. Augustine. From Pythagoras to Dante, 10 means completion, perfection; and the Pythagorean progression, 1, 2, 3, 4, whose sum is 10, is the primary, the fundamental sequence. That Milton should accept this idea seemed incontestible: here I had before me instances of the primary sequence and its reverse — dozens in number scattered through PL — were they not open to any ear to hear and any eye to see? Not only were they present but directionally responsive to context, consistently responsive, whether in cross-rhythmic or linear form.

2

It was when Milton seemed to go beyond this primary series by multiplying it by 2 or by 3 that there was departure from tradition, originality in application. I reexamined the occurrences of primary series in cross-rhythmic construction. In this form Milton could extend the "coverage" of the series either by repeating the construction or by expanding the overlaps, or by both processes together. But to multiply a cross-rhythmic series he would have to repeat it in chain form, the number of repetitions being his multiplier.

An excellent example is at PL X, 509-520, where the multiplier of the retrograde series is 3, associated with the triple curse as well as with retributive justice. Notice how series (1) and (2) are expanded in exactly the same way.

[he wonder'd,] but not long	2′—1′
Had leisure, wond'ring at himself now more;	4′+5+3
His visage drawn he felt to sharp and spare,	. . . (1)
His arms clung to his ribs, his legs entwining	2'—1'
Each other, till supplanted down he fell	4′-5+3
A monstrous serpent on his belly prone,	. . . (2)
Reluctant, but in vain, a greater power	2—1'
Now rul'd him, punish'd in the shape he sinn'd,	4′—3
According to his doom: he would have spoke,	2+5—5—1 . . . (3)
But hiss for hiss return'd with forked tongue	
To forked tongue, for now were all transform'd	
Alike,	

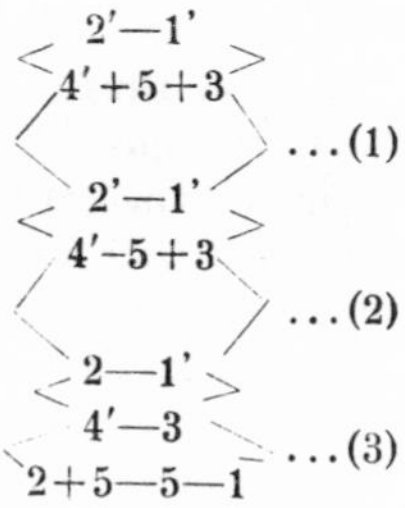

If it is all but impossible to account for these three successive sinister series as chance products, what shall we say of lines 515-516 and their demarcated intervals, which, occurring in the very midst of a negative, descending chain of responsive series, comprise an ascending, positive linear sequence: 1', 2′, 3', 4′ —

Reluctant, but in vain, a greater power
Now rul'd him, punish'd in the shape he sinn'd,

symbolizing the immanence and omnipotence of God? This affirmative progression is enmeshed in a negative rhythmic configuration which symbolizes the punishment administered by God's power. AP 1 —➤ (see above, p. 59) is here superposed on the cross-rhythmic chain (relevant intervals are italicized):

4′-5+*3*	*3*	[1'+2′]	1', 2′	513-515
2—1'	*2—1'*		3'	515-516
4′—3	*4′*		4′	516-517

Similar maneuvers of symbolic envelopment could be found elsewhere in Milton, but not with just these patterns, for the present intention is to gloss a uniquely responsive context. Incidentally, the ascending linear series explains and justifies the commas after "Reluctant" and after "in vain."[1]

3

A much simpler way of extending the coverage of a series would be to multiply a linear 1, 2, 3, 4 or 4, 3, 2, 1 by 2 or by 3, as in the examples cited at the beginning of this chapter. Suppose, however, the multiplier were 4, i.e., there were pauses to demarcate the intervals 4, 8, 12, 16 or 16, 12, 8, 4; must the context, I asked myself, necessarily contain a literal 4, or might 4 carry some symbolic meaning?

According to Philo (*On the Creation,* xvi,xvii) 4 is the number of creation, especially of the heavenly bodies, and specifically the creation of light. "4 was made the starting-point of heaven and the whole world. . . . It was a matter of course that the Maker arrayed the heaven on the fourth day with the light-giving bodies."

Even while I was examining the ancients for traditional meanings, I came on a passage in PL that might have been composed expressly to illustrate Philo. At III, 710-725 Uriel gives an eyewitness report of how at creation darkness and chaos make way for the starry universe. Then "light shone," and with light came order.

At the words, "Confusion heard his voice," begins the downward progression 16, 12, 8', 4′. But the final term, the base-term ("spirited with various forms,"), is simultaneously the first term of the upward progression 4′, 8, 12, 16, which ends appropriately with the words: " . . .. that light / His day," (725).

Where is the sceptic mind that such a sequence would not startle, if not disconcert? First a retrograde, negative response to context, then a direct, positive response, each progression based on Philo's Scriptural number for light: can a sequence like this — 16, 12, 8', 4', 8, 12, 16 — be accident? But if not accident, what is it? The sole alternative seemed to be this: Milton adjusts rhetoric to fit a sequence of intervals — here seven in all — whose numerical values conform to traditional numerology to gloss an expressive context.

Surely something far from trivial was at stake. Surely my hand was near the latch to an unsuspected crypt in the vast mansion of Milton's mind and art. But go warily! Passageways are dim. No hasty judgments or assumptions. First find other multipliers symbolically responsive — find them or forget the quest.

I had not far to look. Less than twenty lines ahead, Book IV begins with a cry, "O for that warning voice!"

The voice is Jehovah's, and Jehovah's number in Scripture is 7. For Philo and St. Augustine the sanctity of 7 is ineffable. Immediately succeeding these five words, and starting with "which he who saw . . .," are pauses that demarcate the following sequence of intervals: 7, 14, 21, 28. Then, after a 7-beat interval, comes a second sequence: 7, 14, 21, 28, starting with "And like a devilish engine . . ." (17—). These two ascending series, separated by 7, fill the entire 31-line paragraph except for the first three beats and the final metric line. Thus the positive cry for Jehovah is prolonged in symbol to cover the whole paragraph. Or put it this way: the paragraph is glossed and re-glossed with the direct number sacred to Jehovah.

Again the question: could pure chance produce this reduplicated sequence — 7, 14, 21, 28 + 7 + 7, 14, 21, 28 — seemingly so perfect a response to context? Between the paragraph's beginning and end are 40 pauses, of which 10, or a fourth of the whole, come at just the right points to define nine intervals arranged in a meaningful, rational pattern. I made a rapid survey of all the intervals contained in Milton's epic verse. Neither of the sequences — 16, 12, 8, 4, 8, 12, 16 nor 7, 14, 21, 28 + 7 + 7, 14, 21, 28 ever recurs. In over 12500 lines each sequence is unique. As mere random number-groups, I reasoned, these sequences could unquestionably be fortuitous. But they are not mere random number-groups. Each is a rational sequence, an opportune mathematical event. Opportune, for each tallies precisely with a contextual situation that seems consciously timed to receive the gloss of a traditional numerical symbol. Moreover, each is an expansion of the primary Pythagorean progressions 1, 2, 3, 4 or 4, 3, 2, 1, whose directional response elsewhere in Milton's verse is so consistent as to be explainable only as conscious adjustment of rhetoric to symbolic progression.

4

Chance, I knew, if given enough scope among unlimited random sequences of numbers, can inevitably, sooner or later, effect any sort of number-grouping whatsoever. But such products of chance are unrelated to any world but the world of random numbers.

Suppose a given limited sequence *s* occurs by chance in a random procession of numbers *(Rr)* produced in some way devoid of meaningful context. Suddenly, however, let us suppose that this random procession is revealed as derived from a context *Rc* created by a purposive mind. If *s* should now be found responsive to a contextual situation in *Rc,* it is *possible,* if the procession of numbers is vast enough, that we might again have a chance-occurrence. But if the odds are against *s* occurring in a limited procession *Rr,* they are much greater against a responsive occurrence in *Rc.* Hence there are double odds against the responsive occurrence of symbolic **16, 12, 8, 4, 8, 12, 16** or symbolic **7, 14, 21, 28** + **7** + **7, 14, 21, 28** merely on the basis of pure chance.

The problem before us, then, is by no means a matter of the mere occurrence of a numerical sequence in a progression of random numbers. We cannot exclude the fact that all rhythmic intervals of an epic poem are involved in the presiding activity of a creative human mind that links context with context, a mind as careful of the management of rhythms as it is of every choice of image and every delineation of character. There is nothing random about this presiding mind. It operates according to motive. It clarifies and orders. It emends and revises and adjusts not only once, but repeatedly, and for reasons known only to itself. This being so, the issue is: Could chance effect a simultaneous conjunction of a uniquely ordered numerical sequence and a contextual situation to which it bears a symbolically responsive relation? Even if we were willing to concede that chance could do it once, could it do it more than once within the limited totality of intervals in Milton's epic verse? Could it do it, as in the present instance, within the compass of 50 lines? Is there not a high probability that the mind that so successfully adjusted the sequence 16, 12, 8, 4, 8, 12, 16 symbolically to a responsive context would try as soon as possible to adjust some other sequence with equal success?

5

But why should numerical symbol be present at all? Why should Milton indulge in it? Without some plausible answer to this question I, for one, would not dare to suggest that these progressions might be a deliberately scribed product of the poet's will. What is the motive? Why take the trouble to adjust rhetoric to a computed sequence that seems meant to transcend both rhetoric and prosody?

In no spirit of assertiveness, I submit that these progressions, and many other examples I shall cite later, are related to the structural rhythmic ideal of Milton's epic paragraph. As we have seen, this rhythmic ideal is that of the polyphonic music which was his lifelong delight, his study and his practice. The researches of Sigmund Spaeth and Ernest Brennecke have made clear how familiar he must have been with every sort of contrapuntal device used in canonic and free fugal music. A man's deepest interests and habits go into all he does, especially if his work includes a masterpiece that occupies the best years of his maturity. If he is schooled in polyphony, look for some of its science in his written style. If he is blessed with a father worthy of all praise and reverence, and that father is not only a creative musician but an admirable business man whose success as scrivener and money-lender must have owed much to a facility in quick arithmetical calculation, why, the son would almost inevitably excel in both music and arithmetic.

Known facts agree with this statement. During Milton's school-days logarithms were invented and enthusiastically explained in textbooks on arithmetic. He tells us that after leaving college he would take trips to London expressly to learn what was new in mathematics and music. We may be sure that the elder Milton was adept in "mensurable music," and imparted what he knew to his precocious son — mensurable music with its application of mathematical proportions to variable tempi of voice-parts in motet and madrigal. Indeed one biographer reports that "by the help of his mathematics he could compose a song . . . ." Unfortunately no such composition by the younger Milton is extant.

Today it is hard to associate these two activities of music and mathematical computation until we realize the arithmetical precision that seems to underlie many of Bach's triumphs in fugue. And remember how the boy Mozart was ablaze with joy not only over fugal music but arithmetical processes. It is recorded that "the house erupted with figures scribbled on every bit of space — walls, floors, tables and chairs. This passion for mathematics is plainly in close alliance with his great contrapuntal facility" (Marcia Davenport: *Mozart,* N. Y., 1932, p. 16).

As for Milton, he was aware not only of Kepler's laws of planetary motion but Kepler's rationalization of the Music of the Spheres. Though he never mentions Descartes, he could not escape a spirit that swept over Europe — Cartesianism — *l'esprit géométrique* — with its faith in mathematics as the guarantor of excellence in art as well as in all clear thinking. For Milton this spirit would be but a reinforcement of Pythagoras' and Plato's apotheosis of mathematics. Why be surprised then if Milton's consummated rhythmic style in measured verse should contain an occasional fusion of two loves: his love for contrapuntal music and his love for mathematical processes?

His problem would be: Just how might such a fusion be brought about? How might mathematical studies be made to serve rhythmic analogues to free polyphony? The answer was: symbol.

A mathematical progression holds together a rational sequence of numbers. If each term in the sequence is a demarcated interval in a Miltonic paragraph, the total metric space covered by a series depends on base-number and type of progression. A progression is an identifiable entity, and it is in motion, moving from low to high or from high to low. If its base-number is 1, it may have only directional significance. If its base is more than 1, it offers an opportunity to the symbolist to endow it with ethical or religious meanings. Some of these meanings may be traditional, older than Holy Writ. Others may be the symbolist's arbitrary assignment, justified, among numerologists, if consistently employed.

Well may the reader smile or sneer at the vagaries of numerical symbolists. Yet when we consider that whole periods of history have been shaken and molded by passionate defenders of certain numerical symbols, we must regard the subject as worthy of serious thought. Part of the Jewish Cabala, and many places in both Jewish and Christian Scripture are intensely concerned with symbolic numbers. Milton was aware of that concern. As a poet with a sacred theme, he was ready to exploit it. His attitude would have been confirmed by the mystic cults of Greek philosophy, especially that of Pythagoras, who ascribed special meanings to all numbers from 1 to 10.

But I suspect it was a subject which an "enlightened" man of Milton's era did not care to discuss at large. If, like Milton, he believed Scripture to be literal and all-sufficient revelation of the divine, he could not help pondering mystic meanings of numbers scattered up and down the various books. To identify oneself with a pious mind of 1650 is to be automatically something of a numerologist.

Return now to the Miltonic paragraph as a rhythmic analogue to a piece of contrapuntal music. In motet or madrigal a voice can enter at any point and go out at any point. It may move independently of other voices. The rhythmic scheme of its melody may differ entirely from that of other voices it overlaps. As for tempo, it may bear toward the basic measure a different proportion from that of other voices. For instance, the basic measure may be in duple time, and two or three voices may be performing fugally in that time, while across those voices, even singing different words, a voice in triple time may enter and leave. The effect may well be rich, complex, even bewildering. This was the sort of "mensurable music" Milton learned from his father and from available treatises on musical theory.

Entirely plausible therefore would seem the suggestion that a numerical progression, definable by punctuated intervals in the Miltonic paragraph, is the result of conscious adjustment whose purpose is to simulate the presence of an individual cross-rhythmic "voice" performing independently of other cross-rhythmic "voices."

6

The analogue at once justifies and supplies a motive for the joint employment of mathematical progressions and numerical symbol. The multiplier of the primary linear series 1, 2, 3, 4 and 4, 3, 2, 1 makes available a number that causes the progression to have more than directional individuality. The number, if symbolic, endows the progression with an ethic, hence with something like the human personality of a part-singer performing in a skilled musical ensemble round a Bread Street table. If we should find in Milton's paragraphs more than a few progressions based on a variety of numbers, and these numbers should bear a consistent symbolic response to context, we might indeed uncover something like a *system* of symbol.

But not too fast. The very sugestion is over-bold, and should be followed up with the utmost caution. For Milton left us no treatise, and precious few hints, regarding the rhythmic structure of his paragraph. There are secrets in his technique, but we can go no further than inference grounded on indirect evidence.

What we can say with assurance is that the proposed analogue furnishes a motive consistent with Milton's era, with his private studies, his passion for polyphonic music, and his acknowledged interest in mathematics.

What fields of mathematics did Milton study? Why did he study it? What use did he make of it? The present rhythmic phenomena suggest an answer. He studied proportions and progressions, subjects on which every book he knew in mathematics, even more than the treatises he knew on musical theory, would have specially emphasized. More about them later.

What I would repeat here is that the numerical sequences we have found, against whose chance-occurrence the odds seem to be so great, do not exist merely in the impersonal world of pure mathematics, but in a world of human motives, of ideals of art, of ethical values. And to discuss them at all we must first imagine ourselves in the intellectual climate of the England of three hundred years ago.

7

Consider, then, each of Milton's epic paragraphs to be, rhythmically, a finished contrapuntal piece. When we find (i) precisely demarcated intervals that fit a numerical progression, and (ii) its direction and base-number symbolically responsive to context, I suggest that this progression has been consciously scribed as an analogue to a cross-rhythmic voice in polyphonic music. Just as such a voice may enter at any point of pause and depart at any point, so may such a progression. Again, as a musical theme may, in canonic forms, be reversed into retrograde pattern and motion, so a progression may be ascending or descending, or, to use the canonic terms, direct or retrograde. Being a multiple of the primary Pythagorean series 1, 2, 3, 4 or 4, 3, 2, 1, its expected length is four terms. If it goes beyond this number, we must not be surprised to find that it is a functional response to some unusual feature of the context.

Now it would be impossible to regard the Miltonic paragraph as a rhythmic analogue to a contrapuntal piece of music if there were any paragraphs that begin or end in midline. But every one of Milton's four hundred paragraphs starts with the metric line and ends with it. Though this feature has hitherto gone unregarded, it is an important fact, for it evidences more than Milton's incessant care to preserve his basic measure. It proves his determination that the rhythms of the whole paragraph be one unified and completed performance, a congeries of rival cross-rhythms responsive to ever-varying contextual situations. As I showed in a previous chapter, he will at times even give special care to the very count of syllables in response to context. But he never relaxes his hold on the total piece.

To see how perfectly integrated are the rhythms of each paragraph, observe that editors who take liberties with the text never re-paragraph at a point in midline. They are very seldom even tempted. Milton gives them no opportunity. Only two or three paragraphs contain midline pauses that might suggest such a division.

This is a phenomenon that contradicts expectation, for it occurs in verse whose rate of enjambement and consequent frequency of interior pause greatly exceeds the practices of other poets, although many of these poets, especially of the 19th century, often start paragraphs in midline. But Milton's unprecedented rate of enjambement, the studied variety and management of his overlap-lengths, his steady safeguarding of the basic measure by means both direct and indirect — these characteristics, added to an obstinate avoidance even of opportunity to start and end paragraphs in midline, are parts of one consistent rhythmic program. They make little sense apart from that program, whose purpose is to create a rhythmic analogue to a finished contrapuntal piece.

It is Milton's invention. It has proved inimitable. For it is a product of more than rhetoric and prosody, of more than one discipline. It fuses the devices of more than one art. The poet of *Lycidas* and *At a Solemn Music* collaborates with the master of fugal and canonic forms. Milton's unsurpassable definition of fugue at PL XI, 561-563 is surely meant by him to apply to the rhythmic method of his epic style as well as to polyphonic music.

But that style probably contains, I submit, even more of him than the rhetorician, the prosodist, and the skilled contrapuntist. It gives him opportunities to make covert use of his mathematical studies. The reader shall judge if the evidence, limited as it must be in a book necessarily restricted in size, warrants anything more than a probability. The evidence is inferential: it must be sought in certain sequences of rhythm that are related symbolically to context with varying degrees of aptness and consistency, yet with so much aptness and consistency that it seems immeasurably harder to ascribe them to chance than to conscious calculation.

8

Before presenting more of this evidence I must mention another of Milton's opportunities to apply polyphonic analogue to the rhythms of his paragraph.

In many a musical composition of the 16th and 17th centuries the singers do not stop at the end of the score but return to the beginning and continue. Today we still mark such a procedure by D.C. (*da capo*) and show by other signs just how much of the score is to be repeated before the finale. But sometimes a composer of canon is ingenious enough to fashion a theme that can dispense with a finale: three or more overlapping parts may each continue round and round the piece, good taste alone determining the number of repetitions. This is "perpetual canon," or, as musicologists also term it, a "round."

Illustrations are now accessible in most large libraries. One of the elder Milton's friends, Thomas Ravenscroft, published, during the poet's infancy, three books of rounds: *Pammelia* (1609), *Deuteromelia* (1609), and *Melismata* (1611), and the best things in them have been reprinted in *Pammelia and Other Rounds and*

Catches by Peter Warlock (Oxford, 1928). Another and more diversified collection is *Euterpe Round Book, Fifty English Rounds, Catches, and Canons of the 16th and 17th Centuries,* ed. by C. K. Scott (London, 1913).

The words of some of these rounds are of very serious character. Henry Lawes's three-part "I wept and chastened myself" (Scott, No. 36) is based on the same lament for Absolom (2 Sam. xviii. 33) which the elder Milton had set for a five-part anthem. And William Lawes's four-part "She weepeth sore in the night" (Scott, No. 30) is a round based on the same opening dirge of Lamentations which the elder Milton had set for a six-part anthem. Such a relationship of the Lawes brothers' rounds with the elder Milton's most ambitious contrapuntal work is a casual but significant reminder of the poet's intimate association with those whose cultural meat and drink were the rhythmic devices of polyphony.

Illustrations of other serious rounds in Scott's collection are Thomas Ford's "Haste thee, O Lord" (No. 33) and "Look down, O Lord" (No. 34), each for three voices, and William Byrd's canon, "Non nobis Domine" (No. 24). We can almost visualize a group of singers at the elder Milton's table occupied wholeheartedly with this round of Byrd's, which is indeed a marvel of vocal beauty and polyphonic ingenuity, with perhaps the composer present (he lived till 1623), himself directing the repetitions and determining their number. And then, to lighten the atmosphere, he might have the eager singers turn to another round of his, delightful and skilfully wrought, "Hey ho, to the greenwood" (Scott, No. 23).

Now in many a Miltonic paragraph are responsive numerical progressions recognizable only if we think of it as in perpetual canon, i.e., potentially infinite, the first line being regarded as a continuation of the last. Since each paragraph is a self-contained rhythmic entity, Milton does not run progressions over from paragraph to paragraph. Unless therefore he should adopt the analogue of perpetual canon, it would be impossible for a progression, if its base-number should be of any size, to start late in the paragraph.

Observe a few examples.

9

Descriptions of military maneuvers in PL are likely to contain rhythmic groupings of special symmetry. In the short 6-line paragraph at IV, 782-787 Gabriel issues an order to Uzziel: "Half these draw off, . . .". This 2-beat interval starts an ascending arithmetical progression: 2, 4, 6, 8, the last term ending with the words ". . . From these," (786). The process of drawing off half the guard causes the other half to be deployed in the opposite direction, or, as Milton puts it: "Half wheeling to the shield, half to the spear" (785).

Arithmetic parallels the maneuver, but only on the condition that we observe the analogue of perpetual canon, i.e., regard the end and the beginning of the paragraph as continuous. Starting at the same 2-beat interval ("half these draw off,"), and counting backward, we find pauses that demarcate 2, 4, 6, 8. In other words, there is present a retrograde as well as a direct progression, each based on the same number, 2.

Now the retrograde progression, moving from highest to lowest term in the direction of the rhetoric, starts with the fourth term (of 8 beats) — with the words, "As flame they part, etc." (784-). But this is also the fourth term reached by the direct progression. Therefore these two antithetic progressions have two terms in common, the first and the fourth, which are at opposite poles of a circular rhythmic continuum. The antithetic series interlock in such a way as to girdle the paragraph, base-term *a* being at Pole p′, and fourth term *d* at Pole p″.

Let us describe the direct series as $\overrightarrow{a\ b\ c\ d}$, and the retrograde series as $\overleftarrow{d\ c\ b\ a}$. Then they interlock at Pole p′:

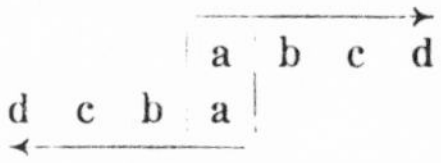

$$\begin{array}{ccccccc} & & & \overrightarrow{a\ \ b\ \ c\ \ d} \\ \overleftarrow{d\ \ c\ \ b\ \ a} & & & \end{array}$$

and at Pole p″:

$$\begin{array}{cc} \overrightarrow{a\ \ b\ \ c\ \ d} & \\ & \overleftarrow{d\ \ c\ \ b\ \ a} \end{array}$$

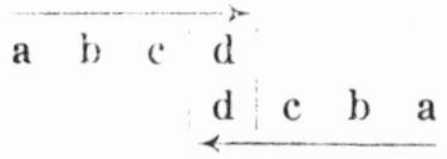

Pole p′ is thus the center of symmetry in the sequence of symmetry 8, 6, 4, 2, 4, 6, 8, and Pole p″ is the center of symmetry in the sequence 2, 4, 6, *8*, 6, 4, 2.

We are led to think of the integrated pattern as circular:

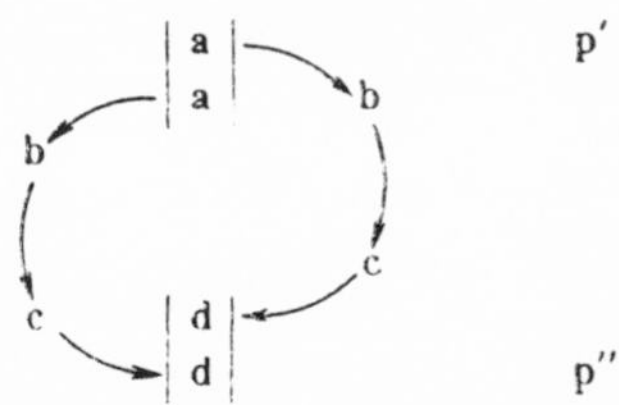

Gabriel's very diction seems indeed to confirm this dynamic configuration, for see how his command, "Our *circuit* meets full west," immediately precedes the *d*-term, which is common area of overlap for each circuiting progression.

Picturing the rhythms thus, we are aware that Gabriel's command, "half these draw off" (term *a*), finds its fulfilment — "As flame they part / Half wheeling . . ." (term *d*) — facing it at the opposite pole, and the words of fulfilment are reached simultaneously by two progressions moving toward it from opposite directions.

Such precision in the ordonnance of rhythms is beyond controversy, is verifiable in any text, and is comprehensible only on the ground that Milton's paragraph is a contrapuntal analogue performing in perpetual canon with mathematical progressions free to begin at any pause and end at any pause. Milton is emulating the cross-rhythmic interplay of voices in motet and madrigal. So responsive are the progressions to the very special context that we are safe in declaring: Milton here chooses a specific paragraph-*length* with a conscious purpose — to effect responsive interlocking of two antithetic progressions. They could not be so managed in a paragraph of 5 lines, say, or 7, or 8. For a short paragraph the lines must number 6 precisely.

Or put the case thus. If we designate paragraph-length as *n*, and the progression as AP, then in this paragraph the girdling interlock AP 2 $\rightleftarrows$> is directly related to — depends on — Milton's choice of *n*. As a function of *n*, the interlock is restricted to the multiplier 2. At the same time *n* may be regarded as a function of the multiplier, for every choice of n may depend on a premeditated plan to scribe an interlock based on a number factorially related to $5n$.

Now if this particular girdling interlock were a unique rhythmic phenomenon, if there were nothing just like it elsewhere in Milton, I would count it a foible of chance, and toss it into the dustbin of curiosa. But when I can lay beside it instances of similar phenomena, I judge it fair, at this stage of our inquiry, to advance the following proposition: At least in *some* of his paragraphs Milton has consciously scribed mathematical series, to which he has adjusted his rhetoric in such a way that the series respond, directionally at least, to the immediate context.

But there is still more to note about the two antithetic series. Each is infinite in extent.

If we start with the words, "half these draw off," we find pauses that accommodate the following intervals: 2, 4, 6, 8, 6, 4, the last four-beat interval returning us to where we started. Let us now reduce this sequence to Pythagorean simplicity by dividing it by 2. We get 1, 2, 3, 4, 3, 2. Since the paragraph is in perpetual canon, this sequence becomes a continuum:

1, 2, 3, 4, 3, 2 1, 2, 3, 4, 3, 2 1, 2, 3, 4, 3, 2 1, 2, 3, . .

which yields continued series both direct and retrograde:

$$1, 2, 3, 4, \quad \overbrace{3, 2,} \quad \overbrace{1, 2, 3,} \quad \overbrace{4, 3,} \quad \overbrace{2, 1, 2, 3,} \; \ldots . \text{ and}$$

$$\ldots . \; \overbrace{3, 2, 1, 2} \quad \overbrace{3, 4,} \quad \overbrace{3, 2, 1,} \quad \overbrace{2, 3,} \quad 4, 3, 2, 1$$

or,

1, 2, 3, 4, 5, 6, 7, 8, ... and . . . . 8, 7, 6, 5, 4, 3, 2, 1.

Multiply by 2 to recover the intervals present in the text:
2, 4, 6, 8, 10, 12, 14, 16, ... and . . . . 16, 14, 12, 10, 8, 6, 4, 2.

Why, in the present paragraph, should Milton scribe infinitely continuous series? Because he is depicting supernatural beings whose modes of motion transcend the finite. These antithetic progressions mirror the manner of Cherubic deployment ("As flame they part"—784): he conceives their winged shapes as separating in flaming arcs capable of perpetual rotation.

Perhaps as a mathematical by-product of this rotatory symmetry is a second sequence of symmetry. Observe that the 5-beat interval, "As flame they part / Half wheeling to the shield," (784—) is a center of symmetry. On each side of it are pauses that demarcate the following intervals: 3,9,1,9,3. Hence the sequence of symmetry:

. . . 5, 3, 9, 1, 9, 3, *5*, 3, 9, 1, 9, 3, . . .

The five intervals on each side of *5* form a symmetrical number-group with 1 ("Uzziel") at the center. The result is bilateral within bilateral symmetry mirroring the military precision of Angelic maneuver.

10

A structural duplicate, almost rhythm by rhythm, of the paragraph just cited is at PL X, 610-615. Sin and Death betake them "several ways"; immediately, at the words "Both to destroy" (611), starts AP 2 ⟶. Simultaneously this 2-beat interval is the base-term of AP 2 ⟵. The antithetic series girdle the paragraph: at Pole p′ is "Both to destroy"; at Pole p″ is the 8-beat term *d*: "which th' Almighty seeing / From his transcendent seat the Saints among," —

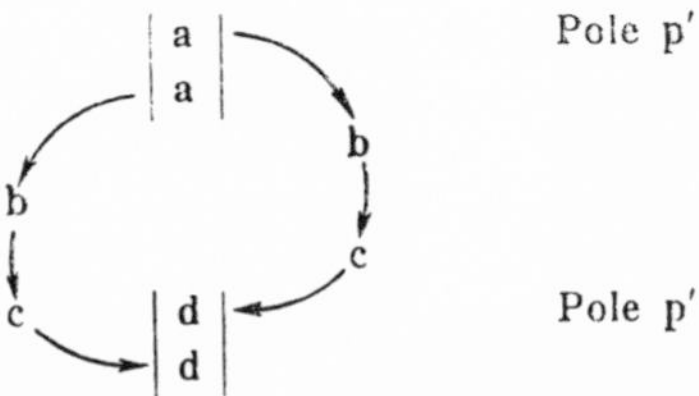

Thus the two arithmetical series "betake them" in opposite directions starting from term *a*, in perfect response to "several ways," "several" here meaning two. Though the base-term may be responsive to "several" and to "Both," there is a computational reason why it would have to be 2, just as in the military paragraph at PL IV, 782-787. Given $n = 6$, no base-number but 2 could effect this design of girdling interlock.

Moreover, each series, as in the military paragraph, is infinite. For, if we start with "Both to destroy," we find pauses that demarcate the following sequence of intervals: 2, 4, 6, 8, 6, 4, the last 4-beat interval returning us to where we started. Now divide by 2, getting 1, 2, 3, 4, 3, 2. Extend to a continuum: 1, 2, 3, 4, 3, 2, 1, 2, 3, 4, 3, 2, 1, ..., whence the unlimited series: 1, 2, 3, 4, 5, 6, 7, . . . and . . . 7, 6, 5, 4, 3, 2, 1; and, multiplying by 2 to recover the intervals in the text: 2, 4, 6, 8, 10, 12, 14, . . . and . . . 14, 12, 10, 8, 6, 4, 2.

Notice that the contextual situations at the opposite poles are antithetic: at *a* are Sin and Death bent on destruction; at *d* the Almighty's observant eye. And Sin and Death are bent on *unlimited* destruction, while "His transcendent seat" implies transcendent reaches on all sides, so that very aptly the retrograde series starts from a quantity exceeding any conceivable value; and if we start at any multiple of the fourth term we start at this very interval expressing the Almighty's inconceivable vision.

Such repetition of paragraph structure with rhythmic response to context all but establishes the proposition that at least in *some* of his paragraphs Milton consciously scribes mathematical series, adjusting his rhetoric to them in such a way that they are directionally responsive to context.

In the present paragraph the directional response is even more artfully apt than in the military paragraph. For the antithetic series respond to (i) the opposite ways taken by Sin and Death, and (ii) the antipodal images of Sin and Death vs. the Almighty observing all they do.

[At this point I prefer to bracket an observation, for its basis is strictly inferential. Its validity, which can be referred back to Scripture, rests on seemingly valid numerical responses in other paragraphs. The observation is this: elsewhere in Milton the number 8 seems to symbolize Providence, or society under God's providence. Here the 8-beat term at Pole p'' certainly expresses God's all-seeing, foreseeing eye. We might expect such a symbolic number to be the *base* of a progression, as indeed it is in certain longer paragraphs of PL. Here it is the head-term of the retrograde progression, and its position in a girdling interlock puts it in polar antithesis to the base-number of the antithetic progression: the all-seeing eye vs. the object of vigilance.]

11

In PL VI are other examples of sequences of symmetry that respond to military action. In the very short paragraph at 127-130 Abdiel, at the sight of Satan in rebellious array, "Forth stepping opposite, half way he met / His daring foe," (128-129). The last seven words (4 beats) are precisely "half way" in the paragraph: backward to the beginning are 8 beats; forward to the end are 8. "Half way he met / His daring foe" is the base-term of both AP 4 ⟶ and AP 4 ⟵, each series girdling the paragraph twice and terminating where it starts. The retrograde series — 16, 12, 8, 4 — starts at "at this prevention . . ." (129—).

At PL VI, 558-567 Satan cries, "Vanguard, to right and left the front unfold." These five beats are a center of symmetry: on each side the same numerical sequence "unfolds," each unfolded sequence containing its own center of symmetry, and repeating itself indefinitely:

. . . . | 1, 4, 3, 4, 6, 4, 3, 2, 3, 3, 4, 6, 4, 3, | 1, 4, 3, 4, 6, 4, 3, 2, 3, 3, 4, 6, 4, 3, | 1, 4, ...

5 (1, 4) . . . *5* (2, 3) . . . *5* (1, 4) . . . *5* (2, 3) . . . *5* (1, 4)

3, 4, *6*, 4, 3	3, 4, *6*, 4, 3	3, 4, *6*, 4, 3	3, 4, *6*, 4, 3
[= 20]	[= 20]	[= 20]	[= 20]

(Vertical lines denote paragraph-beginning.) Notice that not only does each group of 20 beats between the 5's have its own "unfolding" to right and left betokening smart maneuver, but 6 is in each case the center of symmetry — 6 in response to the "hollow" 6-sided "cube" of line 552 in the preceding paragraph.

In this latter paragraph — at VI, 537-557 — Satan's host approaches "in hollow cube / Training his devilish enginery" (552—). The 6-beat interval that succeeds — "impal'd / On every side with shadowing squadrons deep" (553—) — is the center of symmetry: on either side of it radiates the sequence of intervals:

6, 10, 12, 11, 5, 3, 5, 3, 5, 11, 12, 10, 6

which contains its own center of symmetry: *5*. The whole continuum of intervals is:

. . . 10,6,*6*,6,10,12,11,5,3,*5*,3,5,11,12,10,6,*6*,6,10,12,11,5,3,*5*,3,5,11,12,10,6, . . .

(543-544) (553-554) (543-544)

Again bilateral within bilateral symmetry mirroring precision of military movement. Note the prominence of 6's: 6, number of sides to each cube. Not only is it the principal center of symmetry but it flanks each sequence of symmetry on either side.

Accurate counting and placing of intervals is not restricted to the shorter paragraphs. In the 113-line paragraph at PL VIII, 66-178 Raphael gives a lecture on astronomy. "What if the sun / Be center to the World," (122—): this 5-beat interval starts at a point as near to the center of the paragraph as can be calculated. The paragraph contains 565 beats. Exactly 283 beats precede Raphael's remark.

12

We have practically no direct testimonial evidence about the secrets of Milton's craft. The evidence we adduce must be circumstantial, and, to carry conviction, must pass the test of remorseless questions like the following: (1) Can these recurrent rhythmic phenomena be explained away as chance-products? (2) Is the symbolic response of a multiplier of the primary series 1, 2, 3, 4 or 4, 3, 2, 1 consistent with responses of the same multiplier found in other paragraphs?

In the example last given, which involves response not of symbolic number to context but merely of numerical reference in the context to location among beats, the odds against chance would seem overwhelming. If there were an abundance of 113-line paragraphs, and if the contexts of many of these paragraphs were concerned with astronomy, then, given enough paragraphs on astronomy of this precise length — it being understood that the poet entirely ignores numerical response — sooner or later the statement concerning the sun's centrality might be expected to fall at the paragraph's exact center. But there is only one 113-line paragraph in all Milton's blank verse, and this of all paragraphs is a lecture on astronomy. That there should begin, at the exact center of this lecture, the significant words declaring centrality makes it more than probable that an ordering mind willed such an adjustment of numerical count to contextual situation.

We cannot ignore the logic of it: if Milton can be shown beyond all reasonable doubt to have fingered and computed the beats within a single one of his paragraphs for the purpose of effecting response of numbers to context, then we are right, we are compelled, to expect similar fingerings in other paragraphs.

It follows also that if symbolic responses are present, based on progressions covering a goodly number of metric lines, then Milton must have composed his verse — as his biographer says he did — by dictating a more or less sustained group at every sitting, indeed an entire rounded paragraph whenever possible. He did not create as Virgil did, line by line, nor as Shakespeare did, "with that easinesse, that wee have scarce received from him a blot in his papers." Nor are we to understand in any literal sense Milton's tribute to his Muse, who he says "inspires / Easy my unpremeditated verse." Easy — yes, in the morning's outpour of ten to forty lines. But he takes the rest of the day to enrich them with after-thoughts, to file and emend, to "pencil it over with all the curious touches of art, even to the perfection of a faultless picture."

13

One of the commonest concepts inevitably recurrent in such fables as those of PL and PR is power, strength, force (and the antithesis: weakness, impotence). Milton's numerical symbol, based on Pythagorean tradition, is 5 or any multiple of 5.

Numerologists are full of vagaries about 5. The Pythagoreans did not fix it to one meaning. In the first place it was their number for marriage, being the sum of the first masculine number (3) and the first feminine (2). In several striking passages, as we shall see, Milton certainly seems to adopt this meaning. But even more prevalent with the Pythagoreans was a second meaning, derived from a mystic geometric figure, the pentagram (= a pentagon with a five-pointed star inscribed), which served as emblem of their esoteric brotherhood, and symbolized "health."[2] The letters *υ, γ, ι, ει, α* were placed in order at its five outer points. *ὑγίεια* means soundness of body and mind; hence vigor, strength; hence power, force in general.

Perhaps the ease with which progressions based on 5 could be adjusted to cross-rhythmic construction influenced Milton's choice of a symbol for power. Illustrations will make this clear.

The eleven lines at PL VI, 856 ff., climaxing Satan's defeat on the celestial battlefield, contain the only patch of cross-rhythmic construction in the entire 43-line paragraph (see analysis in Appendix II). Messiah's weapons have reduced the Satanic host to impotence. Numerical symbol responds in an arrangement of pauses that demarcate a retrograde arithmetical series based on 5: AP 5 ←.

But the response is very specific rather than merely general. A functional, dramatic flaw in the series is injected at just the narrative point of catastrophe, the culminant point of the paragraph.

[The overthrown he rais'd,]
                                        and as a herd   2—5—4
Of goats or timorous flock together throng'd   20
Drove them before him thunder-struck, pursu'd   1—5—3
With terrors and with furies to the bounds
And crystal wall of Heav'n, which op'ning wide,   2—1'
Roll'd inward, and a spacious gap disclos'd   4'—3   15'
Into the wasteful Deep; the monstrous sight   5'
Strook them with horror backward, but far worse   2'—2
Urg'd them behind; headlong themselves they threw   3—3   10'
Down from the verge of Heav'n, Eternal Wrath   7
Burnt after them to the bottomless pit.

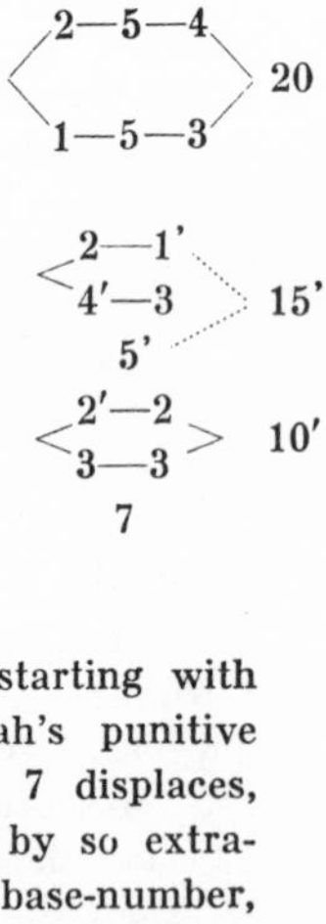

The normal nadir-term would of course be 5, starting with "Eternal Wrath." But "Eternal Wrath" is Jehovah's punitive might, and Jehovah's sacred number is 7. Hence 7 displaces, obliterates 5. Indeed normal descent is interdicted by so extraordinary a context. The series bypasses the expected base-number, becomes suddenly bottomless by virtue of Jehovah's number of eternality. Eternal Wrath burns away the wonted bounds of number and the very laws of proportion.

Thus we can untie the most notorious prosodic knot in Milton, if not in all English verse: How shall we read line 866? Any way we like — is the answer. It doesn't matter how we pronounce "bottomless" — not when the frame of things, words and numbers as well as Satanic legions, are crashing to chaos. Wrench accent to suit metre, or violate metre to preserve accent: in either case anomalous utterance is as inescapable as Satan's fall.

. . . . .

In the 9-line paragraph at PR IV, 551-559 Satan challenges Christ to prove his power as Son of Omnipotence. Let him maintain his stand atop the Temple's highest point. If we start at the exact central beat of the paragraph — at the word "safely" (555), which marks indeed the paragraph's center of symmetry, its "highest pinnacle," we find a sequence of intervals that define an arithmetical series based on 5, a series that continues to ascend without end: 5, 10, 15, 20, 25, . . . Let us express infinity by ∞; the series may then be represented as AP $5 \longrightarrow \infty$.

Again, if we start 4 beats behind the point where AP $5 \longrightarrow \infty$ starts, i.e., at the pause after "progeny" (554), and count backward, we find the very same sequence of intervals: 5, 10, 15, 20, 25, ... Hence there is present the retrograde series AP $5 \longleftarrow \infty$: . . . 25, 20, 15, 10, 5. Its fifth term starts with the words, "in their hands . . ." (557—), its fourth term with the words, "highest is best, . . ." (553—); its base-term is: "highest is best, / Now show thy progeny;" (553-554).

The 4-beat interval between the two base-numbers states the issue: "if not to stand, / Cast thyself down;" (554-555). Has Christ the *power* to stand, or is he so *powerless* as to cast himself down? And if he should do it, has he the power to do it safely?

Now since the power of God is here involved, each series, both direct and retrograde, is appropriately infinite. Let us see how the pause-arrangement brings this result about, and how the antithetic series are interlocked, creating centers of symmetry at opposite poles.

If we start at "safely" (555) we find pauses that demarcate the following sequence of 5 and multiples of 5: 5, 10, 15, 15; and the final 15 returns us to where we started. Reduce this sequence to lowest terms by dividing by 5, and we get 1, 2, 3, 3. Since the paragraph is a rhythmic continuum (in perpetual canon), we extend this sequence indefinitely to: 1, 2, 3, 3, 1, 2, 3, 3, 1, 2, . . . which yields: 1, 2, 3, $\overbrace{3, 1}$, $\overbrace{2, 3}$, $\overbrace{3, 1, 2}$, $\overbrace{3, 3, 1}$, . . ., i.e., the primary

Pythagorean progression extended to ∞: 1, 2, 3, 4, 5, 6, 7, . . . Let us now restore the multiplier 5 to recover the intervals actually present in the text: 5, 10, 15, 20, 25, 30, 35, . . .

In exactly the same way, if we start 4 beats behind where AP 5 $\longrightarrow \infty$ starts, i.e., at the pause after "progeny" (554) and proceed backward, we find the same sequence, but retrograde (AP 5 $\longleftarrow \infty$). Arithmetically, it moves in the opposite direction to AP 5 $\longrightarrow \infty$.

To define either of these progressions in this 9-line paragraph requires a minimum of three terms. $\overrightarrow{\text{a b c}}$ . . . defines AP 5 $\longrightarrow \infty$, and . . . $\overleftarrow{\text{c b a}}$ defines AP 5 $\longleftarrow \infty$. If the reader will trace each of the three-term sequences in the text, he will notice that the two series overlap to the extent of sharing 11 beats in term *c*. We may call the resultant pattern an interlock in which the overlapping term *c* is displaced by 4 beats. Let δ stand for displacement.

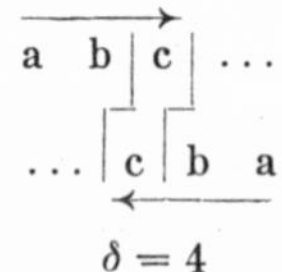

$\delta = 4$

The pattern creates a sequence of symmetry whose center is 11:

S. of Sym.: 5, 6, 4, *11*, 4, 6, 5 (Pole p′)

This *S. of Sym.* starts with the words: "safely if Son . . ." (555).

If there were no displacement, i.e., if all of *c* were shared by both series, the *S. of Sym.* would be 5, 10, *15*, 10, 5, and would exactly girdle the paragraph; term *c* (15) would be at one pole, and at the opposite pole would be the point of tangency between the two base-terms. But the displacement of 4 beats in the direction away from the base-terms leaves an interval of 4 beats between them. Thus the center of symmetry at Pole p″ is this 4-beat interval:

11, 4, 6, 5, *4*, 5, 6, 4, 11

The rotational symmetry of the two interlocking antithetic progressions may be expressed thus:

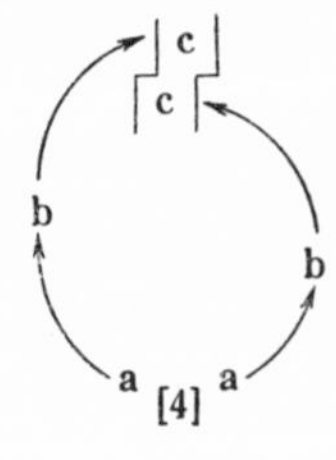

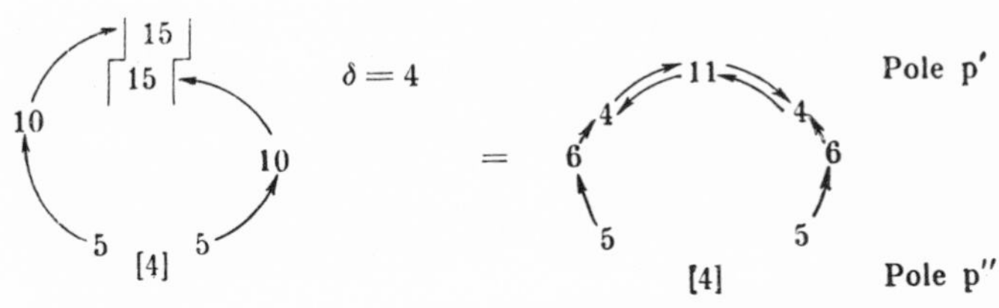

The center of symmetry at Pole p′ is: "lest at any time . . . There stand, if thou wilt stand;" at Pole p″ the center of symmetry is: "if not to stand, / Cast thyself down." Note that the very concepts expressed at opposite poles are antithetic: to stand vs. not to stand.

The reader who has checked the above analysis with the text wonders how much of it Milton was conscious of. Other paragraphs, as in illustrations already cited, show beyond doubt that in ordering his rhythms (i) he sometimes creates sequences of symmetry *as such* in response to appropriate contextual situations; (ii) he sometimes locks antithetic progressions, a process that results in sequences of symmetry as an inevitable by-product; (iii) he regards each paragraph as a finished contrapuntal piece in which numerical progressions perform analogously to cross-rhythmic voices in the rhythmic continuum of a perpetual canon.

In the present paragraph the antithetic series — AP $5 \longrightarrow \infty$ and AP $5 \longleftarrow \infty$ — are adjusted to the rhetoric with such neat precision, and so aptly does the clash of symbolic $5 \longrightarrow$ vs. $5 \longleftarrow$ respond to the contextual clash of power vs. powerlessness, that one more than hesitates to give chance any credit for the configuration. Besides, it should be made known that this is the only AP $5 \genfrac{}{}{0pt}{}{\longrightarrow \infty}{\longleftarrow \infty} >$ which I have found in all Milton's epic verse. That such an interlock should *happen* to occur in just this paragraph where it is symbolically responsive is, to me at least, almost unthinkable.

For a paragraph as short as this we can only surmise what practical method of mental arithmetic Milton employed to fix the places of pause. He might well have blue-printed and visualized the rhythms as a circular E-chain of cross-rhythmic construction. Such construction, starting with "safely if Son of God: . . ." (555), is as follows:

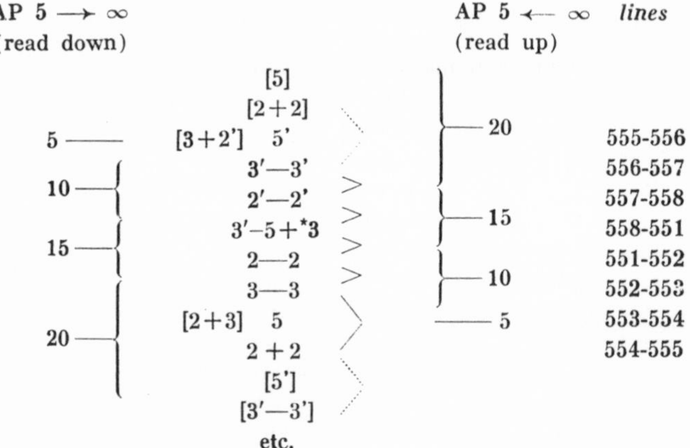

* = start of paragraph.

Inspection of this E-chain shows instantly that pauses are demarcated for AP 5 —→ and AP 5 ←—, with 4 beats separating the base-terms.

14

Mammon's speech at PL II, 229-283 is scribed over with progressions based on multiples of 5. If we start with "him to unthrone . . ." (231—) we find pauses demarcating AP 10 —→ to six terms: 10, 20, 30', 40'', 50', 60, ending with "... magnificence;" (271). Starting 30 beats ahead of where this AP 10 —→ starts, is a second AP 10 —→, also carried to six terms: 10', 20'', 30', 40,

50, 60'. It begins with "Suppose he should relent . . ." (237—) and ends with " . . . peaceful counsels," (279).

As a contrapuntal analogue, the second progression is in flight from — in fugal association with — the first, 30 beats always separating them. The rival progressions are extended beyond the usual four terms, partly perhaps in order to cover most of the paragraph. But a third progression, based on a still larger multiple of 5, more than circuits the paragraph. AP 15 → starts with "ye have what I advise . . ." (283—), goes to seven terms (15, 30, 45', 60'', 75', 90, 105), and ends at the dead stop after "servile pomp" (257).[3]

If these three base-numbers — 10,10, and 15 — symbolize power, as they seem to do in many another progression, they are indeed an appropriate gloss to Mammon's plea: "Let us live to ourselves . . . Free, and to none accountable." Isolationist, pacifist, optimist, he advocates strength that comes from self-reliance. He promises mastery over all circumstance. His thoughts are grandiose: the recurrent expansion of these fugal series seems to be a response to such grandiosity. And there seems to be special significance in the unusual number of terms to which AP 15 → is carried: 7, number of Jehovah himself, whom Mammon would emulate.

. . . .

Inferable from many scattered progressions, the symbolic meaning of 17 is that of 7 aggrandized by 10. In fact it seems to be a rule that when 10 is added to any number it merges the meaning of that number with the Pythagorean meaning of 10 (completeness or perfection). 17 would then symbolize *perfect* divinity or sovereignty. At PL VIII, 561-594 Raphael expounds the transcendent merit of true love as distinguishable from carnal passion, the true love that "hath his seat / In reason . . . and is the scale / By which to heavenly love thou may'st ascend." Such love equates with God: hence the number of God is in the base-number of AP 17 → (17, 34', 51'', 68'), which starts with the first word of the paragraph and ends with the last.

But a second AP 17 → overlaps the first. It starts at "For what admir'st thou, . . ." (567—), runs to four terms — 17', 34'', 51'', 68' — and ends where it starts. In this symbolic way the angel repeatedly glosses his definition of true love as divine. Each series exactly girdles the paragraph, i.e., everything Raphael has to say on this head comes within the compass of what is fully communicable only by symbol.

15

Though tempted to multiply illustrations, I shall give space only to a sufficient number to establish a probability that Milton consciously demarcates pauses to accommodate symbolic progressions. Well do I realize that when we set foot on the hills of symbolic interpretation we exchange security in a land of the conventionally rational for a trail where every next step is a risk. Boldness may lead to the disaster of self-deception. Discreetest circumspection may terminate upon isolated crags of wishful thinking. Even level paths may prove delusions, imagined landmarks turn out to be mockeries of chance.

If we had some direct testimony from Milton himself, or from any man or woman associated with him while he created his epic paragraphs; if we had someone's inadvertent remark that he had a flair for symbolic numbers; then I would not hesitate to offer many pages of examples showing interlocking symbolic series, all of which, without overstraining contextual meanings, would appear more or less consistently responsive. But I prefer merely to put into the reader's hands sufficient material for him to draw his own inferences.

Milton is a 17th-century man versed in Jewish as well as Christian lore, very probably familiar with the Serif Yetsirah of the Jewish Cabala as well as with the speculations of Christian Cabalists of both Italy and England. He knows Plato's excursions into numerical symbol, St. Augustine's, Dante's. He knows Scripture by heart. If Newton, prince of mathematicians, could, a generation later, devote years of pious thought to calculations based on what he firmly believed to be Scriptural revelations, including fiery furnace and Noah's ark, it surely is neither incongruous nor ridiculous for us to keep an open mind to the suggestion that Milton employs a system of numerical symbol not for its own sake but to further an intelligible artistic ideal. Numerology for Milton's age was not the humbug it is for literate Westerners of the 20th century.

The case of John Sebastian Bach is of extraordinary interest and application. Until recent years no one would have dreamt that during his busiest creative period this consummate contrapuntist sometimes superposed upon his most intricate polyphonic designs a system of numerical symbol. But German musicologists are demonstrating that in some of his best-known compositions Bach actually counts the very notes of his melodic themes to make them add up to responsive numbers that gloss the verbal context. His particular method of application is not Milton's. It rather resembles *gematria* of Jewish cabalists. For example, the number 112 stands for Christus, 14 stands for Bach; and he ascribes certain traditional meanings to numbers like 7, 9, and 17. The count may be not only of notes but of bars, and even of subject-entries in a fugue.

A phenomenon so fantastic would be incredible except that in this case we have external evidence — what amounts to direct testimony — that Bach actually practised this sort of numerology. His principal librettist, a postal clerk in Leipzig who wrote under the pseudonym "Picander," was given to printing numerical "puzzles" which are now found to correspond with numerical sequences contained in many of Bach's scores. The two men were on very friendly terms, for they collaborated in many works, including the St. Matthew Passion.[4]

We have no Picander's direct testimony to establish with objective finality Milton's system of numerical symbolism. But the simple fact of Bach's indulgence makes it far easier for us to entertain and appraise every bit of suspected symbol that comes to hand in PL and PR. If Bach, as late as the 18th century, could gloss his creations with a numerology that seems as gratuitous as it is furtive and arbitrary, one finds it less strange that Milton, eighty years earlier, should weave into his rhythms a precisely calculated system rooted in tradition and inspired — as seems not to be the case in Bach — by perfectly plausible artistic motives.

16

Before turning from arithmetical series, let us examine two or three with symbolic multipliers not yet illustrated.

(a) At PL II, 988-1009 Chaos the Anarch addresses Satan. Close to the middle of this 22-line paragraph the words "I upon my frontiers here" (998) start a retrograde AP-progression with 11 as base, i.e., AP 11 ←: 44′, 33', 22′, 11'. The base-term returns us to where we started, so that the progression completely and exactly compasses — glosses — the words of Chaos.

11, as base-number, seems always to mean obeisance, law, proportion, order, peace, composure when in direct series; in retrograde series the opposite: disorder, disproportion, anarchy, agitation. In traditional symbology Milton could have found no number for these concepts. But I am reasonably sure that in Scripture he could have found it: in Joseph's second dream, in which the sun and moon and the *eleven* stars do obeisance to Joseph. For this is the only striking use of 11 in the Old Testament, and it is forever associated with obeisance.

The present retrograde series perfectly responds to a context that implies total disorder. The terrible form and the words of Chaos seem to ask for such a gloss. But with what extraordinary aptness does the base-term start: "Confusion worse confounded;" (996)! The reader will recall that AP 4 ← at PL III, 710 f. begins with "Confusion heard his voice, . . ." and will perceive the consistency with which both retrograde series respond to a negative or sinister concept. But at PL III, 710 f. the emphasis is on the emergence of light and light-giving bodies from Chaos; hence base 4. Here in Book II the emphasis is on the ruin inflicted even upon the very ruler of ruin by Satan's fall from Heaven; hence the number of disorder itself — retrograde 11 — is the base-number.

And be it noted that the direct series, AP 11 →, is not present.

(b) At PL V, 28-94 Eve relates a disturbing dream in which she is tempted to taste the forbidden fruit. She wakes "With tresses discompos'd, and glowing cheek, / As through unquiet rest:" (10-11). This dream of hers is the first threat to the peace of Eden: at her first mention of it to Adam a retrograde series based on 11, AP 11 ← (44', 33′, 22, 11'), starts with the words, "for I this night, . . ." (30—). The context in which the base-term ends contains, appropriately, the very words that express her arrival at the tree of disaster: " . . . . brought me on a sudden to the tree / Of interdicted knowledge:" (52).

But it is not the same tree she has seen by day. The effect is wondrous. Now the number 9, and its aggrandized form 19, as in passages elsewhere, bear the Dantean meaning of miracle, wonder.

Immediately following the end of AP 11 ⟵ begins AP 19 ⟶ (19′, 38, 57′, 76″) with the words, "fair it seem'd, / Much fairer to my fancy than by day: / And as I wond'ring look'd, . . ." (52—), and ends with " . . . wond'ring at my flight and change / To this high exaltation;" (90). She has tasted the fruit and been rapt heavenward — a truly wondrous, a miraculous experience. The series not only begins but ends with a note of wonder, with the very word wonder. And the word that ends the series comes precisely at the point where the series reaches, mathematically, its own "high exaltation."

But at the next word, "suddenly," begins a primary retrograde progression AP 1 ⟵ (normally = 4, 3, 2, 1), but it descends only through the third term, then fails of completion. Why? I suggest the following reason. Eve's guide disappears, and, alone, she sinks from her skiey elevation: she falls — though only metaphorically — asleep. Not a complete, literal fall: hence the base- or nadir-term, which would be a single demarcated beat, is dissolved in her joy of waking and finding it all a dream.

Am I reading into these successive responses more than the immediate contextual situations warrant? Am I interpreting either the directional or symbolic elements wishfully in favor of some premeditated thought-sequence which I myself have imposed on the paragraph? Let him who follows the text and the number-sequences be judge.

This trio of progressions — AP 11 ⟵ + AP 19 ⟶ + AP 1 ⟵ (functionally flawed) — all but covers the entire paragraph. But the combined group, from the start of the first progression to the break-off of the third, is placed with remarkable symmetry inside the paragraph: 13 beats before AP 11 ⟵ is the paragraph's beginning; 13 beats after AP 1 ⟵ is the paragraph's end.

In all Milton's epic verse this is the only paragraph in which AP 19 follows AP 11, or, for that matter, where two series based on these particular numbers are ever tangent in any kind of progression. That one should succeed the other in a paragraph whose very special context yields symbolic responses consistent with meanings recognizable elsewhere — this does seem to be beyond the reach of pure chance.

The paragraph has 67 lines. Let us for a moment ignore context and think of the paragraph as simply a sequence of random interval-numbers. Then, if we had enough such paragraphs of this length, sooner or later we should find one in which the present sequence occurs: 44, 33, 22, 11, 19, 38, 57, 76. But suppose, when we have at last come upon such a sequence, we should be apprised of the fact that all the numbers of the paragraph stand for intervals demarcated by pauses in an expressive verbal context. Is it likely that these eight arithmetically ordered intervals which turned up after so many trials would, again by chance, bear the slightest symbolic response to successive contextual situations?

It is a case of chance within chance, chance multiplied by chance. Nevertheless, if the responsive sequence in this paragraph were the only instance in Milton of the phenomenon, I could dismiss it as an accident. But similar phenomena are demonstrable elsewhere in the same poem, all of whose paragraphs are the work of the same poet. Are we not justified then in relating all of them to a mind consciously calculating, consciously adjusting rhetoric to symbolic progressions?

CHAPTER V

"INSTINCT THROUGH ALL PROPORTIONS"

1

We are now prepared to ask: Are symbolically responsive series in Milton's verse-paragraphs confined to arithmetical progressions? Or do geometrical progressions occur also?

If nothing were known about Milton's intense interest in mathematics, such a question would be senseless. But we have to do with a mind demonstrably encyclopedic in its acquisitive grasp and scope, reaching for light in every science and art, submitting to every discipline that may further an epic enterprise.

Fortunately Edward Phillips tells us just what mathematical treatises he studied under his uncle's supervision. He names the *Elementa Arithmeticae* by Christian Wurstisen (Urstisius), the *Questiones Geometricae* by Peter Ryff, the *Trigonometriae Libri Quinque* by Bartholomew Pitiscus, and the *Sphaera Mundi* by John Sacrobosco. But a teacher as competent as Milton must have been would not only have mastered the contents of these treatises but would have been alert to examine and study any current mathematical works displayed on London bookstalls. By the time he planned *Paradise Lost* he must have had a grasp of arithmetic, algebra, geometry, and trigonometry that would put to shame the mathematics of most present-day graduates in liberal arts.

We are for the moment, however, mostly concerned with his study of arithmetic. Urstisius' *Elementa,* first printed at Basel in 1579, is a very practical treatment, many of its 190 pages being devoted to proportion, especially to the "Rule of Three," and the application of this Rule to commercial problems. It ends with a short chapter on square root and cube root. It certainly would not represent the range of Milton's arithmetical accomplishments.

When he "made excursions" from Horton to London he could have picked up books much more exciting than Urstisius.

We know his sympathetic interest in the work of the celebrated Peter Ramus (1515-1572), so that he would have been familiar with one or more of the "emended" editions of Ramus's arithmetic and geometry. Such an edition was made by Lazarus Schonerus in 1599 and published at Frankfurt in 1627.[1] But the book he would have examined with unusual zest was Edmund Wingate's *Arithmetique Made Easie* (London, 1639), for Wingate presents the first exposition in English of logarithms, or, as they were also called at that time, "artificial numbers" — the most important and useful mathematical tool invented during the four hundred years before Newton.

As a matter of course both Ramus and Wingate handle proportions and progressions at some length, and, like all the earliest expositors of logarithms, Wingate treats them as a development of proportion. He is an enthusiast. His invitation to handle the hugest numbers with minimum calculation, and his detailing of the various sorts of progressions could not have failed to be of absorbing moment to one whose mind from earliest boyhood was at home in the intricacies of mensurable music.

In his Chapter IX Wingate describes a geometrical progression in which "the first number . . . is the roote or first power, the second is the square or second power, the third the cube or third power, the fourth the biquadrate or fourth power, the fift the fift power, the sixt the sixt power, etc." His example is: 3, 9, 27, 81, 243, 729, . . . "each proportionall being multiplyed by the roote produceth the proportionall next above it."

Such a progression as Wingate here describes I called a power series, and designated it PP.

Wingate encourages the invention of new forms. Once he describes a series that truly rockets to the sky: 2, 2^2 [4], 4^2 [16], 16^2 [256], 256^2 [65536], . . . Algebraically this is r^1, r^2, r^4, r^8, . . ., the exponents of successive terms being in geometrical progression. I called this a power-of-power series, and designated it P^P.

But such a progression, given a root-number of any size, involves numbers so huge that at first I hesitated to think Milton could have made any use of it. A less steeply ascending series would be one with successive exponents 1, 3, 5, 7, ..., i.e., r^1, r^3, r^5, r^7, . . . I called such a sequence a superpower series, and designated it PPP.

Still another easily devised progression involving powers is a sequence of squares, in which each term of an arithmetical series is squared; e.g., $1^2, 2^2, 3^2, 4^2, \ldots$ Or it might be $2^2, 4^2, 6^2, 8^2, \ldots$ Designate such a series S Sq. If successive numbers should be cubed, call it a sequence of cubes (S Cu).

Here, then, are five kinds of progression involving powers: power series, superpower series, power-of-power series, sequence of squares, and sequence of cubes: PP, PPP, P^P, S Sq, and S Cu. Each may be direct (e.g., PP $\longrightarrow$) or retrograde (e.g., PP $\longleftarrow$). Anyone reading a work like Wingate's would be stimulated to think about such series and apply them to various root-numbers.

2

Now the very thought of examining a blank verse paragraph for the presence of a series composed of successive powers is, I dare-say, as repugnant to the reader as it was to me. It is as repugnant as counting Bach's notes and bars to uncover symbolic responses. Yet, as a reverent Trinitarian, Bach was, to start with, a convinced numerical symbolist, and Picander's speculations, though at first they might merely have amused, came eventually to engross one corner of a mind incessantly dovetailing and overlapping measured rhythmic sequences in fugal and canonic inventions.

Only one practical difficulty must be surmounted in applying a given power series to the Miltonic paragraph: a certain amount of arithmetical calculation.

Suppose Milton wishes to gloss a context where the concept of power or force is dominant. Suppose his paragraph has 73 lines, and he would demarcate intervals for PP 10 $\longrightarrow$. The series is to go to the Pythagorean four terms. Since it is regarded as an analogue to a cross-rhythmic voice in polyphonic music, the root-term can start at any punctuated pause. And since the paragraph as a whole is regarded as a contrapuntal piece in perpetual canon, any higher powers of 10 simply circuit it for a number of times with a number of beats left over as a remainder.

Hence if we would know at what point a term ends in the paragraph we must divide the term by the number of beats in the whole paragraph. Let us designate the number of lines in the paragraph as n: then the number of beats is $5n$. In the proposed paragraph n = 73, and $5n$ = 365. The proposed series, PP 10 ⟶ = $10^1, 10^2, 10^3, 10^4$, or 10, 100, 1000, 10000. We divide the two largest terms by 365. 1000 = (2×365) + 270. 10000 = (27×365) + 145. The progression may start at any pause in the paragraph.

The first interval, defining *r*, the root-number of the progression, has 10 beats. This is followed by the second interval, defining 10^2, or 100 beats, at the end of which 10^3 begins. To determine where 10^3 ends, we must, after making two circuits of the paragraph, go forward 270 beats. But 270 beats forward lack only 95 beats of a full circuit. Therefore, when we have determined where 10^2 ends, we can, to save time, go *back* 95 rather than forward 270 beats to determine where 10^3 ends. And in recording the procedure we simply change the directional sign: we write a minus sign before 95 instead of a plus sign before 270. (Throughout my analyses the absence of sign means +.)

What we are doing in this process is getting the sequence of remainders accurately computed and in proper order if we are to demarcate PP 10 ⟶ in a paragraph of 73 lines. And we find the sequence of remainders for the first three terms (10^1,10^2,10^3) to be 10,100,-95.

But suppose we do go back 95 beats from the pause where 10^2 ends: then if 10^3 is present the interval for 10^2 (100) is broken into two parts: 5, 95. We can thus simplify the sequence of remainders for the first three terms to *10, 5, 95.* If such a sequence is present in a 73-line paragraph, we are certain that the first three terms of PP 10 ⟶ are present.

As for 10^4, we know it starts at the pause that ends 10^3, and that it circuits the paragraph many times, with a remainder of 145 beats. Hence we must go forward 145 beats from the pause after *5* in the sequence *10, 5, 95,* and this brings us 50 beats beyond the pause after 95. The resultant sequence for all four terms of PP 10 ⟶ is *10, 5, 95, 50.* This sequence is the *formula* for the progression whose full sequence of remainders is 10, 100, -95, 145. The formula is the ultimate simplification of intervals that guarantee the presence of the progression. We always know where the sequence of remainders begins and ends: in the present case it begins before 10 and ends after 145. But with the formula the points of beginning and ending are not evident except as derived from the sequence of remainders. Either of the points *may* be before or after any of the intervals of the formula. It is therefore essential that we indicate points of beginning and ending in any formula. I have found it convenient to place an arrow where the progression starts, and a caret where it ends: thus: $\underset{\uparrow}{\mathit{10}}, \mathit{5}, \mathit{95}, \underset{\wedge}{\mathit{50}}$.

Any series may be retrograde. This means that it starts with the highest term, goes from pause to pause of the constantly diminishing powers, and ends where the root-term ends. The retrograde formula is the exact reverse of the direct. If the direct is $\underset{\uparrow}{\mathit{10}}, \mathit{5}, \mathit{95}, \underset{\wedge}{\mathit{50}}$, its reverse is $\underset{\uparrow}{\mathit{50}}, \mathit{95}, \mathit{5}, \underset{\wedge}{\mathit{10}}$.

This will be doubly clear if we turn again to the sequence of remainders. For PP 10 ⟶ we have found this to be 10, 100, -95, 145, which, reversed, i.e., starting the series with 10^4, is 145, -95, 100, 10. Simple inspection shows that, if we start where the interval of 145 starts, the group, simplified, is 50, 95, 5, 10.

We now have all we need for determining whether PP 10 ⟶ or PP 10 ⟵ is present in a 73-line paragraph. The complete information may be summarized:

PP 10: (10, 100, -95, 145) = $\underset{\uparrow}{\mathit{10}}, \mathit{5}, \mathit{95}, \underset{\wedge}{\mathit{50}}$ [$\underset{\uparrow}{\mathit{50}}, \mathit{95}, \mathit{5}, \underset{\wedge}{\mathit{10}}$]

We put the sequence of remainders for the direct progression in parentheses, and each formula in italics, bracketing the retrograde. But we may omit before the retrograde formula the corresponding sequence of remainders.

3

At PL VI, 189-261 is a 73-line paragraph. Let us scan it for significant sequences of intervals. We find it does *not* contain PP 10 ⟶. But it does contain PP 10 ⟵. If we start at "no thought of flight . . ." (236—), we find pauses to demarcate the intervals $\underset{\uparrow}{\mathit{50}}, \mathit{95}, \mathit{5}, \underset{\wedge}{\mathit{10}}$.

In retrograde series we may expect to find the responsive contextual situation either at the beginning, i.e., the beginning of the head-term, or else in the root- or nadir-term. The root-term of the present series is the 10-beat description:

ten paces huge
He back recoil'd; the next on bended knee
His massy spear upstay'd; (193-195)

So rich is this response that one is tempted to throw all caution away, erase the word probability as to Milton's conscious calculation of symbolic series, and declare it an absolute certainty. Let us rather regard this passage as greatly raising the degree of probability.

The response is fourfold. (i) It is directional. Satan is forced backward under Abdiel's descending sword-stroke, the description of which marks the end of the descending progression. (ii) It is literal. The exact number of backward paces of recoil is paralleled and measured by the number of metric beats in the term that tells it. (iii) It is symbolic. 10, a multiple of 5, means, when the progression is direct, power — an inference based on responses in many other paragraphs. Here, in retrograde progression, it means the reverse: impotence. The response to Satan's state of temporary helplessness is uncannily perfect. (iv) It is finite. Satan recovers quickly from Abdiel's "noble stroke"; hence the progression is one that extends only to four terms.

. . . .

But in this celestial battle are elements that reach beyond the finite. Let us now turn to calculations involving the infinite, and see how a certain kind of infinite series responds to concepts of the infinite expressed in this same paragraph.

If, given $n = 73$, we take 10 as root of what I have called a superpower series, i.e., $r^1, r^3, r^5, r^7, \ldots$ ($10^1, 10^3, 10^5, 10^7, \ldots$), the sequence of remainders is 10, -95, -10, 95, 10, . . . Let us simplify this sequence to a formula. From the starting-point, wherever it may be, we first go forward 10 beats. The second term (r^3) takes us back 95 beats; the resultant two intervals are 85,10.

The third term (r^5) takes us back 10 beats, resulting in a sequence of three intervals: 10, 85, 10. But the fourth term (r^7) advances 95 beats to a point of pause already marked off. It is the very point where we started. The fifth term (r^9), which advances 10 beats, is likewise already demarcated. We can in fact continue PPP 10 $\longrightarrow$ for an unlimited number of terms, and the three intervals 10,85,10 suffice for them all. The series is therefore infinite. To recapitulate:

$$\text{PPP 10: } (10, -95, -10, 95, 10, \ldots) = \underset{\uparrow}{\mathit{10, 85, 10}}\ \infty\ \underset{\uparrow}{[\mathit{10, 85, 10}]}$$

(The logical place to begin the retrograde series is where the fourth term would begin, or any power of 10 whose ordinal number in the series is a multiple of 4.)

Now apply these formulas to the present battle-piece. Necessarily, if either formula is present, then from the nature of its sequence of numbers both the direct and the retrograde series are present. In other words, if the sequence *10, 85, 10* occurs, PPP 10 $\longrightarrow \infty$ and PPP 10 $\longleftarrow \infty$ perform simultaneously:

$\longrightarrow$

a	b	a
a	b	a

$\longleftarrow$

Carefully scanning this paragraph (PL VI, 189-261), we do find PPP 10 $\genfrac{}{}{0pt}{}{\longrightarrow \infty}{\longleftarrow \infty} >$ present. PPP 10 $\longrightarrow \infty$ starts with the words, "deeds of eternal fame / Were done, but infinite: . . ." (240—). PPP 10 $\longleftarrow \infty$ starts with the words, "how much more of power / Army against army numberless . . ." (223—), and ends with ". . . the least of which could wield / These elements, and arm him with the force / Of all their regions:" (223).

The symbolic response is, in its way, as perfect as for PP 10 $\longleftarrow$. For the beginnings of both PPP 10 $\longrightarrow \infty$ and PPP 10 $\longleftarrow \infty$ are in contextual situations where the indeterminate words "infinite," "eternal," "numberless" dominate. The single use of "infinite" in this paragraph occurs in — seems reserved for — the root-term of PPP 10 $\longrightarrow \infty$; the single use of "numberless" occurs in — seems reserved for — the beginning of PPP 10 $\longleftarrow \infty$. In the simultaneous performance of these antithetic ∞-series, rooted in the number that symbolizes force, we have a mathematical mirror of the interplay and struggle of *unlimited* armies locked in battle.

Let us keep in mind the following facts. (1) Given $n = 73$, 10 is the only small number that yields an infinite progression. (2) The paragraph, long as it is, full of pauses as it is, yields intervals for such a progression once and only once. But the intervals coincide so perfectly with responsive contextual situations that only exact calculation and premeditated adjustment of symbol to context seem capable of explaining their presence.

Is it, then, a torturing of Milton's text, is it a wishful flight of fancy to say that in this battle-piece we have almost indubitable evidence (i) of conscious demarcation and circumspect adjustment of different kinds of power-progressions? (ii) of the symbolic meaning of 10 as power, force? (iii) of Milton's employment of simplified formulas to scribe progressions?

Yet if the progressions here explained were, in spite of their astonishing responses to context, solitary phenomena, if this paragraph were the only one in which such phenomena occurred, I would scrap the whole matter as fortuitous. But similar phenomena occur elsewhere in Milton's epic verse, and in sufficient numbers to hold us to our quest.

Of the many available examples, the first group I shall now present does not require extended explanations or onerous arithmetic to verify. In the case of every progression, I shall give the formula as derived from the sequence of remainders. If the reader is in doubt about the method of derivation, he should turn back to the detailed explanation given in this and the preceding section.

4

(i) At PL VIII, 437-451 God promises Adam a companion,

> thy fit help, thy other self,
> Thy wish, exactly to thy heart's desire. (450-451)

to take the place of the beasts of Eden, a fellowship "unmeet for thee." The creature is to be in Adam's image, hence in God's. Now 7 is the number of God, and this 15-line paragraph is scribed and circumscribed with power and superpower progressions based on the root-number 7.

At the outset be it known that, though thirteen other 15-line paragraphs occur in Milton's epic verse, not one of them contains intervals that define any progression based on 7. A fact like this strengthens, almost beyond probability, the assumption that Milton has deliberately chosen 7 to gloss God's solemn promise.

The words "exactly to thy heart's desire" (451) begin a direct power series: PP 7 $\longrightarrow$. Given $n = 15$,

PP 7: (7, -26, 43, 1) = *19, 7, 17, 1*
↑ ^

Here the last term as scribed in the text interprets the first, for the progression ends with ". . . My image," (441), and it is God's image that is to fulfil Adam's heart's desire, the very height of his need and his longing. The retrograde progression is not present.

Almost all editors drop the comma after "wish" (451), causing the progression to vanish.

(ii) Now notice one very curious fact about pauses in this same paragraph (VIII, 437-451). The precise central beat — the 38th — falls on "still;" (444). If we start at this pause, i.e., with "I, ere thou spak'st, . . ." the following intervals are demarcated as with a ruler: 7, 18, 7, 18, 7, 18, and the last 18 returns us to where we start. What is the significance of such an alternation of 7 and 18?

Given $n = 15$, the formula for a superpower series based on root 7 is thus derived:

PPP 7: (7, -32, 7, -32, 7, -32, . . .) = *7, 18, 7, 18, 7* [*7, 18, 7, 18, 7*]
^ ↑ ^ ↑

I have carried the formula to five terms because after the fifth term all higher terms are demarcated by the pauses already present — provided there is an endless alternation of 7 and 18. There is just such an alternation in this paragraph, and, since $7+18+7+18+7+18 = 75 = 5n$, PPP 7 yields infinite series both direct and retrograde. Three direct series are present, each one beginning with a 7-beat interval.

(*α*) PPP 7 $\longrightarrow \infty$ starts at "I, ere thou . . ." (444—)
(*β*) PPP 7 $\longrightarrow \infty$ " " "be assur'd . . ." (449—)
(*γ*) PPP 7 $\longrightarrow \infty$ " " "but of thyself, . . ." (439—)

[*Note.* Lest any reader go astray in tracing these or any other progressions described in later pages, be it observed that my directive words "starts at" mean: "starts at the punctuated pause *before* the following words." Also, when I use the words "ends at" I mean: "ends at the punctuated pause *after* the following words."]

Theoretically, performing simultaneously with these three direct series are three retrograde series. But it is likely that in this context Milton intends only the direct series to apply: as they go round and round the paragraph, ever ascending to inconceivable powers of 7, they gloss God's infinite attributes, God's guarantee that he will surely fulfil his promise. Of course casuistry can justify the co-presence of three retrograde series, for in God all contradictories are resolved.

Still another PPP ⇄> is present; but it is finite, restricted to the usual four terms.

PPP 7: (7, -32, 7, 43) = 7, *18*, 7, *18* [*18*, 7, *18*, 7]
↑ ^ ↑ ^

PPP 7 → starts at "Thy wish, . . ." (451—)
ends " " . . . the spirit within thee free." (440)
← starts " "And no such company . . ." (446—)
ends " " . . . thy other self," (450)

The words that start ← suggest that the two simultaneous series are meant to contrast the divine attributes of Adam with the undivine state of the beasts he must associate with.

If we trace in the text the intervals that define → and ←, we notice that → is exactly superposed on ←:

→			
7	18	7	18
18	7	18	7
←			

The resultant sequence of intervals that define this interlock is the sequence of symmetry (*S. of Sym.*) — 7, 11, 7, 7, 11, 7 — whose center of symmetry is the point of pause that ends line 450 (" . . . other self,").

(iii) Whenever Deity speaks there seems to be an unusual number of pauses that demarcate progressions. God as the supreme mathematician is of course a Platonic concept, restated in Cartesian terms in the 17th century, anticipating Sir James Jeans's conclusion to *The Mysterious Universe* (1930): " . . . from the intrinsic evidence of his creation, the Great Architect of the Universe now begins to appear as a pure mathematician."

When Deity speaks, progressions often occur in antithetic pairs, creating sequences of symmetry. In the paragraph we have been considering (PL VIII, 437-451), still another pair of series is present. God declares he will give to Adam "thy other self," (450). In Pythagorean numerology the number of woman is 2, the number of man is 3, and their sum, 5, is the number of marriage. Here we are concerned with the number of woman. "thy other self" starts a direct superpower series based on 2. Given $n = 15$,

PPP 2: (2, 8, 32, -22) = *2, 8, 10, 22* [*22, 10, 8, 2*]
↑ under 8, ^ under 22, ↑ under 10, ^ under 2

PFP 2 ⟶ ends at " . . . rightly nam'd" (439).

But PPP 2 ⟵ is also present, starting with "What next I bring shall please thee, . . ." (449—), and ending at " . . . I was pleas'd," (437).

These two series have the second term — *b* — in common, i.e., they are interlocked, creating a sequence of symmetry with 8 the center.

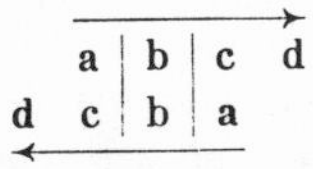

⟶

	a	b	c	d
d	c	b	a	

⟵

S. of Sym.: 22, 8, 2, *8*, 2, 8, 22.

Here the root-term of PPP 2 ⟶ ("thy other self") suggests the nature of the contextual response. The antithetic pair is complementary rather than antagonistic, for their interlocking creates a bilateral symmetry in which we can visualize 2 ⟶ as the mirror-image of 2 ⟵, its likeness, its inseparable other self. Regard term *b* as an axis, then swing either series round through 180 degrees, the other series remaining fixed, and the two series are one.

(iv) It may be thought that with a large variety of formulas available to demarcate PP-, PPP-, and P^P-series, every paragraph would yield almost any formula we might look for. This is not the case. There are paragraphs that have very few or no sequences of intervals which demarcate progressions. Such is the 41-line paragraph at PL I, 84-124, where Satan rallies Beelzebub with words of heroic valor. There is a special fluency in the style, as if Milton were exceptionally concerned with his rhetoric. Present, however, are at least three progressions. They deserve recording.

A direct power series based on 5 (force, strength) is present. Given $n = 41$,

PP 5: (5, 25, -80, 10) = *10, 40, 5, 25.*
^ ↑

PP 5 → starts at "so much the stronger . . ." (92—), and ends with " . . . If thou be'st he;" (84).

Many editors drop comma after "disdain" (98), making this series vanish.

(v) The number 3, as well as its aggrandized form 13, often seems to symbolize justice, righteousness. Now in a 41-line paragraph it is a curious mathematical fact that when 3 is root of a superpower series the series is infinite. A cursory inspection of the sequence of remainders will show how this comes about.

PPP 3: (3, 27, 38, -68, 3, . . .) = *3, 27, 38* ∞ [*38, 27, 3*].
↑ ↑

In the paragraph at PL I, 84-124 both direct and retrograde PPP 3 are present. Not only present, but dramatically present.

Satan is stung with "a sense of injur'd merit" (98). His convictions about justice forbid him to "bow and sue for grace / With suppliant knee." From an outraged heart comes his cry of defiance: "All is not lost," (106). Immediately preceding these words is the root-term of PPP 3 ← ∞: "What though the field be lost?" Immediately following the same cry is the root-term of PPP 3 → ∞: "the unconquerable will." The result is that from "so much the stronger . . ." (92—) to ". . . much advanc'd," (119) we find the following intervals demarcated: 38, 27, 3, 2, 3, 27, 38. This sequence of symmetry is like a numerical graph of depression-recovery.

PPP 3 $\leftarrow \infty$ PPP 3 $\rightarrow \infty$

c	38	"so much the stronger . . ." (92—) ....
b	27	"And to the fierce . . ." (100—) ....
a	3	"What though the field be lost;" (105) ......
[2]		"All is not lost;" (106) ....
a	3	"the unconquerable will," (106) ....
b	27	"And study of . . ." (107—) ....
c	38	"and deify . . ." (112—) ....

On one side of the key-words, "All is not lost," is a descending ∞ -series that defines in symbol an infinite loss wrought by infinite injustice. On the other side is the same numerical pattern but in reverse, being an affirmative decision of infinite will to reestablish justice by recouping infinite loss. The terms on either side of the central 2-beat declaration form a configuration that suggests equilibrium: voussoirs within an inverted arch of adamant.

Nowhere else in Milton's epic verse does the sequence 38, 27, 3, 2, 3, 27, 38 occur. That it should come in a paragraph of just the length for it to tally with a significant progression-formula, and at the same time in just the contextual situation where it can respond with absolute aptness — does this not point to deliberate computation and adjustment rather than to any feat or freak of chance?

(vi) At PL VI, 131-148 Abdiel's words defying Satan are animated by infinite concepts. The Omnipotent, he cries, could create even out of infinitesimals an unlimited host of armies to thwart the towering aspirations of any adversary. "With solitary hand / Reaching beyond all limit" he could defeat Satan (137-141). Now if such a declaration is to be glossed with numerical symbol, the progression ought to be infinite. And it is.

In many other passages the root-number 17, when in direct progression, seems to symbolize God's (7) perfect power (10) or omnipotence. And if the progression is infinite the meaning would be intensified. In retrograde, 17 then might signify the retributive presence of God's omnipotence. In the present paragraph Abdiel is the vocal representative of such retributive presence.

By a seemingly demonic feat of calculation, the beginning of this paragraph is actually the beginning of a retrograde infinite power series based on 17, and the end of the paragraph is the end of that series.

Observe how it is possible. Given $n = 18$,

PP 17: (17, 19, -37, 1, 17, . . .) = *1, 17, 19* ∞ [*19, 17, 1*].
↑ ↑

The retrograde progression therefore starts with a 1-beat interval. It is the word "Proud," that begins the paragraph. This is a most singular substantive, explainable as elliptic Latin, yet somewhat forced and precious. Does it not seem to have been chosen expressly to secure the exacting 1-beat interval of this unusual formula?

A retrograde PP 17 ∞ whose formula is composed of three terms would begin logically, i.e., according to Pythagorean prescription, at the 4th power, or at any power whose exponent is a multiple of 4. Hence, to begin at the 4th power, as here, implies a beginning at a power whose exponent is an unlimited multiple of 4.

The context favors such a place of beginning. For the unlimited size of the starting-term responds to Abdiel's denunciation of Satan, whose "hope was to have reach'd / The highth . . . The throne of God" himself.

Editors sometimes drop comma after "visible" (145), causing the progression to vanish.

(vii) At PL III, 1-55 Milton confides: only by grace of his Muse, giver of Heavenly Light, has it been safe for him to sojourn in Hell,

and up to reascend,
Though hard and rare: thee I revisit safe,
And feel thy sovran vital lamp; (20-22).

These words are the root-term of PPP 12 →, which ends at ". . . Hail, holy Light" (1). PPP 12 ← is not present.

Given $n = 55$,

PPP 12: (12, 78, -43, 133) = *12, 35, 43, 90*.
↑ ^

The meaning of 12, a difficult number to interpret, being a product of symbolic factors, seems determined here by its factor 4, traditional number of heavenly light. And light, both literal and metaphorical, both earthly and heavenly, is the theme. Not only is it in the root-term, but it ends the progression.

5

It is not my intention to fatigue the reader with gratuitous illustrations tedious to verify. But the establishment of a probability that Milton sometimes adjusts rhetoric to measured intervals that define symbolic progressions cannot be accomplished unless a reasonably wide assortment of phenomena is made available. If the reader is determined to disbelieve that Milton ever indulges in numerical symbol for any purpose, then nothing short of direct testimony from the poet or from one close to him can carry weight. Such a reader has my sympathy. I would gladly join him except that the phenomena under investigation are not a matter of faith or of disbelief. If the apparently responsive features of the progressions I am presenting prove to be illusions, and the polyphonic analogues which by hypothesis they are assumed to be are but an ingenious dream related in no vital way to Milton's known life and interests, then the gods of chance have triumphed, and Milton's style remains more inscrutable than ever.

In this section let us examine several paragraphs in which a number of different progressions perform simultaneously.

(i)

At PL II, 871-967 Satan traverses the "wild abyss" of Chaos. Now he is whirled aloft as on a chariot of clouds.

> but that seat soon failing, meets
> A vast vacuity: all unawares
> Flutt'ring his pennons vain plumb down he drops
> Ten thousand fadom deep, . . . (931—)

These words begin a descending power-of-power series based on 8. Given $n = 97$,

P^P 8: (8, 64, -269, 96) = *96, 101, 8, 64* [*64, 8, 101, 96*].
∧ ↑ ∧ ↑

The descending series ends at ". . . Into this wild abyss," (910). The ascending series is not present.

8, in direct series, would be the number of God's providence. But such providence, in the usual sense, Satan has forfeited. In his present peril he is "alone, and without guide," (975). The descending series is therefore responsive symbolically. Also directionally: Satan drops "plumb down," as befits a P^P ←. "Ten thousand fadom," however, is but a round-number concession to man's limited ability to visualize numbers in the millions. For the series actually drops from 16777216 [8^8] to 8 in three stages, the first stage being the most precipitous.

(ii)

Present in this 97-line paragraph are two antithetic superpower series also based on 8.

PPP 8: (8, 27, -212, 12) = *12, 165, 8, 27* [*27, 8, 165, 12*]
∧ ↑ ∧ ↑

→ starts at "nigh founder'd on he fares, . . ." (940—)
ends " " . . . He rules a moment;" (907)
← starts " "Pursues the Arimaspian, . . ." (945—)
ends " " . . . perhaps her grave," (911).

Observe two special features, each an extraordinary response to context.

(a) The formulas for → and ← are exactly superposed one on the other. (Since the second term from the right in the formula for → is the root, let us represent the series thus: $\overrightarrow{\text{d c b a}}$, in order to avoid using c or d as root-term.)

The interlock is:

```
 ———————→
| d  c  b  a |
| a  b  c  d |
←———————
```

$r = b$

It creates the *S. of Sym.*: 12, 15, 8, *142*, 8, 15, 12.

Such a simultaneity of antithetic performers mirrors mathematically the conflicting forces with which Satan contends.

(b) But the conflict is further symbolized, and the symbol doubly intensified, by reason of a most curious — and most rare — mathematical fact, which, considering the contextual situation, tempts one to declare, Impossible for chance to do this!

Given $n = 97$, the formulas for PPP 8 have exactly the same intervals as the formulas for PPP 12 except for one simple difference: their order is reversed.

PPP 12: (12, -212, 27, 8) = *27, 8, 165, 12* [*12, 165, 8, 27*]

Hence PPP 8 → = PPP 12 ←, and PPP 8 ← = PPP 12 →:
i. e., PPP 8 ⇄ = PPP 12 ⇆

```
 ———————→              ———————→
| d  c  b  a |        | d  c  b  a |
| a  b  c  d |        | a  b  c  d |
←———————              ←———————
```

$r = b = 8$ $r = a = 12$

The *S. of Sym.* remains the same for both interlocks.

This rare simultaneous duplication of differently-based antithetic progressions locked in a symmetric design that superimposes the formula for PPP 8 in both directions precisely upon the formula for PPP 12 in both directions — how can pure chance ever effect this necessary sequence of seven symmetrically grouped intervals — **12, 15, 8, 142, 8, 15, 12** — at just the right contextual situation to be a multidirectional response? If the paragraph were of any other length than 97 lines, if the length deviated but slightly, were, say,

96 lines or 98, this mathematical image of complicated struggle across Chaos would be impossible. How can we explain its presence except by assuming that at some time Milton studied the relation of paragraph-lengths to formulas of power progressions? and this before he ever began the final revision of his poem?

But he was blind. Could a blind man do these things? Yes, because all the computing of formulas, all the technique of overlapping and interlocking progressions could have been perfected years before blindness came. Progressions, one more than suspects, were the heart of his mathematical studies, these and how they might be adjuvant, by way of contrapuntal analogues and numerical symbology, to his projected epic. As for the practical method by which, though blind, he fingered his blank verse to adjust rhetoric to prescribed intervals — this could have been routinized by means of some simple and inconspicuous manual device, whose operation would have been easy for hands used to traversing an organ-keyboard. For we know he took daily delight in playing his organ, and the music he played was contrapuntal.

(iii)

Of all Jehovah's allocations as reported by Milton, the most august is at PL V, 600-615. In these 16 lines, in which Father appoints Son to be vicegerent, there are two groups of symbolic series, one based on 3 (justice), and the other on 10 (omnipotence).

Fugal Pair of PPP 3 →'s

Given n = 16,
PPP 3: (3, 27, 3, -53) = *20, 3, 27, 3* [*3, 27, 3, 20*]
^ ↑ ^ ↑

(*a*) PPP 3 → starts at "Progeny of Light, . . ." (600-)
ends " " . . . Mee disobeys," (612)

(*β*) PPP 3 → starts " "which unrevok'd . . ." (602—)
ends " " . . . utter darkness," (614)

The presence of these series implies that Jehovah's act is *just.* 10 beats (10 = power) separate (*a*) → and (*β*) →. Two facts are noteworthy: (1) no retrograde PPP 3 is present; (2) although Milton's epic verse contains nine other 16-line paragraphs, in not one of these nine do we find any superpower series based on 3. PPP 3 ⟶ seems therefore to be reserved for Jehovah's edict, and its fugal repetition seems confirmatory of the poet's conscious purpose.

Consort of PP 10 ∞'s

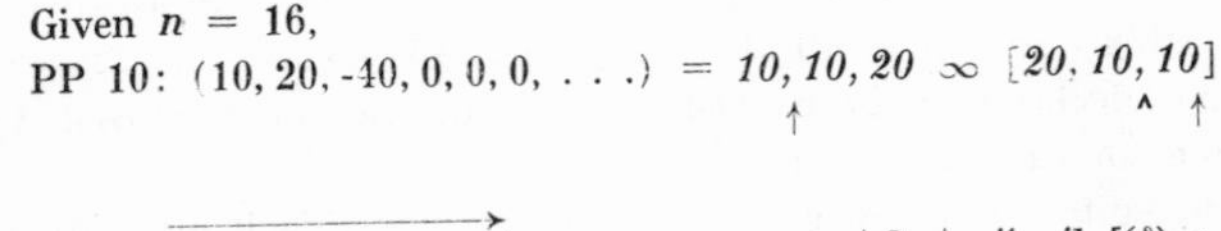

Given n = 16,
PP 10: (10, 20, -40, 0, 0, 0, . . .) = *10, 10, 20* ∞ [*20, 10, 10*]

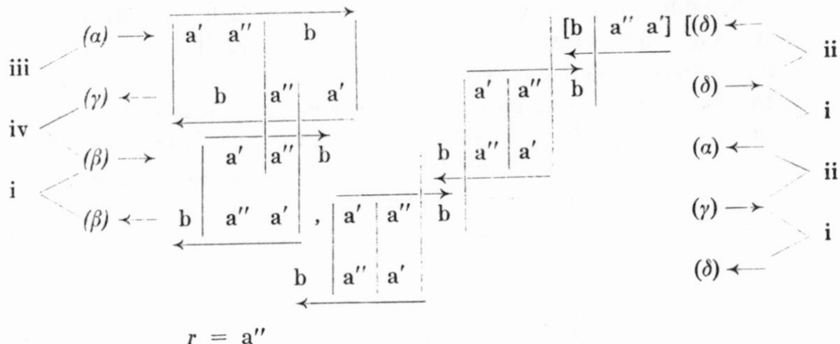

r = a″

Sequences of Symmetry

i. 20, 10, 10, 20
ii. 10, 10, *20,* 10, 10
iii. 10, 10, 10, 10
iv. 10, 10, *10,* 10, 10

(α) ⟶ starts at "progeny of light, . . ." (600—)
⟵ " " same place
ends " " . . . Into utter darkness," (614)
(β) ⟶ starts " "which unrevok'd . . ." (602—)
⟵ " " "and on this holy hill . . ." (604—)
ends " " . . . Hear my decree," (602)

$(\gamma) \longrightarrow$ starts " "your head I him appoint; . . ." (606—)
$\longleftarrow$ " " same place
ends " " . . . My only Son," (604)
$(\delta) \longrightarrow$ starts " "deep ingulft, . . . Hear all ye Angels, . . ." (614—)
$\longleftarrow$ " " "and shall confess him Lord: . . ." (608—)
ends " " . . . At my right hand;" (606)

Observe that $(\beta) \longleftarrow$, $(\gamma) \longrightarrow$ girdle the paragraph, and are tangent at opposite poles (20, 10, 10, 10, 10, 20).

$10\,\infty$ = perfect and infinite power. The edict thus vibrates with alternating currents of PP $10 \longrightarrow \infty$ and PP $10 \longleftarrow \infty$; i.e., the positive declaration is backed by infinite sanctions poised to descend on the disobedient.

Some editors (e.g., Wright) drop comma after "darkness" (614), destroying the consort, for this pause is needed for $(a) \longrightarrow$, $(a) \longleftarrow$, $(\gamma) \longleftarrow$, and $(\delta) \longrightarrow$.

In this consort we seem to have Milton's mathematical duplicate of those words in *Of Reformation* describing the lives of the righteous who live in sight of the "blessed vision": "progressing the dateless and irrevoluble circle of eternity."

. . . . . .

Many are the paragraphs in which root-term or head-term of a power progression responds to 7, number of God, divinity, sovereignty. Sometimes the entire paragraph is girdled with infinite series based on 7, girdled and re-girdled. Here are two or three instances.

(iv)

If any paragraph deserves the presence of repeated and overlapping progressions based on 7 it is Adam and Eve's morning prayer to creation at PL V, 153-208. Given $n = 56$,

$$\text{PPP } 7\!: (7, 63, 7, 63) = \underset{\uparrow}{7}, 63, 7, \underset{\wedge}{63}.$$

If we continue the terms, the sequence of remainders merely alternates 7 and 63; PPP 7: (7, 63, 7, 63, 7, 63, . . .). If these alternations should continue without end, the progression would be infinite. And this is just what they do in this prayer.

If we start at "yet these declare . . ." (158—) we find the following intervals marked off as with a ruler: 7, 63, 7, 63, 7, 63, 7, 63, the last 63 returning us to where we start, so that the alternations continue round and round the paragraph. It is possible mathematically because $4 \times (7 + 63) = 280 = 5n$. The result is that each of the four 7-beat intervals begins an infinite series: PPP $7 \rightarrow \infty$.

(α) → starts at "yet these declare . . ." (158—)
(β) → " " "sound his praise . . ." (172—)
(γ) → " " "dusky or grey, . . ." (186—)
(δ) → " " "and ye that walk . . ." (200—)

. . . .

Performing across these PPP $7\ \infty$'s is a pair of antithetic power series based on 33.

PP 33: (33, -31, 97, 121) = *2, 31, 66, 121* [*121, 66, 31, 2*]

→ starts at "both when thou climb'st, / And when high noon hast gain'd, and when thou fall'st, . . ." (173—)
ends " " . . . Angels, for yee behold him," (161)
← starts where → starts
ends " → ends

33 carries the symbol of its factor 11, which symbolizes obeisance, service, law, order. The sun serves the glory of God and obeys law and order in its punctual rising and setting.

But see the response to lines 173 f. which begin both → and ←. The sun *climbing* parallels →; the sun *falling* parallels ←. Accordingly the antithetic progressions perform simultaneously, one being superposed on the other.

→
a	b	c	d
d	c	b	a
←

$r = a + b$

S. of Sym.: 2, 31, 66, 22, 66, 31, 2

(v)

Girdling by PPP 7 ∞'s, on a smaller scale, is in the paragraph at PL VI, 1-28, where we are close to the mount and throne of God. Given $n = 28$,

PPP 7: (7, 63, 7, -77, 7, . . .) = *7, 63, 7* ∞
↑

(α) ⟶ starts at "from whence a voice . . ." (27—)
(β) ⟶ " " "array'd in gold / Empyreal, . . ." (13—)

The second 7 in the formula of (α) is the root-term of (β), and the second 7 in the formula of (β) is the root-term of (α), this because the two ascending series interlock, having their 7's in common. For $7+63+7+63 = 140 = 5n$.

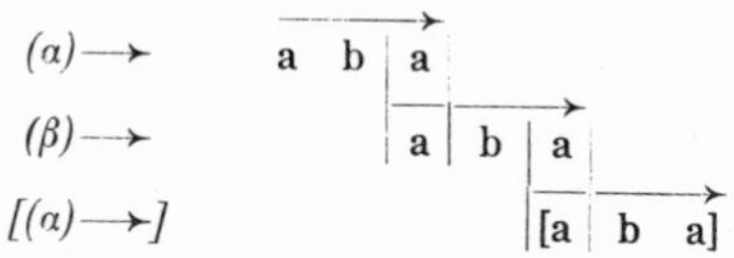

(α)⟶	a	b	a			
(β)⟶			a	b	a	
[(α)⟶]					[a	b a]

Still another progression based on God's number is here present. Given $n = 28$,

PPP 17: (17, 13, -23, 73) = *7, 10, 13, 50*
↑ ^

It starts where (α) 7 ⟶ ∞ starts: "from whence a voice . . ." (27—) — the voice of Jehovah. The reader will recall that a remarkable AP-series based on 7 starts after "O for that warning voice," at the beginning of Book IV (above, p. 67).

The retrograde series (PPP 17 ⟵) is not present.

(vi)

At PL IX, 896-916, motivating Adam's soliloquy, is the issue: to whom does he owe sovereign allegiance, absolute devotion? To Eve, "fairest of creation," or to the Creator himself, whom Eve has just disobeyed? 7 = sovereignty. The paragraph is scribed and circumscribed with PPP 7 ∞'s. Given $n = 21$,

PPP 7: *7, 28, 7, 28* [*28, 7, 28, 7*]
↑ ^ ↑ ^

Several antithetic pairs may be said to be performing in one consort, making the following interlock-design:

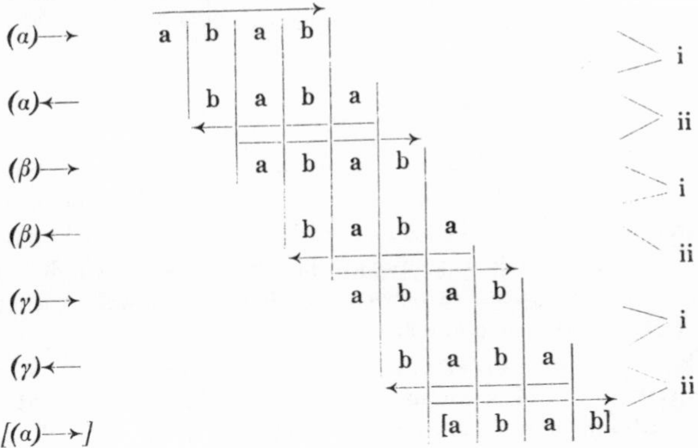

Sequences of Symmetry

i. 7, 28, 7, 28, 7
ii. 28, 7, 28, 7, 28

(α) → starts at "amiable, or sweet! . . ." (899—)
← " " "Defac'd, deflower'd, and now to death devote? . . . (901—)
(β) → " " "for with thee . . ." (907—)
← " " "How can I live without thee, . . ." (908—)
(γ) → " " "no, no, I feel . . ." (913—)
← " " "Bone of my bone thou art, . . ." (915—)

Each series is really infinite, for the sequence of remainders for PPP 7, given $n = 21$, is 7, 28, 7, 28, 7, . . . , and the sum of $7+28+7+28+7+28$ is 105, or $5n$. Hence each series girdles the paragraph and continues indefinitely.

These alternating currents of PPP 7 → ∞ and PPP 7 ← ∞ may be taken as the mathematical mirror of Adam's inner turmoil — of his "thoughts disturb'd."

6

Let us now examine some unusual responses to context, and include progressions that are sequences of squares.

(i)

At PL IX, 494-548 are two paragraphs very critical to the fable, and each has, underneath its metric surface, what looks like an extraordinary symbolic gloss. In the first (494-531) Satan in serpent-form so disports himself before Eve as to catch her eye. In the second (532-548) he catches her ear as well, with words that flatter and astound her.

In the 38-line paragraph at IX, 494-531 the serpent enacts a dumbshow full of grace and blandishment. There is present a pair of antithetic power series whose root is 3. Each series is carried to five terms, i.e., to a redundant term beyond the usual Pythagorean four, in what seems like clear response to "floated redundant" (503) and "tortuous train" (516). At the same time this extension to five terms enables each series to circuit the paragraph, indeed circuit it almost twice. For the sum of the first four powers of 3 is only 120. But if we add 3^5 (243), the total is 363 (=[2×5*n*] minus 17). As will presently appear, if each series were restricted to the usual four terms, the failure of these intervals to make a full circuit would result in a lost opportunity to respond to context.

We can only surmise why the root-number is 3. Is it because the serpent is associated with the triple curse of Genesis? Or, if 3 carries the meaning of justice, is the concurrent performance of PP 3 ⟶ and PP 3 ⟵ meant to reflect the moral ambiguity of the serpent's antics? If 3 means justice, righteousness, and faith, does 3 ⟶ point to the serpent's lustrous beauty that seems incapable of guile, while 3 ⟵ symbolizes the perfidy of Satan's mask?

PP 3 (to five terms):

(3, 9, 27, 81, -137) = ^17, ^3, 9, 27, 81 [*81, 27, 9, 3,* ^*17*^]

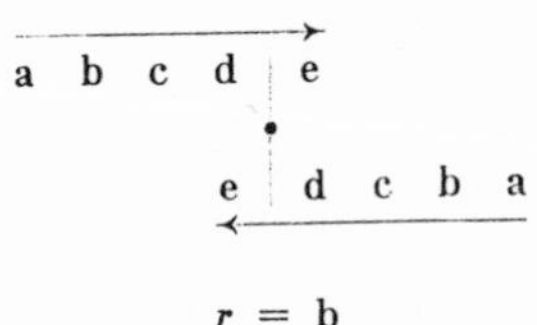

r = b

S. of Sym.: 25, 17, 3, 9, 27, 27, 9, 3, 17, 25

→ starts at "as since, but on his rear, . . ." (497—)
ends " end of paragraph
← starts " "and of his tortuous train . . ." (516—)
ends " " . . . side-long he works his way." (512)

Besides the response to redundance of terms, the progressions of this interlock are related to context in other curious ways.

(a) As in certain paragraphs elsewhere the context may refer obliquely to the mathematical process itself, so here the word "base" (498) instantly follows the base- or root-term of PP 3 →, and "Circular base of rising folds" describes the movement not only of the serpent's body but of the progression rising in numerical value to encircle the paragraph.

(b) Much more extraordinary is the following feature. The vital 3-beat root-term of the retrograde series — "side-long he works his way" (512) — contains a pun that shows how Milton can merge his music with his mathematics.

Sidelong motion is that of a crab. For musicians of the 17th century and earlier, a crab's imagined way of progressing suggested, and confirmed the use of, a technical term, *canon cancrizans,* which still survives in 20th-century books on counterpoint. In canon cancrizans, or "retrograde canon," the melodic theme is reversed. An ingenious composer may make both direct and retrograde forms of the theme overlap — even perform simultaneously. A crab's motion seems to be at once backward as well as forward — an illusion of contrary motions merged into one coordinated act. Polyphonic musicians try to emulate this feat of nature. Masters of canon and fugue, including J. S. Bach, can blend antithetic rhythms and melodies into a harmonious interlock — precisely the rhythmic maneuver of Milton's in locking PP 3 → with PP 3 ← in this paragraph. The intervals that define these contrary progressions overlap and blend into a sequence of symmetry. Likewise the serpent's motion, in the manner of a successful canon cancrizans, creates, for all its devious gyrations, perfect harmony and grace.

In a way secretly insistent, then, Milton glosses this context with references at once mathematical and contrapuntal. I need hardly add that he could not have employed a word that literally denotes a crustacean image. A word like "crablike" would dull and degrade the serpentine object which he wants rather to make imposingly lustrous. So he suppresses "crab" and gives us the more general word "side-long" descriptive of a crab's peculiar gait; then he forces our minds to dwell on the pleasantly beguiling similitude of a sailboat tacking in the wind (513 f.).

This same paragraph contains certain other progressions whose opportune occurrence points to a very special numerical response.

For all his "wanton wreaths in sight of Eve," the serpent fails to arrest her eye until he postures directly in front of her as if in obsequious admiration and worship. "Oft he bow'd / His turret crest," (524-525), and fawned and licked the ground before her.

Try to visualize this encounter, and you will see why Milton should want to gloss it with progressions. Eve is used to the gambolings of Eden's menagerie. Therefore to attract her special attention would require something new and glamorous in the way of bowing and fawning. No wonder the serpent's "turret crest" curtsies in an emphatic variety of gestures. But observe that in so doing the resplendent head must descend from various elevations. And here is opportunity for mathematical response. It takes the form of an astonishing assemblage of retrograde progressions.

Within the compass of the four beats that follow the words, "oft he bow'd / His turret crest," no fewer than four retrograde — *only* retrograde — series start. But each has a different root. Accordingly each must start from a different numerical height and descend at a different rate of speed.

PPP 2 ←— starts at "and sleek enamell'd neck, . . ." (525—)
PPP 3 ←— " " "Fawning, . . ." (526—)
PPP 4 ←— " " "and lick'd the ground . . ." (526—)
PPP 16 ←— " " " " " "

The formulas are thus derived:

PPP 2: (2, 8, 32, -62) = *20, 2, 8, 32* [*32, 8, 2, 20*]
^ ↑ ^ ↑

PPP 3: (3, 27, 53, -93) = *10, 3, 27, 53* [*53, 27, 3, 10*]
^ ↑ ^ ↑

PPP 4: (4, 64, -116, 44) = *44, 4, 4, 64* [*64, 4, 4, 44*]
^ ↑ ^ ↑

PPP 16: (16, 66, -84, -14) = *14, 2, 16, 66* [*66, 16, 2, 14*]
^ ↑ ^ ↑

At no other place in Milton's verse do the beginnings of so many retrograde series of different roots converge so near to the same point. Almost certainly the root-numbers are not meant to bear separate symbolic meanings. Their one significant feature lies in their different downward rates of motion, and their starting from different numerical heights. And be it emphasized: not a single *ascending* series starts in the immediate vicinity of "oft he bow'd / His turret crest."

Some editors drop comma after "access" (511), causing PPP 4 ⟵ to vanish. Some drop comma after "field" (520) or after "crest" (525), causing PPP 2 ⟵ to vanish.

(ii)

The serpent's ensuing speech in the paragraph at IX, 532-548, crammed with successful flattery, is very slow-paced, loaded with stops, as if Satan were alertly pausing again and again to gauge the effect of his phrases. So many are these pauses that the *chance*-occurrence of a certain number of interval-sequences defining power-series is inevitable. We are compelled therefore to ask: What progressions must we discard because they seem beyond doubt fortuitous? Which may we retain with any assurance as responsive?

At the same time inexorable logic declares: Once concede that in any paragraph, long or short, Milton consciously scribes a sequence of intervals to demarcate any mathematical progression, you cannot then deny the probable presence of symbolic sequences in other paragraphs. And logic, just as inexorably, tells us that in any paragraph, solely by chance, may occur a sequence of progression-intervals which Milton himself was entirely unaware of.

For us there is only one way of telling chance-progression from planned progression: indubitable response to context. Symbolic and directional responses are the heart of the matter. The present paragraph at PL IX, 532-548, with all its points of pause, probably contains a number of chance-progressions. But I shall now submit evidence for the presence of some exceptionally responsive progressions that point to conscious scribing.

10 is not only the Pythagorean number of perfection, but, as multiple of 5, the number of power. Satan contrasts the power of Eve's perfect beauty (10 ⟶), fit to ravish the gods, with the waste and impotence of that beauty (10 ⟵) confined "in this enclosure wild." Given $n = 17$,

PP 10: (10, 15, -20, -30) = *25, 5, 5, 15* [*15, 5, 5, 25*]

But let us carry the progression to seven terms.

PP 10 (to seven terms) : (10, 15, -20, -30, 40, -25, 5) =
15, 5, 5, 5, 5, 5, 10 [*10, 5, 5, 5, 5, 5, 15*]

Both PP 10 ⟶ and PP 10 ⟵ are present, each carried to seven terms.

⟶ starts at "thy daily train . . ." (548—)
ends " " . . . A goddess among gods," (547)
⟵ starts " "if perhaps . . ." (532—)
ends " " . . . angels numberless," (548)

⟶ is exactly superposed on ⟵:

a	b^v	b^w	b^x	b^y	b^z c
c b^z	b^y	b^x	b^w	b^v	a

$r = b^x + b^y$

S. of Sym. : 10, 5, 5, 5, 5, 5, 5, 10

Since neither series stops at the sixth term, and neither goes to the eighth, the fact that each goes to the seventh seems truly significant. 7 = godhead, divinity, celestial sovereignty. The full symbolic meaning of PP 10 ⟶ (to seven terms) is therefore a conflation of the meanings of 10 and 7: "the sovereign power of [Eve's] perfect and celestial beauty."

But the paragraph is still further scribed with PP 10's. If we restrict series to the usual four terms, we find a second interlock, and the two interlocks are locked into a consort that creates four sequences of symmetry.

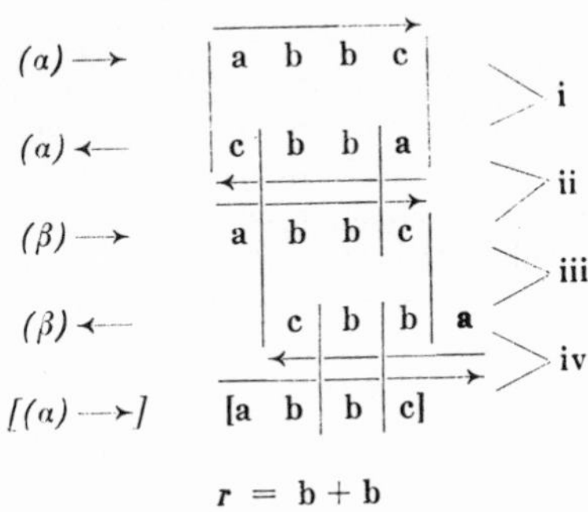

r = b + b

Sequences of Symmetry

i. 15, 5, 5, 5, 5, 15
ii. 10, 15, 5, 5, 15, 10
iii. 25, 5, 5, 5, 5, 5, 25
iv. 15, 10, 5, 5, 5, 10, 15

(α) ⟶ starts at "thy daily train . . ." (458—)
ends " " . . . in this enclosure wild," (543)
(α) ⟵ starts " "nor have fear'd / That awful brow . . ." (536—)
ends " " . . . angels numberless," (548)
(β) ⟶ starts " "who should'st be seen . . ." (546 —)
ends " " . . . with ravishment beheld," (541)
(β) ⟵ starts " "all things thine / By gift, . . ." (539—)
ends " " . . . the heaven of mildness," (534)

(iii)

One of the puns in Satan's derisive speech at PL VI, 609-619 is mathematical. In the statement, "[we] propounded terms / Of composition" (612-613), "terms" hints of a cluster of significant progressions "composed" to gloss the ironic context. But before describing Satan's sally of mathematical wit — worthy of Isaac Newton — I must allay the reader's possible suspicion of illicit ingenuity on my part. I have not selected certain formula-intervals out of some available large number present in this paragraph, for the fact is that it contains no progressions based on any other roots than those that here serve Satan's purpose.

These progressions are two PPP's (PPP 6 —➤ and PPP 9 —➤), a P^P (P^P 8 —➤), and a S Sq. No need to consider here the symbolic meanings of roots, for Satan selects his roots simply because they alone, given *n* = 11, offer places of beginning and ending to suit his particular maneuver.

Now the formulas for PPP 6 —➤ and PPP 9 —➤, given *n* = 11, are extraordinary in that they are almost identical. Such near-identity of formulas, occurring in any table of formulas based on any value of *n*, is so rare as to be a mathematical freak. The explanation of it we can leave to the professional mathematician. What we are chiefly interested in now are matters like the following: (1) PPP 6 —➤ and PPP 9 —➤ have the very same sequence of intervals; (2) each starts at the same point in the sequence; (3) in only one respect do they differ: they end at different points of pause; (4) the startling response to context of so unusual a pair of formulas is a signal reminder of Milton's close study of progressions and his ability to adjust them to paragraph-length.

Given *n* = 11,

PPP 6: (6, -4, 21, -14) = *2, 4, 3, 14*
↑ ^

PPP 9: (9, 14, -21, 4) = *2, 4, 3, 14*
↑ ^

PPP 6 —➤ starts at "(what could we more?) . . ." (612—)
ends " " . . . straight they chang'd their minds;" (613)

PPP 9 —➤ starts where PPP 6 —➤ starts
ends at " . . . terms / Of composition," (613)

With the text before him, let the reader verify also the presence of P^p 8 ⟶. Given $n = 11$,

P^p 8: *8, 9, 26, 16*
↑ ^

P^p 8 ⟶ starts at "straight they chang'd their minds. . . ." (613—)
ends " " . . . Flew off," (614)

We are now equipped to discern each point in Satan's mathematical jesting. With his cry, "What could we more?" both PPP's begin, each rooted in a different number. He couldn't do more with numerical calculation than that! — when the double-headed beginning gives to the words immediately preceding, "open front / And breast" (611-612), an appropriate ironic gloss of ambiguity, paralleling the ambiguous nature of those "pillars laid / On wheels" which proved so deceptively different from hollow oaks.

PPP 9 ⟶ ends with " . . . propounded terms Of composition," but immediately following these words comes the statement, "straight they chang'd their minds," which ends PPP 6 ⟶. Thus there is a "change of mind" as to where progressions end. Shift three beats ahead of one ending and there's another ending, in spite of the fact that both progressions have begun simultaneously.

But the "change of mind" is much more drastic. For with the very words, "straight they chang'd their minds," which end PPP 6 ⟶, an entirely different series starts, rooted in a different number: root 9 gives way to root 8 in a power-of-power series.

But notice the words that terminate P^p 8 ⟶: "Flew off." The 4th term of P^p 8 ⟶ is 8^8, or 16777216: certainly high enough for a flight off!

And a radically new feature begins with this 1-beat interval, "Flew off." These words begin a kind of progression different from any of the others: a S Sq ⟶: 1^2, 2^2, 3^2, 4^2, 5^2, which Satan's punning words describe as a fall (from the top of P^p 8 ⟶!) "into strange vagaries" —

> As they would dance, yet for a dance they seem'd
> Somewhat extravagant and wild, (615-616).

This S Sq $\rightarrow$ does indeed, by an uncanny calculation and adjustment of its first five terms, dance forward. It encircles and exactly girdles the paragraph. The end of the fifth term returns it to where it starts, for $1+4+9+16+25 = 55 = 5n$.

Commentators ascribe this ironic dance to the influence of Homer. But it is both Homeric and Cartesian. It is the creation of a satanic mathematician's sense of humor.

(iv)

In the paragraph at PL IX, 834-855 is the S Sq $\rightarrow$: $2^2, 4^2, 6^2, 8^2, 10^2$. Start at "Great joy he promis'd . . ." (843—) and end " . . . their harvest queen." (842) When reduced to formula, this sequence requires only four intervals to demarcate it. Given $n = 22$,

$$4, 16, 36, 64, 100 = (4, 16, 36, -46, -10) = 4, 6, 10, 36$$

2 = woman, here Eve, who entirely possesses Adam's thought. Hence the successive numbers squared not only start with 2 but ascend by additions of 2. The progression goes through the fifth term because (i) 5 = marriage; (ii) $2^2 + 4^2 + 6^2 + 8^2 + 10^2 = 220 = 2 \times 5n$. Carried through five terms, this S Sq $\rightarrow$ makes therefore exactly two circuits of the paragraph, ending where it begins.

In summary: the number of terms is the number of marriage; the series girdles the paragraph as many times as the number of woman; and the number of woman is (i) the starting-base, (ii) the amount by which successive base-numbers expand, and (iii) the exponent of the progressive involution.

S Sq $\rightarrow$ opens with Adam's joyous prospect of reunion with Eve. It culminates in his vision of her beauty crowned like a rural queen.

. . . . . .

But simultaneously performing with this wholly affirmative "voice" is a consort of progressions that respond to Adam's misgiving, to the ambiguity of his feelings. 4, the root-number, is probably the number of woman squared: hence = woman.

PP 4: (4, 16, -46, 36) = *26, 4, 6, 10* [*10, 6, 4, 26*]
↑ ^ ↑ ^

S. of Sym.

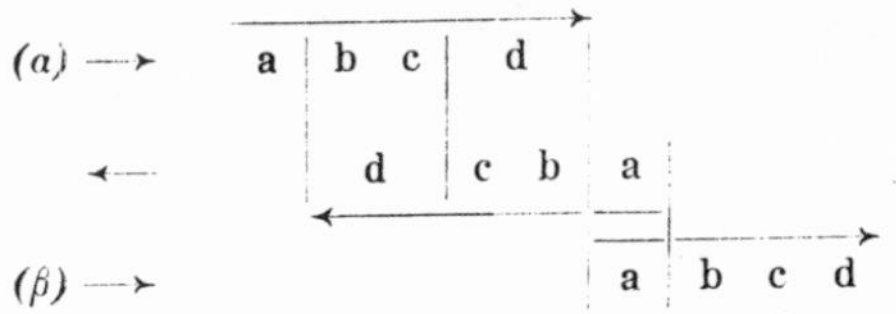

(*a*) ⟶	a | b c | d		26, 4, 6, 6, 4, 26
⟵	d | c b a		10, 6, 4, *26*, 4, 6, 10
(*β*) ⟶		a b c d	

r = b

(*a*) ⟶ starts at "Great joy he promis'd . . ." (843—)
ends " " . . . so long delay'd;" (844)
⟵ starts " "Yet oft his heart . . ." (845—)
ends " " . . . hee the falt'ring measure felt;" (846)
(*β*) ⟶ starts " "and ambrosial smell diffus'd . . ." (852—)
ends " " . . . Came prologue," (854)

Observe the perfect responses of all the head-terms, and especially the extraordinarily apt response of the terminal or root-term of ⟵. One is tempted to surmise that since Adam's joy of anticipation exceeds his misgiving, the consort is so devised that two ⟶'s are locked with only one ⟵.

(v)

A sequence of cubes rarely occurs. The best instance is in the 13-line paragraph at PR IV, 486-498, in which the following series is present: S Cu ⟵: 9^3, 7^3, 5^3, 3^3, 1^3 [729, 343, 125, 27, 1]. The simplest way to trace it is by way of a sequence of remainders reduced to formula; thus:

(14, 18, -5, 27, 1) = *14, 13, 5, 22, 1*
↑ ^

Start at "other harm . . ." (486—). Down from your proud height, ambitious spirit! says Jesus, and the descending progression parallels the thought, flashing with final clarity on the magisterial word, "desist," (497). The progression desists, though Satan is not yet willing to do so.

This sequence 14, 13, 5, 22, 1 does not occur in any of the other eleven 13-line paragraphs which are in PL and PR. Nor is a five-term series of this kind to be found anywhere else in Milton's epic verse. The inference seems irresistible: Milton computes and scribes it to fit the dramatic nadir-term "desist."

(vi)

A progression may be invented to gloss some graphic representation or description of a theological dogma. The case I now present may at first strain credulity. But in representations of Father and Son, in paragraphs where they speak or act, mathematics seems more than usually active. One comes to expect ingenious responses. And in the very short 5-line paragraph at PL X, 63-67 there seems to be such a response. Here, immediately after the Father has commissioned the Son to be man's judge and mediator, the Son is revealed as the express image of the Father's glory.

But how can mere words, however phrased and metred, suffice to tell so celestial a relationship, transcending human understanding? Every pious Christian reveres the verse in Hebrews here paraphrased, and would despair of improving on it. Milton seems here to have the baroque artist's confidence in mathematically exact proportioning and scaffolding that may enable him to infuse into the texture of his language something of the transcendental.

First of all, he wants an unusual kind of progression. If the Son can manifest the Father in full resplendence, then God is not one but two. Would it not be logical, then, to start the progression with the number 2 as base? So he invents the following series which occurs nowhere else in his verse:

$$2^2,\ 3^3,\ 4^4,\ 5^5,\ 6^6$$

Before we try to trace it, let us reduce it to a sequence of remainders. Given $n = 5$, we have:

$$(4, 27, 256, 3125, 46656) = 4, 2, 6, 0, 6$$

Start 2^2 at "and thus divinely answer'd mild" (67), and the five terms carry us to the semicolon ending the words, " . . . Blaz'd forth unclouded Deity;" (65).

But the progression does not go to 7^7 [823543], which would be demarcated by a pause 7 beats behind "Deity." There is no such pause present, i.e., -7 is not present. But observe that +7 *is* present. If we want a 7 in the series we must go *forward* from "Deity." Following 6^6, then, is 7^1. And if we reread the text we realize why the ascending progression halts at 6^6.

Jehovah's sacred number is 7. But 7 raised to any power beyond 7^1 ceases to be a 7 "manifest" to eye or ear. Nor can Jehovah be raised to any higher power than he is. Hence in this progression the 1st power is reserved for the Father *manifest,* and its position is exalted to the culminant place: 2^2, 3^3, 4^4, 5^5, 6^6, 7^1.

Perhaps, however, a more plausible way of explaining this anomalous progression is to start it with the "manifest 7." The complete sequence of remainders would then be: 7,4,2,6,0,6. The sum of these intervals is remarkable: it exactly girdles the paragraph, making a perfect circuit. For $7+4+2+6+0+6 = 25 = 5n$. If the terms are thus arranged, their order is determined by the order of their exponents. It is an exponential series, the only one I have found. The Father comes first, his sacred number manifest. He is Unity, incapable of rising to any power higher than himself. The reader can quickly check my analysis by starting the series (7^1, 2^2, 3^3, 4^4, 5^5, 6^6) with the words, "he full . . ." (65).

We are here impinging on the esoteric. But the text is before us, and the context. The intervals are unalterable. The inference seems inescapable that Milton is here identifying God with the Platonic Idea of pure mathematician uttering the ineffable in a unique progression that traces a geometric figure the most perfect conceivable — a closed circle. It is certainly a curious and significant fact that *all* the pauses in this paragraph — five, including the end-period — participate in demarcating the series. If the anomalous first term were any number but 7, I would scrap it all as fortuitous. But this term parallels one of the mysteries of orthodox Christian dogma, one that has a central place in the immediate context, inviting and satisfying a traditionally symbolic interpretation.

CHAPTER VI

L' ESPRIT GÉOMÉTRIQUE

1

If it is a fact that Milton consciously incorporates in his paragraphs such progressions as I have described, then he must have studied mathematical series as such, calculated their relation to various paragraph-lengths, and learned to adjust them unobtrusively to his rhetoric. The reader should reexamine especially the examples in which (i) two antithetic power-progressions based on the same root are locked together to produce a sequence of symmetry; (ii) the interlocking pair exactly girdles the paragraph, with locked terms at opposite poles (opposite centers of symmetry); and (iii) more than two series, each based on the same root, are locked in what I call a consort. Be it noted that the resultant geometric configurations correspond to the three recognized types of two-dimensional symmetry: (i) bilateral, (ii) rotational, and (iii) ornamental.[1]

Again, if consciously scribed interlocks are a fact, not only was Milton aware that he was creating sequences of symmetry as a by-product of such interlocking, but — and this corollary seems of utmost importance — he knew that in many a paragraph other progression-sequences, wholly fortuitous, were certain to be present. He knew that with every increase in the number of pauses to accommodate a symbolic series there would be an increased opportunity for chance to demarcate progression-sequences which he never calculated and never intended, and which therefore bear no symbolic relation to context except by rarest chance.

A priori, up and down Milton's epic verse such fortuitous sequences are sure to be irregularly present — hundreds of them, including interlocks. But does it follow that *all* sequences that tally with progression-formulas are necessarily fortuitous? Logic replies no. As I have shown, not only is the symbolic response of many a progression too precise and opportune to be conceivable as fortuitous, but behind it is a demonstrable motive — the fulfilment of a contrapuntal ideal.

There was a time when I did regard as fortuitous all sequences that tally with progression-formulas. Because many such sequences must inevitably occur by chance I assumed that all must so occur. I felt I could dismiss symbolic series forever. But my joy was short-lived. Too many phenomena in the form of seemingly indubitable symbolic responses kept forcing themselves on me. Some of them I have explained in the last two chapters. I could not dodge the cold logic of the case: to concede the presence of a consciously designed symbolic progression in any *one* of Milton's paragraphs is to concede the possible presence of a similar phenomenon in some other paragraph. Any other alternative must be an uncompromising, dogged denial of all.

If PL were the work of a 20th century contemporary, then perhaps an obstinate and total scepticism towards the existence of numerical symbol in mathematical progressions, a scepticism of absolute incredulousness, might be justifiable. But we are dealing with a 17th-century mind environed by influences that persist from medieval times. It is neither improbable nor absurd that, for the purpose of furthering a unique artistic ideal, Milton should secretly indulge in numerical symbol. With verifiable and what seems to me irrefutable evidence, I am compelled to accept as very probable products of conscious design a substantial number of numerical progressions in PL and PR. Chance can account for random progression-sequences, even for random interlocks, but, given the limited number of paragraphs in PL and PR, chance simply has not scope enough to effect a whole assemblage of remarkable responses between progressions and specific contextual situations.

At this point let us review a number of facts that will keep the whole problem before us.

2

No other blank verse — as prosodists wonderingly tell — can compare with Milton's in the frequency of interior line-pause. And this, too, coexistent with an unprecedented rate of enjambement. The critics venture no explanation except that it just *is*.

But, underlying this style is an ideal drawn from a sister art: from Milton's passionate study and love from childhood: contrapuntal music — the rhythmic method of canon and free fugue. In its rhythmic structure his epic unit, the paragraph, is an analogue to a finished contrapuntal piece. Essential to it are overlappings of the metric base by different lengths of iambic and trochaic rhythms; at the same time a jealous safeguarding of that base from obliteration under non-pentameter overlaps. In furtherance of both practices he extends blank-verse prosody to include the technique of cross-rhythmic construction. It is a new technique. It at once complicates and controls the movement of highly enjambed passages. As an invention it is inimitable in the variety of cross-rhythmic patterns that integrate to multiples of the norm. Its intermittent presence goes far to explain what we all feel in Milton's style: alternations of rhythmic tension and relief. Shakespeare and John Fletcher, when they indulge in cross-rhythmic construction, give scarcely a hint of .the variety and ingenuity of the patterns that Milton systematizes and employs.[2]

His contrapuntal ideal, inasfar as it includes his perfecting of cross-rhythmic construction, can in itself account for a high frequency of interior line-pause. Yet, as I have tried to show step by step, there is impressive evidence that he has invented an even bolder way to support and implement his ideal. At times he incorporates into his rhythms an extraprosodic, extrarhetorical — in truth a transcendental — element: symbol. I have tried to show how in at least *some* of his paragraphs he glosses the rhythms with numerical progressions whose direction and base-numbers respond symbolically to contextual situations, playing the contrapuntal role of personalized cross-rhythmic "voices." I have shown how these progressions are first noticeable in the primary Pythagorean series 1, 2, 3, 4 and 4, 3, 2, 1 occurring in both cross-rhythmic and linear form, with consistent directional response to context. But they occur oftener in linear form, for then they may have a significant number as multiplier. And one perceives a consistency of response to context that seems to outstrip the busiest workings, the widest ambit, of chance.

Since Milton's general contrapuntal method of free overlapping must of itself bring into being fortuitous interval-sequences that tally with formulas for power-progressions, creating an unusual amount of interior line-pause, then any additional motive for increasing the points of pause, like the contrapuntal motive for scribing symbolic progressions, tends to give chance more and more opportunity to demarcate progressions never intended.

A mathematical analyst, unfamiliar with Milton's blank verse, if told it has an unprecedented number of pauses, merely says: As pauses increase, so would chance-sequences of any four random numbers. There are indeed some paragraphs which at first seem to confirm such a generalization as the whole truth. Consider the paragraph at PL V, 28-94, whose context includes slow-moving, even halting utterance: Eve tells Adam, point by point, her disturbing dream. Actually a third of all the possible places of pause are punctuated. If we scan for progression-sequences, we find so many that at first we declare: "Here surely Milton has not adjusted his rhetoric to fix any particular progressions, or, if he has done so, it's hopeless to discriminate between chance and design."

Not so hasty: even in this paragraph — the extreme instance — one finds certain series and interlocks whose significant base-numbers and whose patterns do point to conscious design. In a previous chapter I used this very paragraph to show the presence of a sequence of AP's almost incredibly responsive to context. Let us remember that this sequence — AP 11 ← (44, 33, 22, 11) + AP 19 → (19, 38, 57, 76) + AP 1 ← (4, 3, 2) — does not begin just anywhere at random in the paragraph, but at the precise point where successive base-numbers will tally, symbolically, with change of thought. A mathematician who says offhand that in any paragraph containing an unusual number of pauses we can find any series whatsoever if we keep looking for it would be right if the number of pauses actually equalled 5*n*, the total number of beats — an impossibility. The number of pauses in the most pointed of the paragraphs of PL does reach, however, a full third of 5*n*, as here. Yet the intervals demarcated by these pauses are not a procession of random numbers underived from, and unattached to, contextual situations. The sequence of AP's at PL V,30-92 occurs nowhere else in the paragraph, nowhere else in Milton's epic verse; where they do occur is just where their head-terms or base-terms respond to immediate context according to symbolic meanings recurrent elsewhere in the poem. Hence the assumption that these AP's are consciously scribed seems founded on the highest probability.

But certain sequences demarcating power-progressions in this same paragraph can also be demonstrated as having been scribed with just as high a probability. I shall trace them with a minimum of detail, but enough to enable any reader to verify their presence.

3

7 is the number of godhead. 11 is the number of obeisance or worship. In this 67-line paragraph (PL V, 28-94) the concepts of godhead and of obeisance are vital. And both PP 7 and PP 11 occur in almost identical consort-pattern.

So unusual a duplication of so complex a configuration, with — at the same time, observe — head- or root-terms of all constituent progressions responsive to immediate context — can this be anything but conscious design? It is as if, after scribing the pattern with a certain root-number and formula, Milton found it comparatively easy to adjust it again, this time with a different root-number and formula, keeping its constituent progressions responsive to context. In no other paragraph does the duplication of this particular consort-pattern occur.

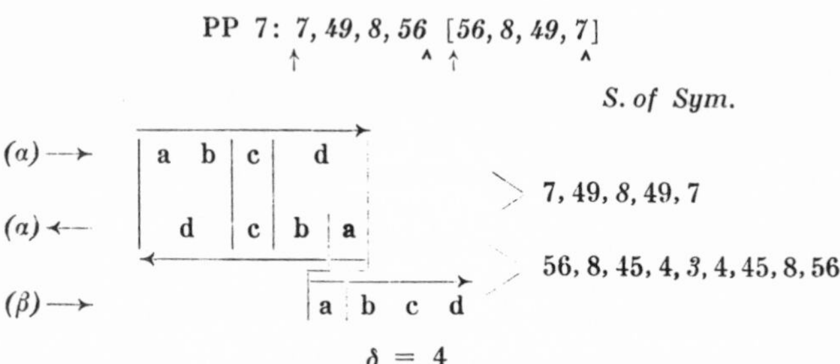

(α) → starts at "Deigns none to ease thy load and taste thy sweet, / Nor God, nor man;" (59—)
ends " "... and to me held," (82)

(α) ← starts where (α) → starts
ends " " ends

(β) → starts at "and see / What life the gods live there . . ." (80—)
ends " "... I thought it thine;" (37)

Notice that the disjunction in the root-term of (α)⟶ ("Nor God, nor man;") seems to dictate the simultaneity of ⟶ and ⟵. The same disjunction is in the 8-beat center of symmetry: "yet able to make gods of men: / And why not gods of men, since good," (70-71).

The head-term of (β)⟶ also starts with words perfectly responsive to the traditional symbolic meaning of 7.

. . . . . .

PP 11: (11, 121, -9, -99) = *11, 13, 99, 9* [*9, 99, 13, 11*]

S. of Sym.

(α)⟶	a b c d	9, 2, 13, *84*, 13, 2, 9
(α)⟵	d c b a	9, 99, 13, 8, *3*, 8, 13, 99, 9
(β)⟶	a b c d	

δ = 8

(α) ⟶ starts at "in vain, / If none regard; Heaven wakes . . ." (43—)
ends " ". . . I rose as at thy call;" (48)
(α) ⟵ starts " "mee damp horror chill'd . . ." (65—)
ends " ". . . only fit / For gods," (70)
(β) ⟶ starts " "as only fit / For gods, . . ." (69—)
ends " ". . . happy creature," (74)

4

But the paragraph in question is so full of pauses that a dozen other progression-intervals, inevitably present as chance-products of sheer frequency of pause, could easily be pointed out. If Milton was aware of their presence, even though he could not specifically define them, not having scribed them, how is he likely to have regarded them?

He would have welcomed them. Even though undefined and

unintended, they would be background-"voices" or *ripieni,* helping to swell the total harmony of cross-rhythmic progressions in a grandly unified contrapuntal performance. He would favor all possibilities of mathematical proportion and progression informing the texture of his verse.

Such an inference, once we posit his contrapuntal ideal, is inescapable. Besides, such an attitude comports with the largest aspect of his epic style. It is baroque, baroque not only in adapting the ideals of a sister-art to produce astonishingly expressive rhythmic effects but in requisitioning the science of mathematics to build up calculated progressions behind a facade of measured rhetoric. To such an art-medium mathematics had never before been thus applied.

I submit that when Milton consciously scribes definite symbolic progressions, at the same time acquiescing in the inevitable chance-presence of unpremeditated progressions, he is not only motivated by a contrapuntal ideal of paragraph-construction but by the baroque faith in mathematics to stabilize, formalize, energize its rhythmic design and texture.

Let us for a moment consider a consciously scribed interlock of antithetic series. The progressions, as directional series, move. And when the root-number is a responsive gloss on the context, they have more than directional meaning. But the very fact of motion, of ⟶ and ⟵ going in contrary directions numerically and locking one or more common terms, creates a symmetrically ordered sequence of numbers that seems meant to arrest and reconcile the opposing motions and the antithetic concepts they symbolize. Contradictories are thus resolved into a configuration at once dynamic and stable.

The fact that ancient philosophy from the time of Pythagoras reduced music to progressions and proportions would alone have spurred Milton to study them with passionate zeal. But such study was unavoidable. It was the spirit of the age that produced Galileo, Kepler, and Descartes. Contemporary with Milton was Father Mersenne, the theme of whose widely influential *Harmonie Universelle* (1636) is that all music is but a part of mathematics. Even in the next generation Newton himself was sympathetic to the leading tenet of Pythagoras. "He was profoundly affected," says his biographer, Louis T. More (*Isaac Newton,* N. Y., 1934, p. 475), "by the significance of the constant and unaccountable occurrence of simple geometrical ratios in physical phenomena. He found in musical harmony the principle of law and order in the cosmos, and believed that the Creator revealed Himself to us through our appreciation of those mathematical ratios. . . . In the advocacy of the Pythagorean-Platonic philosophy, he was following the ideas of his great predecessors, Copernicus, Kepler, and Galileo. But he went even further than they: 'He thought Pythagoras' music of the spheres was intended to typify gravity, and, as he makes the sounds and notes depend on the size of the strings, so gravity depends on the density of matter.'"

All artists, including writers, architects, sculptors, painters, musicians, recognized in "universal mathematics" a reservoir of means and methods for rivaling, even excelling Nature, certainly for interpreting her. Charles Lebrun, the leading organizer of the French Academy of Painting and Sculpture, and official painter in the palace of Versailles, "demanded that painting be founded on geometry" (Carl Sachs: *Rhythm and Tempo*, N.Y., 1953, p. 265). We today, eager to characterize historical periods, call this allegiance to mathematics a symptom of the baroque.

Concerning the art of Frans Hals, the historian Carl Friedrich comments: "It has now been shown that underlying his dash and naturalistic vivacity there was a hard geometric core of structure and rationalist rigidity" (*The Age of the Baroque*, p. 79). He goes on to mention city-planning, then Bernini's stage-designs, then grand opera as "the culmination of that spirit of extravagant vitality and complex mathematical design, or overweening sense of unity and power as the meaning and significance of creative effort. In creating them, man truly worked in the image of God, the Almighty . . . 'But you have ordered everything according to measure, number and weight.' This line from the Wisdom of Solomon (11 : 21) was a favorite quotation in the early seventeenth century" (pp. 85, 93). And this concerning Milton and post-Renaissance writers: "*Paradise Lost* was the Protestant response to the challenge of the Italian *dramma di musica* as Milton had experienced it on his Italian journey. . . . The *Divine Comedy* was the true inspiration of Milton, as St. Augustine and St. Thomas had been of Luther, Calvin, and their followers. . . . In all these writers [Milton, Corneille, Calderon, Vondel, Opitz, Gryphius, Gerhardt, Grimmelshausen, Pascal] Renaissance elements were present to some extent, but basically that was true of all baroque forms:

they sought to combine somehow the formal perfection of the preceding age with the sense of the working of supernatural powers, within and without man. Deeply metaphysical, the baroque poets and writers strained to the utmost their powers of formal art to capture the sense of these dynamic forces" (p. 48).

Is it illusory to maintain, then, that when Milton incorporates symbolic progressions in his verse, he is challenging mortality with mathematics in the very spirit of the baroque, as it has never been challenged in either prose or "numerous verse"? His supple and versatile rhetoric can fix certain significant intervals with a precision rivaling the concealed calculations of Bernini.

In such a situation his whole mind is engaged, or, rather, three overlapping areas of it. One area is a medieval inheritance — symbol; one is the purest of the disciplines sustaining modern science; one is a bequest from Tudor music.

The father's madrigals and anthems determine the son's adaptation of contrapuntal device. The epic paragraph shall contain analogues to the fugal method of voices overlapping voices, yet all harmoniously "concenting." Each competing part "through all proportions low and high" shall possess a rhythmic individuality. Hence the occasional scribing of progressions that move up or down, backward or forward, but move — for motion is their essence. And as they move in cross-rhythm, they can intersect rival progressions whose rate of motion may be slower or faster after the manner of augmented or diminished canon. If the rates are equal, and the directions of movement antithetic, the pair may interlock, creating bilateral symmetry: a static phenomenon, a stabilizer in the midst of incessant motion, true manifestation of *l'esprit géométrique,* a pledge of the imperishable, a winged configuration symbolizing Pegasus.

Nor must it be overlooked that the analogue of perpetual canon, achieved by regarding the start of a paragraph as but a continuation of the end, makes every paragraph a continuum potentially infinite. Thus Milton manages to have the infinite *pervade* the rhythms of his sacred song. I have already adduced signal instances of infinite series that perpetually circuit the paragraph in response to concepts of the infinite. But these two phenomena — perpetual canon and infinite series — are just what every thinker on the subject of the baroque stresses: all the baroque masters are characterized by incessant movement serving aspirations toward the infinite. Curt

Sachs is the latest expounder. "The Baroque aimed at the infinite as opposite to the finite of the Renaissance" (*op. cit.,* p. 266). "Ceaseless movement is one of the first characteristics of rhythm and tempo in the Baroque" (p. 281).

If precisely scribed series, interlocks, and consorts are marks of the Cartesian, scientific area in Milton's many-provinced mind, his endowing of their root-numbers with symbolic meanings is in spirit Dantean, however independent or eclectic may be the symbolic ascriptions. Such an alliance of Descartes with Dante, or renaissance with medieval, an alliance that seems so incongruous, has been fostered, we now perceive, by the cultural climate of the age. Such violent incongruity is an aspect of the baroque.

But the alliance does not exist for its own sake; it is a means to an ideal end. It is the servant of a sublimely conceived polyphony whose voices are etherealized to rhythms, to numbers — in every sense of the word. The subsurface texture of an undetermined amount of Milton's epic verse is pure baroque.

If this reasoning is correct, we should not be surprised to find extraordinary responses of progressions to context, responses that may even be called cabalistic. I now invite the reader to examine with me an instance or two of Milton's adaptation of a geometric spiral to a symbolic numerical progression.

5

In the paragraph at PL IV, 720-735 we listen to Adam and Eve at their evening prayer. If we spread out the intervals consecutively from mark to mark of punctuation as given in Ed. 1 (not Ed. 2), we find them very strangely ordered. Indeed the sequence, found nowhere else in Milton, contains an ordonnance of rhythmic lengths so appealingly rational that not even the most resistant sceptic can call it fortuitous.

Before we trace it, however, let us observe that the statement at lines 721-723 —

> and under open sky ador'd
> The God that made both sky, air, earth and heaven
> Which they beheld,

is an integral unit of 11 beats. The two interior commas do not fractionate it. The words "sky, air, earth and heaven" are a compendious inventory of things beheld, which necessarily demands two commas, neither of which breaks the double overlap into subordinate currents. Absence of a comma after "heaven" suggests that Milton truly regards it as a continuous interval of 11 beats.

In this paragraph, then, the successive intervals are:

(a) 4, 1, 1, 11, 5, 3, 3, 2, 12, 5, 5, 4, 4, 7, 6, 2, 2, 1, 2

Each number from 1 through 5 is paired once and only once, and no other numbers are paired; and, except where 4's immediately follow 5's, we find, between one pair and another, two non-significant intervals, and only two. Let 0 represent a non-significant interval: then we have:

(b) 0 1 1 0 0 3 3 0 0 5 5 4 4 0 0 2 2 0 0

Notice how, to elude easy detection, each pair, wherever possible, straddles the metric line:

(c) 0 *1/1* 0 0 *3/3* 0 0 *3-/-2* *3-/-2* *3-/-1* 4 0 0 *2/2* 0 0

What is the meaning of such an ordonnance? A spiral. This prayer gyres heavenward on wings, even as other prayers of Adam and Eve are described as doing: "To Heaven their prayers / Flew up, nor miss'd the way . . . in they pass'd . . . through heavenly doors" — PL XI, 14-17. Sequence (b), like the key to a graph, permits us to trace a spiral in either clockwise or counterclockwise direction. Clockwise:

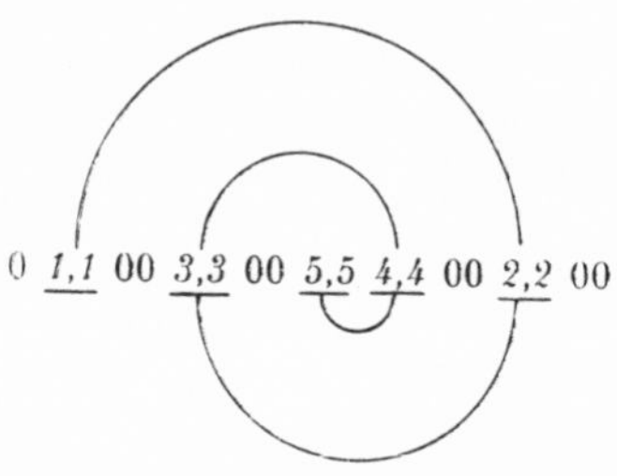

We may, then, conceive this paragraph's rhythmic texture, like the prayer itself, as forming something flexible and in motion, a symmetrical hypostasis of spiral or conical shape determined by numerical stages of ascent, with 5, 5 at the apex.

Now 10 is the Pythagorean number of perfection, being the sum of 1, 2, 3, 4; and 5 is the Pythagorean number of marriage. The primary Pythagorean progression advances in doubled numbers for perhaps two reasons. (i) Man and woman are acting as a pair, yet simultaneously as one petitioner: "both stood, / Both turn'd." Two act as one. (ii) Paired numbers suggest paired wings of the ascending prayer.

This spiral configuration signifies two perfect beings in perfect wedded union engaged in a joint act of aspiration.

As befits heart-to-heart converse of man with his Maker, the gloss is very private. Only by transcending prosody and rhetoric can it be apprehended. But as the pair turn from adoration of God to communion with each other, Milton starts another numerical gloss, almost as concealed.

Keep in mind that the prayer is here the prelude to entrance into the nuptial bower. The paragraph of prayer is therefore very closely connected in thought with what follows in the paragraph of the nuptial bower, so closely indeed that, for once, Milton actually extends a progression from one paragraph to the next: from the prayer-piece to the bower-piece. I know of no other primary Pythagorean series thus carried over. And it is this very maneuver that conceals it.

Sequence (a) ends with 2, 2, 1, 2. For the purpose of exhibiting the spiral in sequence (b), I represented the last two intervals as non-significant: 2 2 0 0. But 1, 2 — "as now, thy gift of sleep." — though non-significant for the spiral, are significant terms of a new progression. They begin an AP 1 $\longrightarrow$ carried to five terms with the 5th term doubled: an AP that continues across from paragraph to paragraph, from the prayer to the bower. The series 1, 2, 3, 4, 5, 5 ends with "into their inmost bower / Handed they went;" (738—).

Why is 5 doubled? Merely to repeat the double-5 of the preceding spiral series? Unlikely, since the other terms are not doubled. But Milton's careful phrasing of the second 5 suggests his purpose: "Handed they went;" — five fingers touching five fingers. The dominant stress falls on "Handed," an unforgettable word, curious and unusual for the sense it bears. It makes us stop and consider. There seems to be no record of its use before Milton, and only one record of its use elsewhere in Milton: in the Preface to his first divorce-tract.

This ascending spiral, immediately succeeded by an ascending linear series, is a unique configuration invented to gloss a unique context. Chance, if given sufficient scope, could produce this complete sequence — *qua* sequence of random numbers. But, out of the four hundred paragraphs in PL and PR, only at this place in PL does the sequence occur. In a procession of random numbers chance could do it. But the crucial question is: How many number-processions, each the length of PL, would chance require to produce this sequence at a contextual situation offering a responsive interpretation, a rational warranty for a rationally ordered grouping of numbers? We need no La Place or Gauss or Einstein to estimate such odds.

Editors, almost without exception, tamper with the punctuation of the prayer-paragraph as given in Ed. 1, thus destroying the rhythmic scheme. Ed. 2 is certainly in error in dropping comma after "stood" (720).

6

Five books away from the prayer-piece is another spiral configuration quite as interesting for its cryptic precision. When Milton scribed one he may well have been thinking of the other.

PL VIII, 644-651 is a paragraph so short that Milton ventures to compute intervals that require exactly ten spiral revolutions. And they spiral downward, not upward, passing through the successive terms of a descending AP 5, starting with the fifth term: 25, 20, 15, 10, 5. In contrast to the prayer-spiral, this one can be demonstrated only by regarding the intervals of the paragraph as continuous, i.e., the paragraph is in perpetual canon.

Adam, bidding farewell to Raphael, says: "Gentle to me and affable hath been / Thy condescension" (648-649). This 7-beat interval starts the (con)descending series. To see how the spiral compasses successive terms, take the sequence of intervals just as they occur in Ed. 1, and spread them out, extending them across the vertical lines that represent paragraph-bounds:

. . . 3 5 7 6 5 2 | 1 2 5 2 2 3 5 7 6 5 2 | 1 2 5 2 2 3 5 7 6 . . .

Raphael has come from God's presence. Appropriately therefore we start the descent with God's number 7.

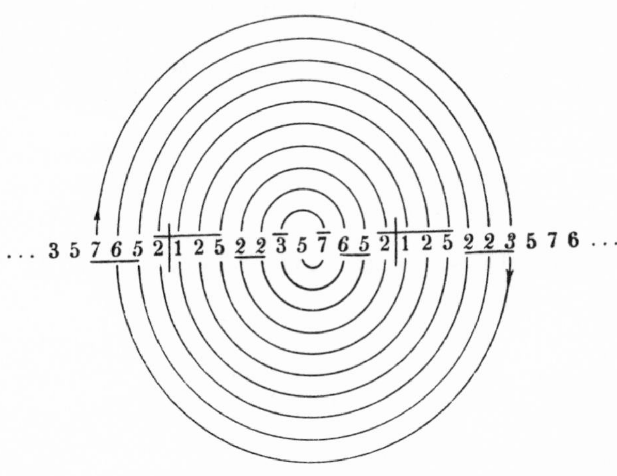

We pass through 7 + 3 + 6 + 2 + 5 + 2 in compassing 25; through 2 + 5 + 1 + 2 + 2 + 1 + 5 + 2 in compassing 20; through 2 + 5 + 2 + 6 in compassing 15; through 3 + 7 in compassing 10; finally reaching 5: "Sent from whose sovran goodness I adore" (647), which takes us to where we started. The series has indeed sent Raphael down from the "sovran goodness" of God — from the starting-number 7; he arrives at the adoring married pair (5) whose conjugal welfare is his mission.

The series has started in wide circuits and has gradually (cf. "Gentle . . . Thy condescension") diminished in order to arrive at a relatively tiny spot of earth. Perhaps Milton intends to equate the number of circuits, 10, with the number of the spheres, or means it to symbolize perfection; or both. The base-number 5 seems to have the same meaning as in the evening prayer.

Indeed Raphael's spiral appears to be an answer to that prayer. An Archangel comes down from 7 (Heaven) to 5 (human married life) even while the human pair wafts words of adoration upward as evidence of their perfect wedded bliss.

The presence of such a spiral suggests again that Milton must have employed some sort of manual device not only for counting intervals in a paragraph backward as well as forward, but even for aggregating groups of intervals separately situated.

There is further reason for believing that Milton the arithmetician has given special thought to Adam's farewell to Raphael, with ironic terminal words, "and oft return." For the paragraph contains a significant power series which, also retrograde, starts where the spiral starts, but, unlike the spiral, which ends where it begins, ends with the paragraph.

PPP 7 ←— glosses Raphael's divine (7) (con)descension (←—).

PPP 7: (7, -17, 7, -17) = *10, 7, 3, 7* [*7, 3, 7, 10*]
^ ↑ ^ ↑

←— starts at "Gentle to me . . . / Thy condescension, . ." (648—)
ends " " . . . . and oft return." (651)

7

I shall presently propose that it was Milton's early and steadfast plan to divide PL into twelve books, and that this division was actually at hand when he authorized — for a sufficient reason — the first published division of ten books. Here I would remind the reader that the only changes really required for the repartitioning of Ed. 2 involve merely the splitting of Books VII and X of Ed. 1, adding three new lines to start Book VIII (Ed. 2), and five new lines to start Book XII (Ed. 2). But notice that, though the added lines of XII are set off as a separate paragraph, this is not the case with the added lines of VIII. The result is that the first paragraph of VIII (Ed. 2) runs to 38 lines. If the transition-lines of VIII were, consistently with those of XII, separately paragraphed, the first two paragraphs of VIII (Ed. 2) would be of 4 and 34 lines. I would here submit evidence that Milton did intend to set off the first four lines of VIII (Ed. 2) consistently with the way he set off the first five lines of XII (Ed. 2), but that, by a printer's oversight, line 5 of Book VIII has been left unindented. Indent the line, and the second paragraph is one of 34 lines. The corresponding paragraph of Ed. 1, observe, has 35 lines (VII, 641-675 of Ed. 1), and begins with "To whom thus Adam gratefully repli'd."

Note a further fact concerning both this 35-line paragraph of Ed. 1 and its altered form, the 38-line paragraph that starts Book VIII (Ed. 2): each is comparatively void of progressions. But if the beginning of Book VIII (Ed. 2) is paragraphed in a way consistent with the beginning of XII, the resultant 34-line paragraph (5-38) will be found to contain an assemblage of symbolic series so extraordinary that it seems altogether improbable, if not incredible, that anything but conscious design can account for them. We can thus justify the host of editors who indent line 5. Let us examine these symbolic series.

The proposed paragraph (VIII, 5-38) consists entirely of Adam's statement of thanks and of perplexity. The words, "to describe whose swiftness number fails . . ." (38—), begin the direct series of a PP-interlock based on root 33, each series being infinite.

Given n = 34,

PP 33: (33, 69, -103, 1, 33, 69, . . .) = *1, 33, 69* ∞ [*69, 33, 1*]
↑ ↑

PP 33 ← starts at "and, . . ." (11—)

→
a | b | c
c | b | a
→

r = b δ = 4

S. of Sym.· 64, 1, 4, *29*, 4, 1, 64

If, however, we attempt to trace this precise interlock — PP 33 $\genfrac{}{}{0pt}{}{\rightarrow\infty}{\leftarrow\infty}>$, we do not find it present. Instead, each antithetic series is *flawed,* and flawed to exactly the same extent. From term *c* a single beat is clipped. As scribed in the text, the formulas are *1, 33, 68* ∞ [*68, 33, 1*]. The resultant *S. of Sym.* now becomes:
↑ ↑
63, 1, 4, *29*, 4, 1, 63. Thus Milton *makes number fail.* Arithmetic responds to the challenging words in the head-term of PP 33 $\rightarrow$.

33 (3 × 11) = law, order, propriety, proportion. Hence the flawing of series rooted in the number that symbolizes perfect proportion is to commit a "disproportion" (27) as objectionable as any that can be imputed to Nature.

Confirmatory of Milton's conscious incorporation of a numerical flaw responsive to context is another instance in this same paragraph. And it comes pat at the very words that evoke it.

Adam is puzzled. Why should all the stars move in their vast spheres, spreading their light merely to serve this atom of an earth? Why should frugal Nature "commit / Such disproportions?" (27). Start at the first word of the paragraph (line 5) and trace an AP based on 11. It ascends: 11, 22, 33. But there's no 44. Instead, there's 46 — two beats too many. But these two beats — mark them well: they come at the words, "Such disproportions." This 4th term seems traced "with superfluous hand," and the very words that perpetrate a disproportion are the expression of it! If they could be removed, the series would be 11, 22, 33, 44, based on the very number that symbolizes right proportion.

. . . . . .

But there is present another, and a subtler, mathematical mirror of Adam's state of mind. It so happens that, given $n = 34$, the sequence of terms for PPP 2 $\genfrac{}{}{0pt}{}{\rightarrow\infty}{\leftarrow\infty}>$ is exactly the same as for PPP 8 $\genfrac{}{}{0pt}{}{\rightarrow\infty}{\leftarrow\infty}>$ except that the directional order of one is the reverse of the other. The root-numbers themselves have probably no symbolic significance. It is the reversibility of their formulas that creates an ambiguous mathematical situation to parallel human dubiety and embarrassed speculation. Any other two root-numbers would have served Milton's purpose if he could have found such numbers involved in a similar numerical paradox — like the following:

PPP 2: (2, 8, 32, -42, 2, . . .) = *2, 8, 32* ∞ [*32, 8, 2*]
↑ ↑

PPP 8: (8, 2, -42, 32, 8, . . .) = *32, 8, 2* ∞ [*2, 8, 32*]
↑ ↑

It follows that if intervals are present for PPP 2 ⟶ ∞ and PPP 2 ⟵ ∞, automatically present are PPP 8 ⟵ ∞ and PPP 8 ⟶ ∞. Thus two pairs of contradictories can perform together, creating the same sequence of symmetry, though the pairs are based on different roots. I have pointed to similar maneuvers elsewhere; the extreme rarity of such formulas greatly strengthens one's conviction that Milton gave close study to the relations of root-numbers to paragraph-length.

PPP 2 ⟶ ∞ / ⟵ ∞ >

a b c ⟶
c b a ⟵

δ = 13

S. of Sym.: 13, 2, 8, *9*, 8, 2, 13

PPP 8 ⟶ ∞ / ⟵ ∞ >

c b a ⟶
a b c ⟵

r = b δ = 13

S. of Sym.: the same

PPP 2 ⟶ starts at "but delight, . . ." (11—)
2 ⟵ " " "Their magnitudes, . . ." (17—)

PPP 8 ⟶ " " "When I behold . . ." (15—)
8 ⟵ " " "something yet of doubt . . ." (13—)

We perceive that the common *S. of Sym.* is a *sequence of uncertainty,* for it defines the presence now of PPP 2, now of PPP 8. The parallel and simultaneous performance of two different →'s and two different ←'s is thus a mathematical reflection of the pros and cons which cause Adam's boundless (∞) bewilderment.

Notice the center of symmetry — 9 beats: "Something yet of doubt remains, / Which only thy solution can resolve" (13—). This concept of doubt is justly the center. At the same time the number 9 may carry the Dantean meaning of miracle and wonder, a concept stressed in "reasoning I oft admire" (25) and "wonder," which immediately precedes the beginning of PPP 2→.

Almost without exception, editors, following Tickell and Bentley, drop comma after "compute" (16). Thereby vanish both PPP 2← and PPP 8 →, and the whole rhythmic maneuver is thwarted.

. . . . . .

Adam is a computing cosmologist whose serious talk is inwoven with mathematical responses. Still others — at least two — are present.

(i) Among things that perplex him is the apparent subservience of all the heavenly bodies revolving round so insignificant "a spot, a grain" as this earth — "while the sedentary earth," he says, ". . . attains / Her end without least motion," (32-35).

From "while . . ." to ". . . motion" are 17 beats.

Now certain root-numbers may be factorially related to $5n$ in such a way that the formula for an infinite progression contains only one term. Given $n = 34$, the sequence of remainders for PPP 17 is 17, -17, 17, -17, . . ., whence the formula *17* ∞ [*17*].
↑ ↑

Therefore the pauses which demarcate successive powers of PPP 17 → simply oscillate forever back and forth across 17. The same is true of PPP 17 ←: if we start the descent from the 4th term, or from any term whose ordinal number in the series is a multiple of 4, the places of pause oscillate back and forth, but always in contrary motion with the powers of PPP 17→. We are compelled, then, to picture 17 as a "sedentary" term or interval, generating, all by itself, the entire infinite progression, and without the least motion to or from any companion term or terms.

17 (10 + 7) = sovereignty, in the sense here of being "Serv'd by more noble than herself," (34).

(ii) PP 34 ∞ is also present. Its formula is also restricted to one term: *34* ∞ [*34*]. It starts where PPP 17 ⟶ starts and ends
↑ ↑
with the words that end the paragraph: "Speed, to describe which number fails." 34 also = sovereignty (2 × 17).

How nicely the last two words define a power-series that reaches beyond any number humanly conceivable!

8

Is it absurd or unreasonable to maintain that such a group is the poet's virtual directive that we detach the first four lines of Book VIII (Ed. 2) from the thirty-four that follow? Or have I merely "dreamt it all up"? Here are pauses and intervals anyone can verify. Here are responses to immediate context which are unmistakably opportune. And always in the background is Milton's motive, a sufficient motive: the fulfilment of an artistic ideal in which mathematics and symbol unite to create a rhythmic style analogous to that of polyphonic music. Why not employ this same tool to check the validity of other doubtful paragraphs?

Immediately one thinks of those three huge unbroken passages at PL I, 331-621, III, 416-653, and IV, 172-357, which nearly all editors fractionate in various ways. I hasten to confess I have not scanned these passages for power progressions. The prolonged calculations involved would have monopolized all my time for an indefinite period. They are the only parts of Milton's epic verse I have had to ignore in this way. Indeed they come so early in PL that sometimes I've been tempted to suspect that Milton wants them to be decoys, sure to lead astray any curious reader who might stumble on symbolic progressions and seek Milton's manner of incorporating them.

The longest paragraph I have scanned for power series is that of 191 lines at PL XII, 79-269, whose integrity as a single paragraph cannot be questioned. All editors find it unfractionable. As far as I have gone with it, it does yield a limited assemblage of interlocking progressions quite responsive to context. But the thought of adjusting calculated pauses within a paragraph of this great length is so awesome that, although such adjustment is entirely possible, and, in view of feats of symbolic response in other paragraphs, practicable, I would suspend judgment till further responses can be demonstrated in it.

There are certain shorter paragraphs to which my proposed length-test might be applied as advantageously as to the paragraph at VIII, 5-38. An example is at PL I, 128-156. It yields no progressions, at least not any of the kinds I have found elsewhere. But let us alter it slightly — from 29 to 28 lines.

Beelzebub's words occupy all the lines except the last, which is: "Whereto with speedy words th' Arch-fiend repli'd." If we take away this line, as in fact many editors do, the paragraph yields a consort of infinite series, some of which make continuous girdles, each series being based on the number of Jehovah, whose "high supremacy" is contrasted with the objects of his "vengeful ire" who seem fated "to undergo eternal punishment."

PPP 7: (7, 63, 7, -77, 7, 63, . . .) = *7, 63, 7* ∞ [*7, 63, 7*]
↑ ↑

(α) ⟶ ∞ starts at "That with sad overthrow . . ." (135—)
⟵ ∞ " " "whate'er his business . . ." (150—)
ends " " . . . his thralls / By right of war," (150)
(β) ⟶ ∞ starts at "Or do him mightier service . . ." (149—)
⟵ ∞ " " "and all this mighty host . . . laid thus low," (136—)
ends " " . . . Hath lost us Heav'n," (136)

PP 14: (14, 56, -56, 56, -56, . . .) = *14, 56* ∞ [*56, 14*]
↑ ↑ ^

14 ⟶ ∞ starts at "and all this mighty host . . ." (136—)
(α) 14 ⟵ ∞ " " "whate'er his business . . ." (150—)
ends " " . . . Hath lost us Heav'n," (136)
(β) 14 ⟵ ∞ starts " "That we may now suffice . . ." (148—)
ends " " . . . or chance, or fate;" (133)

Both 7 and 14 (2 × 7) = Jehovah, sovereignty. The sovereignty of "Heaven's perpetual king" is the theme: contrasted with the fallen Angel's sovereign ability to "suffer and support" Jehovah's vengeance.

Observe: (1) that the third term in the formula for $(\alpha)\, 7 \longrightarrow \infty$ is the root-term of $(\beta)\, 7 \longrightarrow \infty$, and the third term in the formula for $(\beta)\, 7 \longrightarrow \infty$ is the root-term of $(\alpha)\, 7 \longrightarrow \infty$, i.e., (α) and (β) are interlocked, and girdle the paragraph continuously; (2) that the formulas for $14 \longrightarrow \infty$ and $(\alpha)\, 14 \longleftarrow \infty$ are tangent with points of tangency at opposite poles, i. e., the intervals for the antithetic series exactly fill the paragraph $(14 + 56 + 56 + 14 = 140 = 5n)$, effecting a perfect girdle; (3) that the nadir-terms of the $\longleftarrow$'s are quite responsive.

Does not the presence of such a "choir" make it probable that Milton intends a paragraph of just the length required for their performance? Note also that the line proposed for separation (156) contains an alteration in the Morgan MS written in Edward Phillips' hand (see Miss Darbishire's note). Perhaps Milton's momentary state of uncertainty when he dictated the first reading "the Fiend" for "th' Arch-fiend" has something to do with the scribe's failure to indent.

Editors who drop comma after "event" (134) destroy the girdling PPP $7\ \infty$'s.

9

When we assign symbolic meanings to certain numbers, we cannot overlook two possibilities. In a unique context Milton may intend more meanings than one, each traceable to pagan or Scriptural tradition. Again, because some special configuration depends entirely on the choice of a certain root-number, he may intend to subordinate a precise symbolic meaning to an extraordinary directional response, or he may be stressing some unique feature of the configuration.

In the 15-line paragraph at PL IX, 780-794 such possibilities must be considered. The number 13 seems usually to signify perfect justice or righteousness $(10 + 3)$. Here it may be rather, or be in addition, the number of Eve — her specific self as the notorious 13th rib. At the same time the directional responses in the interlock-configuration of PP 13's are unusually important.

This is the climactic paragraph of the whole epic. Only one

interlock is present, but it has notable features. The number of terms in both series is increased beyond four, thereby intensifying the antithesis between Eve's self-centered joy in the forbidden fruit and the tragic import of her luckless indulgence.

PP 13 (to 4 terms only): (13, 19, 22, -14) = *13, 19, 8, 14* [*14, 8, 19, 13*]
↑ ^ ↑ ^

(5 terms): (13, 19, 22, -14, -32) = *8, 5, 19, 8, 14* [*14, 8, 19, 5, 8*]
↑ ^ ↑ ^

(6 terms): (13, 19, 22, -14, -32, 34) = *8, 5, 19, 8, 2, 12*
↑ ^
[*12, 2, 8, 19, 5, 8*]
↑ ^

PP 13 ⟶ (6 terms) | a′ b c | a″ d e

PP 13 ⟵ (5 terms) d a″ | c b a′ |

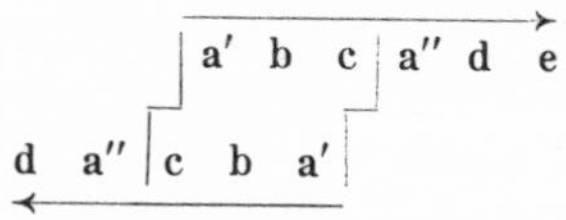

r = a + b δ = 4

S. of Sym.: 14, 8, 4, 8, 5, *2*, 5, 8, 4, 8, [2, 12]

⟶ starts at "Greedily she ingorg'd without restraint, . . ." (791—)
ends " " . . . That all was lost." (784)
⟵ starts " start of paragraph
ends " " . . . reaching to the fruit," (781)

Why is ⟶ extended to six terms, a term beyond ⟵'s five? In response to Eve's positive pleasure of indulgence *without restraint* (791). And when the series does end, observe that it is timed to end at the full midline stop with words that express the consequences of indulgence: "all was lost."

Now if ⟵ also should go to six terms it could not start the paragraph. With five terms, as inspection of the formulas shows, ⟵ must start the paragraph, thereby echoing the note of disaster at the very first line, yes, in response to the very first words.

Some editors drop comma after "woe" (783), destroying the extension of PP 13 ⟶ to six terms.

. . . .

Exactly the same *r, n,* and PP occur together in another 15-line paragraph at PL XI, 84-98. Again there is a PP 13-interlock with each series expanded, but this time each is expanded to six terms. Indeed the way the formula for PP 13 (four terms) is transferred to PP 13 (six terms) probably appealed to Milton as *simplex munditiis.* In the first case, PP 13 ⟶ yields *13, 19, 8, 14;* in the
↑ ^ (↑ under *8*, ^ under *14*)

second it yields *8, 5, 19, 8, 2, 12;* i.e., the two end-terms of the first
↑ ^ (↑ under the first *8*, ^ under *2*)

formula simply break into segments without affecting the relative positions of starting and ending. Let us call these formulas PP 13 (IV) and PP 13 (VI).

Clearly, 13 here means perfect justice. Man, declares the Almighty, has by his crime elevated himself to a creature "like one of us" (⟶). Still, because he has violated "defended fruit," "to remove him I decree," (⟵).

Milton's God is a cunning mathematician. To carry the series to six terms is further to emphasize justice (2 × 3).

Both PP 13 (IV) and PP 13 (VI) form interlocks. The sum of the intervals of either interlock misses a full girdle of the paragraph by 7 beats; or, put more comprehensively, either interlock creates two centers of symmetry, with 14 at one pole and 7 at the other. Which is entirely fitting, for both 7 and 14 (7 doubled) are sacred to the speaker. God's word (7) emanates from both poles, and his word is perfect justice (10 + 3; 2 × 3).

PP 13 (IV) ⇄ >

⟶
a b c d
d c b a
⟵

S. of Sym.: 14, 8, 5, *14*, 5, 8, 14

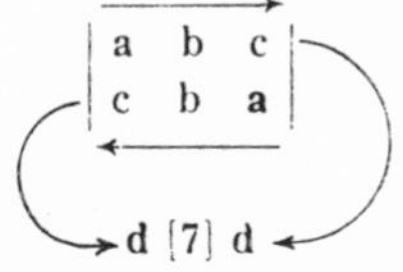

⟶ starts at start of paragraph
ends " " . . . longer than they move," (91)

⟵ starts at start of paragraph
ends where ⟶ ends

PP 13 (VI) $\rightleftarrows >$

		a′	b	c	a″	d	e
e	d	a″	c	b	a′		

$r = a' + b$

S. of Sym.: 12, 2, 8, 5, *14*, 5, 8, 2, 12

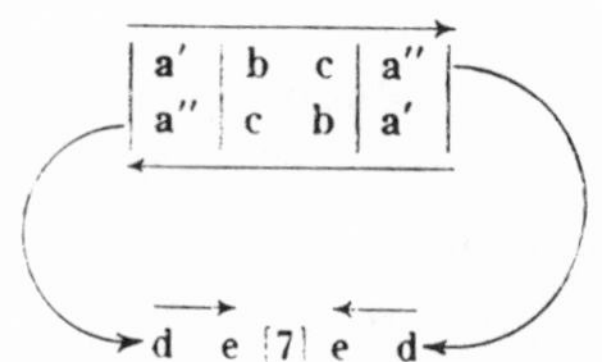

→ starts at start of paragraph
ends " ". . . His heart I know," (92)
← starts " "fitter soil . . ." (98—)
ends " ". . . longer than they move," (91)

The possible advantages of PP 13 (IV) $\rightleftarrows >$ are: (a) simultaneity of beginnings and endings; (b) simultaneity of beginnings of both series with beginning of paragraph.

. . . .

My concluding illustration is an ensemble of symbolic progressions whose response to context seems altogether dramatic. To begin with, the 52-line paragraph at PL IV, 440-491 contains a consort of PPP 5 ∞-interlocks that girdle the paragraph, with locked terms at opposite poles.

PPP 5: (5, 125, 5, -135, 5, . . .) = *5, 125, 5* ∞ [*5, 125, 5*]
↑ ↑

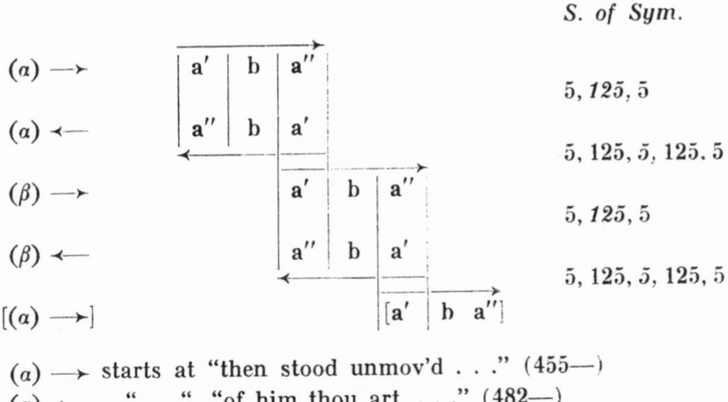

(α) → starts at "then stood unmov'd . . ." (455—)
(α) ← " " "of him thou art, . . ." (482—)
(β) → " " "Return fair Eve, . . ." (481—)
(β) ← " " "I thither went . . ." (456—)

Root-number 5 here carries the Pythagorean meaning of marriage (2 [woman] + 3 [man]). For simultaneously performing are significant series based on 2 as well as on 3. These are finite, i.e., 4-term, and are so disposed as to suggest analogy with rival themes in a fugue. 3 (male) is demonstrably in pursuit of 2 (female). Given $n = 52$,

PPP 3: (3, 27, -17, 107) = *3, 10, 17, 90* [*90, 17, 10, 3*]

(α) PPP 3 ← starts at "I thither went . . ." (456—)
ends " " . . . that smooth watery image;" (480)

5 beats in front of this series, i.e., preceding it by 5 beats (5 = marriage), is a duplicate of it: (β) PPP 3 ←.

(β) PPP 3 ← starts at "and laid me down . . ." (457—)
ends " " . . . Thou following cri'd'st aloud," (481)

(α) performs on the very heels of (β). Contrapuntally, they are in fugal relation, 5 beats always separating their terms. Symbolically, each reinforces the other as they move in swift descent (from 2187 to 3 in three stages).

But now for a remarkable feature. (β), the series in front, ends in a root-term whose very words specifically identify it as symbolizing the pursuing male: "Thou following cri'd'st aloud," (481). And 5 beats in advance of these words begins the root-term of PPP 2 ←, a "female progression," which, pursued, moves in the same direction (←) as the pursuer (β).

PPP 2: *2, 8, 32, 128* [*128, 32, 8, 2*]
↑ ^ ↑ ^

PPP 2 ← starts at "That day I oft remember . . ." (449—)
ends " " . . . of him thou art," (482)

Let us keep lines 481-482 before us:

(a) Thou following cri'd'st aloud, (b) Return fair Eve, (c)
Whom fli'st thou? whom thou fli'st, (d) of him thou art, (e)

(a)—(b) is the root-term of (β) PPP 3 ←. (d)—(e) is the root-term of PPP 2←. Between (b) and (e), terminal points of the two series, are 7 beats. Between (b) and (d), the interval which separates the two root-terms, are 5 beats.

Such an arrangement is interpretable as follows: If these 5 beats that separate pursuer (3) and pursued (2) could only be overcome, (β) 3 ← would catch up with PPP 2 ←, and marriage would be consummated. And if those 7 beats (7 = sovereignty) that separate the terminal points of PPP 3 ← and PPP 2 ← could be overcome, Adam would establish his sovereignty over Eve.

But there is present another PPP 2, this time a direct series, and it forms an interlock with PPP 2 ←. PPP 2 → starts with the words, "What thou see'st . . ." (467—). What Eve sees is a woman. 2 accordingly is the responsive head-term. The series ends at " . . . That day I oft remember," (449). Now these are the very words that start the descending series, PPP 2 ←: their three beats are the amount of overlap of d-terms at Pole p″. For the interlock girdles the paragraph, its center of symmetry at Pole p′ being the 7-beat interval, "and thence be call'd / Mother of human race: what could I do," (474-475). This is indeed a most responsive center of symmetry at one pole of a girdling interlock rooted in the number of woman.

PPP 2 ⇄ >

a b c | d
d | c b a

$\delta = 7$

S. of Sym.: 3, 90, 2, 8, 25, 7, 25, 8, 2, 90, 3 (Pole p′)

A rotational representation must show the displacement at each pole, making it easy for the reader to trace the interlock:

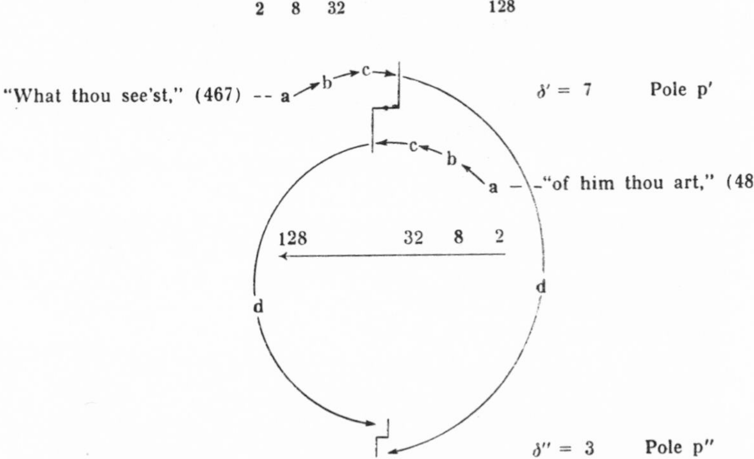

S. of Sym. at Pole p″: 7, 25, 8, 2, 90, *3*, 90, 2, 8, 25, 7

This enveloping of the paragraph by symbolic 2 fits the general enveloping theme: the story of woman (2). With equal aptness the paragraph is girdled by symbolic 5, for the specific theme is marriage (5). All the 2's and 3's are in finite series, for Eve's flight and Adam's pursuit come to an end. But the PPP 5's are endless (∞): Eve cannot imagine her union with Adam as anything but eternal.

Many editors drop comma after "do" (475), causing PPP 2 ⟶ to vanish, and impairing the symbolist strategy.

CHAPTER VII

EPILOGUE: WHY ONLY TEN BOOKS IN THE FIRST EDITION OF *PARADISE LOST?*

1

Milton's epic verse is a manifestation of that same "free" spirit which refused to adhere to any denominational church, but instead drew up in secret a complete dogmatic system. And how, after Shakespeare, could any blank-verse poet express himself in an original, personalized way? Milton reasoned it could not be done unless it were based on some new rhythmic principle. This is a fair inference from *Comus*. Technically, the blank verse of *Comus* is so echoic of the Elizabethans that any repetition of it by the mature Milton, inveterate experimenter, is unthinkable. God gives us, he says, "minds that can wander beyond all limit and satiety." He dreamt of a new austerity for blank verse. The new medium must unite Homer with Euclid, Virgil with Pythagoras. It must incorporate inerrable mathematical proportions. Even as a boy, he had given thoughtful heed to the Pythagorean tenet that number is the essence of the universe, imcompatible with falsehood, bringing truth to light, yet hiding it from the unworthy, parent and nurse of harmony, both human and divine.

The formal extension of Cartesianism to the art of writing is generally attributed to Boileau. But PL antedates the prescriptions of Boileau. For Milton the spirit of the age was but a confirmation of what he read in Plato. "If arithmetic and the sciences of measurement and weighing," says Socrates in *Philebus* (55 E, 64 E, tr. H. N. Fowler, Loeb Library), "were taken away from all arts, what was left of any of them would be pretty worthless. . . . Measure and proportion are everywhere identified with beauty and virtue." If Milton took such words to heart, it should come as no surprise that he sought ways of scribing mathematical progressions not only in the rhythms of individual blank-verse paragraphs but in the overall planning of his epic.

2

Pure chance, declares the mathematician, can cause any numerical group whatever to occur in a sequence of random numbers — *if* the group is applied often enough to a sequence sufficiently extended. But when we find certain exact sequences of intervals haunting the rhythms of this or that paragraph, and responsive, both directionally and symbolically, to contextual situations, pure chance seems impotent. It is called on to satisfy more than a random occurrence in a random grouping. The sequences we have been considering are not impersonal dice-throws but rational patterns in number-sequences created by a purposive mind. It is a mind that weds expressive rhythms to narrative theme and situation.

Of course the intrusion of ethical symbol is repugnant to the pure mathematician, who, in the absence of the poet's signed affidavit, rejects it out of hand, and is inclined to regard as moonshine the analogy of Milton's paragraph to a rounded piece of contrapuntal music. He has no patience with the artist who does not explicitly give away the secrets of his craft, but who strives for his effects by difficult and devious means. If only the case of Milton were as simple as the pure mathematician likes to think. But Milton meditated his work in an age hospitable to mystic influences and irrational beliefs, an age in which, paradoxically, some of the foremost artists had even more faith in the efficacy of mathematics than has the professional mathematician today.

Milton's rhythmic style in PL and PR is distinguishable from that of all other blank verse in that it often leads a double life. It cannot always be grasped at one level, the level of obvious rhetoric and accessible prosody, including that extension of prosody which I have defined as cross-rhythmic construction. Underneath the surface may move a persistent mathematics interpretable in terms of symbol. The result is what we have always known: we often feel in this verse an element of sculptured, even granitic, precision, regardless of the rate of enjambement, or of how suspensively or how loosely wrought is the rhetoric, regardless of the presence or absence of cross-rhythmic construction.

A cryptic element like radium. Its never-ceasing rhythmic radiations in certain paragraphs account for many a strange effect on readers aware of but one rhythmic level. Such readers, in the very act of reading about a paradise lost and a paradise found, are all the while being invited — if they but knew it — to enter a paradise of symbol. The invitation goes unheeded, for it is uttered in mathematical language muffled behind the metric frame.

There is need of further inquiry, of answers to questions like the following. How many of Milton's paragraphs lead this double rhythmic life? What works in mathematics, besides those I mention in Chapter V, did Milton probably study? May he not have made occasional use of certain kinds of progression different from any we have discussed? Is it not possible to learn more about a few of Milton's ingenious friends, like, say, Cyriac Skinner, who might have shared an interest not only in mathematical progressions but in numerical symbolism?

3

Based on the evidence given, at least two general conclusions seem more than plausible. One is negative, the other affirmative.

Neither syntax nor rhetoric nor prosody nor appeals to classical influences, can, singly or in combination, account for the rhythmic style of many of Milton's epic paragraphs.

Keats, while declaring PL to be "the most remarkable production of the world," regards it nevertheless as "a corruption of our language," imagining its characteristic style to be conditioned chiefly by surface features of diction, syntax, and prosody. No wonder he thinks he is imitating that style too closely when he finds in *Hyperion* many of Milton's tricks of word-order. But *Hyperion* lacks the rhythmic method of PL not only at the second but at the first level. For at the first level the rhythmic method must include, some of the time, for every ear to hear, cross-rhythmic construction, of which Keats's blank verse has only an accidental trace.

This omission suggests an affirmative pronouncement. On the first level we can differentiate two distinct styles, although — and this is a grave qualification — each of them is only intermittently present. *A paragraph textured with cross-rhythmic construction has, and is felt to have, a far different weave and movement from one in which such construction is scant or absent.*

Thus, in general, we can distinguish the rhythmic style of PR from that of PL. Cross-rhythmic construction is far less active in PR. In Appendix II I have included the cross-rhythmic construction in one book of PR, and given the frequencies of occurrence of E and T in all the books of both poems.

More specifically, we can distinguish among paragraphs. Let the reader compare PL V, 153-208 with PL X, 504-590, and though he may recognize that each paragraph is inimitably Miltonic, he will find the pace and surface-tensions of one to be worlds away from the other. The first is almost void of cross-rhythmic construction; the second is textured completely with it. In both paragraphs symbolic series are present. But in the second (see notes in Appendix II) the very patterns of cross-rhythmic construction are so managed as to contain symbolic progressions which it needs little analysis for both ear and eye to perceive. These contrasting styles are of course responses to context: contexts more violently different are inconceivable.

Even within a single extended paragraph the two different rhythmic movements may be found in successive passages. Perhaps the clearest example is in the long paragraph at PL X, 720-844, whose extraordinary cross-rhythmic section I have already cited (above pp. 36-37).

But these two styles are felt as disparate only when a crowded abundance of cross-rhythmic construction is set beside a relative paucity. Such construction is indeed characteristic, but it is distributed unevenly, involving only 42 per cent of the lines of PL and only 17 per cent of PR.

Occasionally some post-Miltonic poet has caught the method of cross-rhythmic construction, though never with Milton's variety of pattern, and of course not with his occasional ordering of overlapping segments to effect responsive symbolic series. *Tintern Abbey* is a good example. Here, more than anywhere else in Wordsworth, the rhythms are patterned, in conscious or unconscious imitation of Milton, to contain cross-rhythmic construction. But who would dream of calling the verse Miltonic? The first books of both the *Prelude* and the *Excursion* have a sprinkling of such construction, but it very soon fades in later books, and the verse becomes only measured rhetoric.

The largest differentiating feature of Milton's paragraph is neither cross-rhythmic construction nor the presence of symbolic series, but its adaptation of the rhythmic method of contrapuntal music. It is to serve this contrapuntal ideal that Milton perfects cross-rhythmic construction and scribes numerical progressions. Not only is he the sole discoverer of the opportunity, but the one man on record whose dual equipment as poet and musician qualifies him as capable of exploiting it. Certain of his sustained paragraphs are like buildings of startling design into which many skills unite to produce effects at once dynamic and static. A work of collaboration: rhetor, musician, mathematician, and symbolist have taken counsel together, each with his blueprints. The product is a "monument of fame, / And strength and art" like that "ascending pile" of the baroque called Pandemonium, for both structures have risen like organ-music breathed from daemonic keyboards.

The analogy is close, for, animating many a paragraph, is an unheard polyrhythmic "sound / Of dulcet symphonies and voices sweet." As if he would have his architecture stand like frozen music, Milton sometimes designs his paragraph to be not only haunted by mathematical progressions but held in equilibrium by invisible sequences and centers of symmetry brought into being by conflicting tensions of interlocked antithetic series. The structure which we, "the hasty multitude, / Admiring enter," has been "in many cells prepared." In the present inquiry we have explored a few which have served the secret aims of the world's greatest craftsman of ordered words.

But what master-builder waves aloft his blueprints and broadcasts his working calculus? Raphael's words are to the point:

> the great architect
> Did wisely to conceal, and not divulge
> His secrets to be scann'd by those who ought
> Rather admire. (PL VIII, 72-75)

Hence the evasions of that note on "the verse" to lull the curiosity of readers restive because "the poem rimes not."

4

In the world of PL the artist's will moves from invention to invention, each not only a victory of technique but a victory over technique. For the first time in Western Europe an artist's mind is equipped with more than the accumulated rhetoric and poetic of past verse-masters and critics. His poetic ideal outsoars obedience to literary tradition. Upon a new and different concept he creates the structure of his lays. They are song, but their rhythms are too intricate to find explanation in analogy with previous hexameter, alexandrine, or pentameter. Milton has a new organon, the fruit of a new opportunity available only to a singer equally at home with Shakespeare and with the inspirations of Palestrina and Morley. He does not dare to begin his theme till he has developed a rhythmic medium through which he feels he may emulate the very modes of harp and voice which he believes are in perpetual polyphonic jubilee round the Beatific Throne.

His blank verse invites and rewards prosodic analysis — up to a point. Beyond that point conventional prosody is helpless to expound his method. Nevertheless prosodic analysis can clear the way; Milton himself mastered it in every important Western tongue before he transcended it. We need have no fear of profaning shrines, for he was himself a microscopic observer of technical arcana.

If symbolic series in certain paragraphs are a fact, then we may do more than admire. We may now understand why the movement of Milton's epic verse often requires a special analysis at two levels even to describe. We may now understand why no post-Miltonic poet has ever imitated that movement successfully, or ever will. Moreover, we may have a key to Milton's paragraphing, to some of the strange punctuation of the earliest editions, and, I now venture to submit, to his reason for dividing Ed. 1 of PL into ten and not twelve books.

5

Vain is the search for any evidence that PL contains one sign of hasty planning or of hasty composition. To attempt to explain the change from ten to twelve books has hitherto inevitably tangled the expositor in absurdities. For how could he escape being forced to make the following assumption: that, though Milton bestowed decades of the most intensive and comprehensive thought on his work, still its major outlining, its overall planning, remained clouded and obscure? PL may be formally perfect in all details, its every vowel and every turn of rhythm adjusted with refinements of foresight that can hardly be paralleled in any literature; yet in the largest concern of all — the grand partitioning into books — Milton makes a blunder it takes him seven years to rectify.

So monstrous a supposition has not been advanced by cautious biographers and commentators. They merely state the simple fact of repartitioning, and wisely decline even to suggest a reason. Beholding the monumental edifice complete to last touches of mortar under flagstone and finial — think of declaring that the builder can't make up his mind about the number and arrangement of the main walls!

But our present inquiry suggests a solution that does no violence to the facts of Milton's life-interests and habits, or to his stature as an artist. It involves three propositions.

(i) The division into ten books in 1667 is all prepared to shift to a division into twelve. The fact requires no arguing. Two books of Ed. 1 are disproportionately long: Book VII has almost 1300 lines, Book X has 1540 lines. VII splits into 640 and 650, with three tag-lines added to the new Book VIII. X splits into 901 and 644, with five tag-lines added to the new Book XII. Absolutely no more change is necessary to make twelve books — the Virgilian number — out of ten.

Milton must indeed have some very peculiar, very private reason for issuing this work in a manner that seems in Ed. 1 to outrage one of the instincts of his nature — right proportioning.

(ii) But his indulgence in numerical symbol introduces us here to a rival, though subsurface, concept of proportioning. Mere division into books is not the only actuating motive. The presence of symbol within the books, within the paragraphs, sheds more than a ray of light across the grand partitioning of Ed. 1.

The number 10 has as rich a meaning for Milton as for Pythagoras or Dante. It is not only the number of completeness and perfection but the number of the Spheres, whose harmony touched the imagination of Milton's greatest contemporaries, especially Kepler, and cast a spell over Milton's own mind from earliest schooldays. For him 10 became associated with contrapuntal music, for the Music of the Spheres was, as he several times describes it, contrapuntal.

Now if the rhythmic ideal of his paragraph, and consequently of his entire epic work, is contrapuntal, and if the numerical symbol of that ideal is 10, then it is the symbol of his inspiration in PL. An overall 10-fold division would therefore be a tribute to his Muse.

(iii) Such a line of thought now prepares us for a startling bit of evidence, for an incontrovertible phenomenon which cannot be dismissed as accidental.

Of the ten books of Ed. 1 the first four form a thematic group. The next three — V, VI, VII — form a group even more integral than the first four. The next two — VIII, IX — recount the Fall and its immediate consequences, and logically belong together. This leaves Book X, the Vision of the Future, which, though pointing the way to redemption, ends with man's tragic eviction from Eden and the dissolution of Paradise.

The corresponding division in Ed. 2 — (I, II, III, IV) + (V, VI, VII, VIII) + (IX, X) + (XI, XII) — entirely masks this symbolic grouping of the ten books of Ed. 1.

The division of Ed. 1 is meant to effect a descending primary Pythagorean progression by the thematic groupings of its successive books. Its directional significance is unmistakable. It is consistent with the identical retrograde series 4, 3, 2, 1 scattered through the rhythms of PL, where it always responds to contextual situations involving disaster, defeat, moral obliquity, loss, sorrow.

Numerical symbol therefore explains the *temporary* partitioning of Ed. 1.

But in 1667 Milton's poem was just as ready for partitioning into twelve books as into ten. Knowing his reverence for Virgil and the Virgilian tradition, we are entirely reasonable in thinking that from the day he decided to compose a vast work in epic form he planned it for twelve parts. The subsequent facile splitting of Books VII and X bears witness.

Now Milton knew the merit of his work, knew that a second edition was sure to be called for. It is reasonable to infer that he even gave Simmons instructions for a redistribution of books whenever Ed. 1 should be exhausted. The division of 1667 is temporary tribute to his Muse by way of Pythagorean symbol; that of 1674 is permanent tribute to epic tradition and its most inspired exemplar.

6

If symbolic series are *not* a fact, then I, for one, am in a state of paradisal innocence concerning the workings both of chance and of the designing mind. Not only must I confess that Milton put his study of mathematics to no known use, but that his unsurpassable description of the contrapuntal master of the organ —

who mov'd
Their stops and chords was seen: his volant touch
Instinct through all proportions low and high
Fled and pursu'd transverse the resonant fugue.
(PL XI, 560-563)

suggests analogy only to surface features of his verse.

If I reject plenary allegiance to chance, yet reject also a premeditated method of incorporating symbolic series, I am left to explain them in terms of a misty demiurgic "inspiration," of some divinely unconscious endowment able to create consistent numerical responses of symbol to context. Milton himself might prefer that I meet him on these terms, take him literally when he declares that his "celestial Patroness"

dictates to me slumbering, or inspires
Easy my unpremeditated verse:

as if this acknowledgment applied to anything but the first drafting of any paragraph.

But this way of thinking comes to a halt when I remember a few of the many examples of symbolic response such as I have introduced into previous chapters. They show the virtuoso excelling himself in mid-passage of his song. They show the contrapuntist-mathematician-symbolist a co-worker with the rhetorician-rhapsode. Were this not so, the rhythmic structure and movement of Milton's epic paragraph would long ago have been an open book to prosodic and rhetorical analysis.

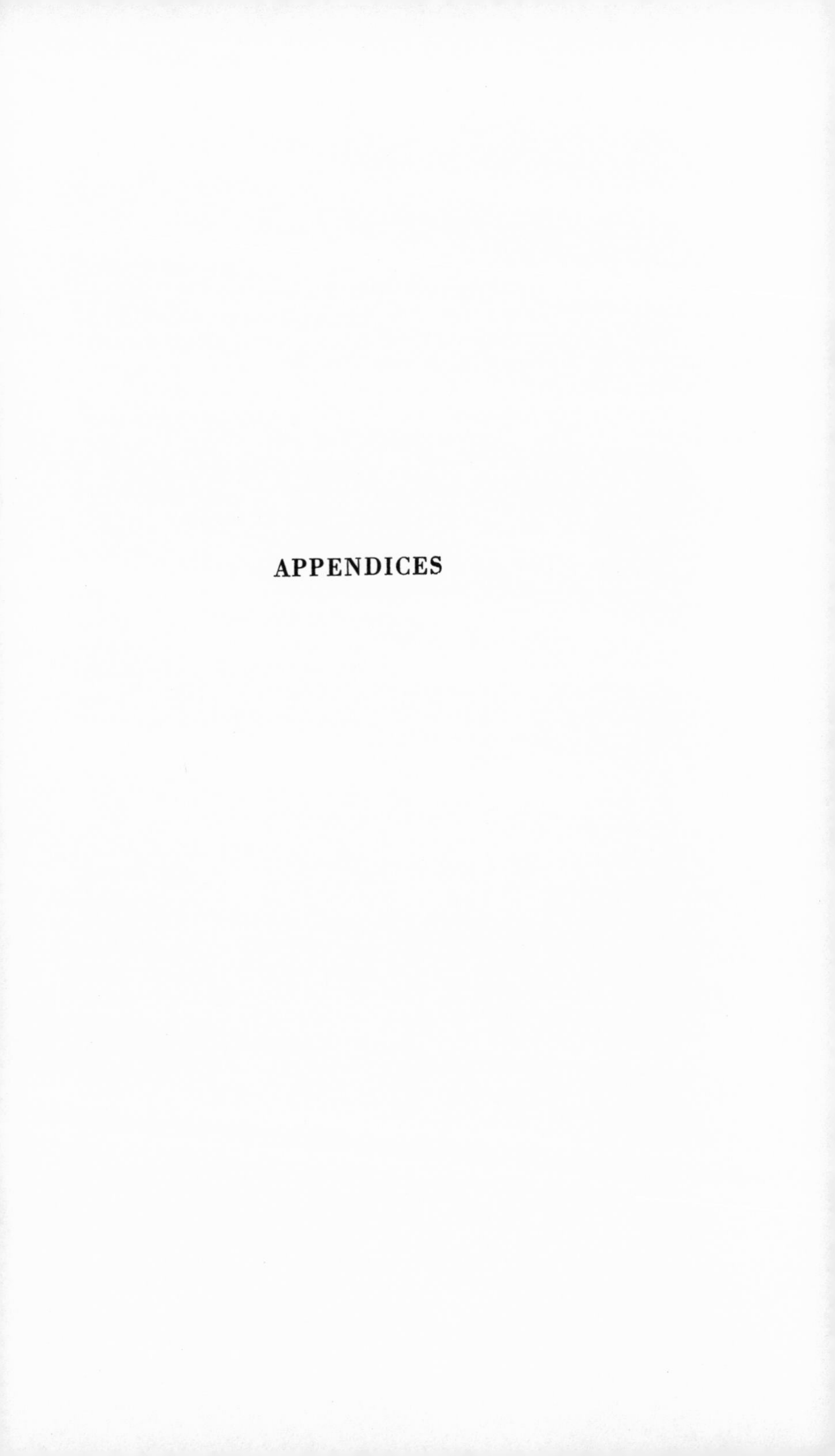

APPENDICES

APPENDIX I

PATTERNS OF QUICK-PACED INTEGRAL PENTAMETERS

In general, a slow-paced pentameter line is one without any interior light-stressed foot. It may or may not have an interior pause strong enough to be pointed. Five main stresses are distinctly felt in it.

A quick-paced line, on the other hand, almost always contains a light-stressed foot, or more than one, so that there are only four, or fewer, main stresses. It contains a weak yet perceptible interior pause, in rare cases determinable only by the reader's judgment of syntactic elements. Its pace may be further accelerated by first-foot inversion, by artful choice of polysyllabic words, or by judicious alliteration and assonance.

Counting from the beginning of a line, let us indicate with a roman numeral the place of the light-stressed foot, and add as an arabic superscript the number of the syllable that precedes the pause. Thus

My exaltation and my whole delight (PL VI, 727)

is represented as III^{5}. The third foot is light-stressed, and a perceptible pause comes after the fifth syllable. Other examples:

And easily transgress the sole command (PL III, 94)	II^{4}
Innumerable as the stars of night (PL III, 565)	II III^{5}
Nor this unvoyageable gulf obscure (PL X, 366)	III^{8}
Such pleasure took the serpent to behold (PL IX, 455)	IV^{3}

Indicate first-foot inversion by i:

Harmony to behold in wedded pair (PL VIII, 605)	II i^{3}
Cherub and Seraph rolling in the flood (PL I, 324)	IV i^{5}

In rare cases a line is felt to be quick-paced even though an interior foot is inverted. Indicate such a foot by adding a roman superscript to i, this numeral telling which foot is inverted.

And all things in best order to invite (PL IX, 402) IV i^{II} ^{7}

Here the second foot is inverted, and a slight syntactic pause follows the seventh syllable.

Many a line is felt to be quick-paced even though it contains a spondaic or near-spondaic foot. In this case we show the position of the spondee or near-spondee by placing a dot in one of five situations round the letter s. ṡ = spondee in 1st foot; ·s = s in 2nd foot; .s = s in 3rd; ṣ = s in 4th; s. = s in 5th. Thus:

Who first seduc'd them to that foul revolt? (PL I, 33) III ṡ^{5}

A quick-paced line may have a pyrrhic + a spondee substituted for two successive iambic feet. Call the substitute e (equivalence) and put a roman numeral before e to mark the place of the first foot involved. Thus:

But longer in that Paradise to dwell (PL XI, 48) II e^{3}
And high permission of all-ruling Heaven (PL I, 212) III e^{5}
Bright effluence of bright essence increate (PL III, 6) II e ṡ^{3}
But the hot Hell that always in him burns (IX, 467) I e IV^{4}
With reason hath deep silence and demur (II, 431) II e IV^{3}

To repeat: if the roman numeral is without e, it marks the place of a light-stressed foot. But if e is appended to the roman numeral, it marks the beginning of a pyrrhic-spondee substitution.

One more kind of quick-paced line, though not common, must be recognized. Sheer mellifluousness of verbal texture can make it irresistibly quick-paced, though it may not contain a light-stressed foot. Indicate such a line simply as O. Thus:

In adamantine chains and penal fire (I, 48) O^{6}
Looks through the horizontal misty air (I, 595) O i^{1}

PATTERNS OF QUICK-PACED INTEGRAL PENTAMETERS IN *PARADISE LOST* and *PARADISE REGAINED*

(References are to Columbia ed. References to PR in italics)

I^{4}	1 : 673; 10 : 218.
I^{5}	1 : 391; 3 : 480; *2 : 168; 3 : 436; 4 : 229.*
I^{6}	1 : 148; 2 : 87, 576, 680, 885, 917· 4 : 76, 620; 5 : 109, 390, 393, 906; 9 : 277, 550, 1189; *4 : 505.*
I^{7}	1 : 100, 793; 2 : 75, 103; 3 : 114, 197, 732; 4 : 213; 6 : 851; 8 : 356; 9 : 144, 276; *2 : 257.*
I^{8}	1 : 120.
I^{9}	10 : 718.
$I\,i^{4}$	*1 : 248, 461; 2 : 420.*
$I\,i\,i^{III\,4}$	11 : 143.
$I\,i^{5}$	1 : 9; 12 : 37, 96.
$I\,i^{III}\,s.^{5}$	2 : 225.
$I\,i^{6}$	2 : 105; 12 : 406; *4 : 15.*
$I\,i^{7}$	3 : 712.
$I\,i^{III\,9}$	11 : 118.
$I\,e^{4}$	2 : 150.
$I\,e^{5}$	4 : 622.
$I\,e^{6}$	1 : 135.
$I\,e^{7}$	1 : 322; 6 : 650; 7 : 193.
II^{1}	8 : 243.
II^{2}	3 : 505; 5 : 382; 6 : 364; 10 : 29; 11 : 216; *1 : 396; 2 : 266; 4 : 67.*
$II^{2,\,8}$	4 : 461; 12 : 7.
II^{3}	1 : 289, 427, 773, 778; 2 : 661, 956, 967; 3 : 48, 403, 666; 4 : 673, 821, 909; 5 : 264, 767; 6 : 408, 491; 7 : 16, 460, 537; 8 : 436; 9 : 443, 11 : 880; 12 : 47, 110, 447, 506, 513, 635; *1 · 51, 200, 243, 245, 306; 2 : 134; 3 : 221, 322, 343; 4 : 74, 356, 393, 455.*
$II^{3,\,7}$	8 : 207.
$II^{3,\,8}$	7 : 580.
$II^{3,\,9}$	2 : 611.
II^{4}	2 : 98; 3 : 94, 506, 587, 657; 4 : 318; 5 : 130, 151; 6 : 505, 807, 883; 7 : 511; 8 : 220, 545; 10 : 625, 1015;

11 : 885; 12 : 399, 570; *1 : 23, 111, 112, 289, 480; 2 : 298; 3 : 367; 4 : 609.*

II^{5} 9 : 976; 10 : 1014.

II^{6} 1 : 101, 177; 2 : 23, 140, 452, 840, 860; 3 : 300, 310, 408, 601, 662, 702; 4 : 138, 490, 745; 5 : 117, 235; 6 : 599; 7 : 149; 8 : 95, 266, 294; 9 : 11, 20, 742; 10 : 749, 845; 11 : 544; 12 : 93; *1 : 108, 238, 401, 445; 2 : 139, 239, 294; 4 : 182, 381.*

II^{7} 1 : 760; 2 : 179, 862, 966; 3 : 249; 4 : 90, 868; 5 : 47, 529, 784, 808; 6 : 649; 7 : 367; 8 : 83, 85, 554; 9 : 22, 155, 362, 531, 966; 10 : 61, 84; 11 : 254; 12 : 1, 27, 514, 532, 573; *1 : 195; 2 : 142, 402; 3 : 129, 186; 4 : 326.*

II^{8} 2 : 673; 6 : 587; 7 : 158, 246; 8 : 598; 9 : 898; 10 : 390, 956; 11 : 259, 881; *4 : 447, 566.*

II^{9} 3 : 364; 5 : 188, 766; 6 : 347; 11 : 241, 274, 690; *1 : 93.*

II i^{2} 8 : 226; 11 : 644; *2 : 217.*

II i^{3} 8 : 605.

II i^{6} 1 : 689; 2 : 469.

II i^{7} 6 : 411.

II ṡ^{3} 1 : 239; 4 : 407, 826; *3 : 94.*

II s.^{3} 9 : 140.

II ṣ.^{3} 7 : 144.

II ṡ^{5} *1 : 387.*

II ṣ^{6} 1 : 204.

II ṡ.^{6} 4 : 87.

II ṡ^{7} 1 : 64; 4 : 77.

II s.^{7} 1 : 137.

II s.^{8} *4 : 206.*

II ṩ^{1,9} 3 : 562.

II e^{3} 3 : 229; 4 : 98; 8 : 104; 10 : 920; 11 : 48; 12 : 113.

II e$^{3, 9}$ 3 : 16; 4 : 292.

II e ṡ^{3} 3 : 6.

II e^{4} 3 : 559.

II e^{6} 1 : 160; 3 : 166, 700; 4 : 317; 7 : 593; 9 : 919; 11 : 176; *1 : 123; 2 : 135.*

II e^{7} 1 : 265; 3 : 50; 5 : 123, 142, 232; 6 : 48; 8 : 107; 9 : 649; *4 : 465.*

II e ṡ^{7} — *4 : 266.*

II e^{8} — 12 : 282.

III^{2} — 2 : 148, 171; 6 : 759; 8 : 451; 9 : 25; 10 : 367; 11 : 432; *4 : 376.*

III^{3} — 1 : 108; 2 : 479, 1051; 3 : 525; 9 : 828; *1 : 244, 464; 2 : 237; 4 : 252.*

III^{4} — 2 : 442, 505; 4 : 4, 30, 186; 5 : 652, 775; 8 : 238, 321; 9 : 1026; 11 : 310; *3 : 54.*

III^{5} — 1 : 104, 152, 168, 190, 206, 355, 363, 366, 411, 448, 450, 454, 653, 654; 2 : 80, 99, 102, 125, 161, 192, 245, 274, 569, 571, 628, 911, 916; 3 : 18, 63, 93, 542, 659; 4 : 55, 89, 162, 168, 239, 278, 290, 365, 682, 760, 906, 998; 5 : 349, 511, 838; 6 : 55, 66, 257, 280, 377, 507, 619, 727; 8 : 315, 326, 446, 551; 9 : 235, 361, 961; 10 : 328, 431, 514, 957, 961; 11 : 215, 339, 383, 519, 555, 637, 701, 775; 12 : 121, 293, 435, 512, 605; *1 : 107, 110, 134, 141, 156, 163, 167, 217, 257, 427, 440, 441, 454; 2 : 92, 267, 273, 349, 384, 434; 3 : 12, 47, 49, 158, 202, 426; 4 : 1, 72, 79, 214, 282, 349, 462, 540, 603, 630.*

III^{6} — 1 : 317, 426, 497, 712; 2 : 71, 104, 513, 548, 751, 1012; 3 : 55, 462; 4 : 84, 621, 910, 954; 5 : 573; 6 : 102, 136, 390, 401, 465, 604; 7 : 54, 124; 8 : 601; 9 : 39, 156, 1151; 10 : 379; 11 : 652, 886; 12 : 337, 348; *1 : 242; 2 : 304, 423, 438; 3 : 105, 287, 418; 4 : 283.*

III^{7} — 1 : 699; 8 : 293; *1 : 421; 2 : 390.*

III^{8} — 2 : 406; 9 : 689; 10 : 366, 1077; 11 : 839; *1 : 367; 4 : 293.*

III$^{2, 8}$ — 10 : 357.

III i^{1} — 3 : 692; 5 : 363.

III i$^{1, 6}$ — 8 : 427.

III i^{2} — 5 : 121, 420; 9 : 328.

III i ·s^{2} — 1 : 21.

III i^{4} — 2 : 28, 528; 4 : 46, 396; 9 : 1046; *2 : 203.*

III i ·s^{4} — *2 : 216.*

III i^{5} — 1 : 175, 241, 291, 313, 397, 486, 520, 544, 609, 669, 745; 2 : 63, 123; 3 : 165, 183, 192, 247, 537, 605, 652; 4 : 100, 390, 498, 585; 6 : 718; 7 : 220; 9 : 345, 639, 814;

	10 : 3; 11 : 708, 778; 12 : 215, 484, 557, 630; *1 : 173, 305; 2 : 473; 3 : 230, 290, 344; 4 : 316, 578, 595.*
III i ·s^{5}	3 : 198; 11 : 833.
III i^{6}	2 : 412; 3 : 640; 5 : 16; 6 : 363, 365; 9 : 340, 774; 12 : 39, 138, 550; *4 : 13, 377, 543.*
III i ·s^{6}	*1 : 341.*
III i^{8}	1 : 147; 4 : 267.
III i^{9}	*2 : 262.*
III ṡ^{3}	1 : 45; 5 : 873.
III ·s^{3}	*4 : 507.*
III ṡ^{4}	2 : 133, 854; *1 : 481.*
III s.^{4}	9 : 350.
III ṡ^{5}	1: 33, 266; 3 : 77; 5 : 690; 6 : 811; 9 : 338, 549; *2 : 85.*
III ·s^{5}	2 : 444; 10 : 964; 11 : 122, 334; *2 : 303.*
III s.^{5}	3 : 612; 4 : 233; 8 : 106.
III ·s.^{5}	10 : 963.
III ṡ^{6}	2 : 745; *1 : 196.*
III ·s^{6}	*1 : 45; 3 : 116.*
IIIi^{IV} ṡ^{6}	2 : 138.
III ·s^{8}	12 : 432.
III s.^{8}	9 : 98.
III e i^{1}	1 : 118.
III e^{2}	3 : 292; 7 : 327.
III e ·s^{3}	11 : 659.
III e^{4}	*1 : 7.*
III e i^{4}	1 : 213.
III e^{5}	1 : 184, 581; 2 : 89, 593; 8 : 430, 600; *1 : 160; 2 : 69; 3 : 197; 4 : 129.*
III e i^{5}	1 : 182, 280, 377, 687; 6 : 49; 9 : 538; 10 : 356; 11 : 179, 549.
III e ṡ^{2}	3 : 75.
III e ṡ^{5}	9 : 439.
III e^{6}	*2 : 456.*
III e^{8}	4 : 11, 732; 8 : 643; 12 : 580.
III e i$^{1, 8}$	1 : 113.

IV^{2} 1 : 70; 2 : 88, 408; 3 : 313, 635, 716; 6 : 164, 476; 7 : 78; 8 : 469; 9 : 270; 11 : 201; 12 : 331, 540.

IV$^{2, 8}$ 7 : 637.

IV^{3} 1 : 57; 3 : 60; 4 : 825; 11 : 370; 12 : 560, 649; *2 : 463; 3 : 258; 4 : 260.*

IV^{4} 1 : 42, 49; 2 : 38, 649, 709, 1049; 3 : 37, 121, 205, 550, 658; 4 : 1003; 5 : 126, 333; 7 : 4, 211, 292; 8 : 477; 9 : 302, 339, 576, 989; 10 : 1079; 12 : 470; *1 : 87, 466; 2 : 302; 3 : 57, 179, 228, 312, 427; 4 : 94, 308.*

IV^{5} 1: 545; 2 : 298, 405; 3 : 141; 4 : 901; 6 : 577; 7 : 197; 8 : 489; 9 : 597, 956, 1153; 11 : 151; *1 : 90, 348; 2 : 367.*

IV^{6} 6 : 291; 8 : 211; *1 : 186.*

IV^{7} 1 : 95; 2 : 2, 342; 3 : 194, 636, 673, 676; 4 : 964; 5 : 263, 768; 6 : 138, 294, 445, 872; 7 : 104, 113; 8 : 14, 28; 9 : 820; 10 : 500, 840; 11 : 510, 634; *1 : 96, 149, 165, 265, 363; 2 : 472; 3 : 380; 4 : 330, 351.*

IV^{8} 1 : 129, 431, 447, 479; 2 : 512; 5 : 408, 763; 8 : 455; 9 : 360, 604; 11 : 684; *3 : 277.*

IV^{9} 2 : 803.

IV i^{1} 1 : 695; 11 : 65.

IV i$^{1, 8}$ 7 : 229.

IV i^{2} 2 : 1054; 9 : 24; *2 : 435; 4 : 157.*

IV i^{3} 6 : 682; *3 : 360.*

IV i^{4} 1 : 485, 506; 3 : 137; 4 : 74; 6 : 99, 681, 741; 8 : 445; 9 : 794; 10 : 857, 942; 12 : 486, 545; *1 : 199, 383, 394; 2 : 108, 209, 314, 471; 3 : 372.*

IV i .s^{4} 6 : 39; 9 : 977.

IV i^{5} 1 : 324, 537; 2 : 671, 752; 4 : 88; 9 : 1019; 10 : 365; *1 : 131.*

IV i .s^{5} 12 : 539 (Ed. 2).

IV i^{6} *4 : 631.*

IV i^{7} 1 : 319; 2 : 93, 180; 3 : 34, 56; 5 : 330, 557; 7 : 81, 134; 9 : 624, 637, 723; 10 : 247; 11 : 314; 12 : 29, 208; *1 : 119, 185, 450; 2 : 421.*

IV i .s^{7} *1 : 250.*

IV i^{8} 2 : 566, 861; 3 : 209; 4 : 58; 5 : 460; 7 : 487; 8 : 641; *3 : 137; 4 : 267.*

IV i$^{II\ 7}$ 9 : 402.

IV i^{IV} ṡ$^{4, 6}$ 4 : 187.

IV ṡ ^{2} — 11 : 714; *4 : 345.*
IV ·s ^{2} — 1 : 191.
IV .s ^{2} — *1 : 145.*
IV ṡ ^{3} — 1 : 124; 6 : 420; 12 : 622.
IV ṡ ^{4} — 4 : 124; 6 : 398, 907; *3 : 144; 4 : 100, 327.*
IV ṡ ^{6} — *1 : 420.*
IV ṡ ^{7} — 9 : 318; 12 : 531; *3 : 308.*
IV ·s ^{7} — 12 : 459.
IV .s ^{7} — *1 : 290, 372.*
IV ṡ ^{8} — 4 : 951.

IV e ^{2} — *3 : 250.*
IV e ^{3} — 1 : 379.
IV e ^{4} — 11 : 632; *1 : 353.*
IV e i ^{5} — 3 : 216.
IV e ṡ ^{5} — 1 : 217.
IV e i ^{6} — *4 : 448.*
IV e ^{7} — 1 : 453; 2 : 718; 3 : 207; 5 : 820; 7 : 20; 8 : 124; 11 : 617, 774; *2 : 396.*
IV e i ^{7} — 1 : 543; 5 : 517; *1 : 213; 3 : 383.*
IV e ^{8} — 6 : 841.
IV e i $^{1, 8}$ — 6 : 760.

V ^{4} — 1 : 430.
V i ^{4} — 3 : 12; *1 : 460; 4 : 269.*
V ṡ ^{4} — 1 : 142, 189.
V i .s ^{6} — 6 : 82.

O ^{2} — 1 : 541; 2 : 951.
O ^{3} — *1 : 40.*
O ^{4} — 1 : 155, 456, 608; 2 : 329, 401, 823, 856; 3 : 336; 4 : 322, 506; 5 : 413; 6 : 213; 8 : 250; 9 : 658; 10 : 1019; *1 : 222, 412; 2 : 356, 410, 461.*
O ^{5} — 4 : 639; 5 : 364, 882; 8 : 150; 11 : 592; *1 : 223; 4 : 102.*
O ^{6} — 1 : 48, 796; 4 : 744; 5 : 747; 6 : 611; *4 : 613.*
O ^{7} — 1 : 60, 69, 236; 2 : 10, 173, 802, 859, 915; 3 : 11, 351, 672; 5 : 834; 8 : 61; *1 : 148; 3 : 100.*
O ^{8} — 1 : 26; 7 : 257.

O i^{1}	1 : 595; 5 : 500; 12 : 314; ***2 : 204.***
O i$^{1, 6}$	3 : 260.
O i^{2}	3 : 479.
O i^{3}	*4 : 207.*
O i^{4}	2 : 184; 10 : 943.
O i·s^{4}	5 : 700.
O i^{5}	11 : 728; *2 : 289, 430; 3 : 79.*
O i^{6}	1 : 151; 2 : 855; 3 : 13; 5 : 431; 10 : 58; ***2 : 416.***
O i^{7}	3 : 219, 547, 714; 8 : 639; 12 : 187; ***4 : 148.***
O i^{8}	5 : 477.
O ṡ^{4}	12 : 209.
O ṡ^{6}	1 : 16.
O ṡ^{7}	9 : 1012.
O s.^{5}	3 : 404.
O i s.^{5}	1 : 163.
O .s^{8}	3 : 679.
I II^{5}	6 : 765.
I II^{6}	10 : 270.
I II^{9}	5 : 125.
I III^{4}	1 : 364; *2 : 238; 4 : 149.*
I III^{5}	3 : 431; 5 : 234; 12 : 36.
I III^{6}	2 : 812; 7 : 22; *2 : 38.*
I III^{8}	1 : 214.
I III^{9}	2 : 266; 9 : 1047; 10 : 807.
I III i^{6}	1 : 55.
I III s.^{5}	*4 : 151.*
I e III^{3}	*1 : 411.*
I e III^{6}	5 : 422, 466.
I III e^{4}	2 : 529.
I III e^{5}	*1 : 428; 2 : 274; 3 : 253.*
I III e^{6}	8 : 575.
I e III e^{6}	12 : 313.
I IV^{4}	9 : 287, 670.
I IV^{5}	1 : 99; 2 : 793; 5 : 625.
I IV^{6}	9 : 401.

I IV^{7}	9 : 1168; 10 : 932; *1 : 98, 371; 2 : 278; 4 : 39, 215.*
I IV^{8}	2 : 946; 8 : 509.
I IV i^{4}	2 : 858; 5 : 421; 6 : 905.
I IV i^{5}	3 : 208.
I IV i^{6}	8 : 142.
I IV i^{8}	8 : 109; 9 : 167.
I IV .s^{7}	*4 : 456.*
Ie IV^{4}	9 : 467, 1008; *3 : 168.*
Ie IV^{5}	11 : 109.
Ie IV^{7}	2 : 641.
Ie IV^{8}	12 : 510; *4 : 24.*
I IV e^{4}	10 : 995.
I IV e^{7}	5 : 769.
I V^{5}	2 : 943; 10 : 982; *4 : 544.*
I V^{6}	10 : 794, 992.
I V i^{4}	1 : 25; 12 : 415; *3 : 420.*
I V i ṣ^{4}	1 : 24.
II III^{4}	2 : 926; 6 : 721.
II III^{5}	5 : 745.
II III ṡ^{5}	9 : 320; *4 : 339.*
II III ṡ^{8}	9 : 955.
II III e^{4}	3 : 589.
II IV^{1}	12 : 217.
II IV^{2}	2 : 46; 4 : 435; 10 : 10; 12 : 572.
II IV^{3}	1 : 170; 2 : 425; 6 : 134; 7 : 349, 607; 8 : 502; 9 : 166; 10 : 44; 12 : 223; *1 : 398; 4 : 627.*
II IV^{4}	6 : 169; 10 : 623; 11 : 112; 12 : 87.
II IV^{6}	2 : 971; 7 : 48, 312.
II IV^{7}	1 : 570; 4 : 740; 5 : 53, 244, 901; 8 : 9, 42, 236, 282; 9 : 419; 10 : 658, 662, 676, 1006; 11 : 167, 470, 618, 773; *1 : 247, 415; 3 : 369, 384.*
II IV^{8}	8 : 586; 9 : 396; 10 : 907.
II IV^{3,7}	3 : 113; 11 : 301.
II IV^{3,8}	5 : 749.
II IV i^{2}	*1 : 468.*
II IV i i$^{II\ 2}$	11 : 88.
II IV ṡ^{3}	1 : 473; 2 : 1013.

II IV ṡ^{6} *2 : 153.*
II IV ṡ^{7} 7 : 180.
II e IV^{3} 2 : 431; 3 : 118; 10 : 36, 928; *1 : 392.*
II e IV^{6} 11 : 616.
II e IV^{7} 3 : 235; 7 : 281; 10 : 865.
II e IV^{8} 2 : 59.
II IV e^{2} 4 : 586.
II IV e ṡ^{2} 2 : 1036.
II IV e^{3} 1 : 40, 329.
II IV e^{6} 9 : 148.
II IV e^{7} 4 : 520; 9 : 129; 10 : 281; *4 : 617.*
II e IV e^{6} 2 : 16.

II V^{3} 1 : 307, 373; 6 : 750; 9 : 420; 12 : 32, 100; *2 : 196.*
II V^{4} 2 : 563; 6 : 434; 8 : 195, 501; *4 : 525.*
II V^{4,7} 3 : 373.
II V^{6} 3 : 502; 4 : 415; 8 : 279.

II V ṣ^{6} 4 : 923.
II e V^{3} 9 : 150.

III IV^{7} *1 : 282.*
III IV e^{6} 1 : 122.

III V^{3} *3 : 13.*
III V ṡ^{5} *4 : 594.*
III e V i^{5} 2 : 39.

I e III IV e^{5} *1 : 241.*

I III V^{4} 5 : 827.

II III V i^{3} 11 : 100.

RELATIVE FREQUENCY OF QUICK-PACED PATTERNS

In PL 22 patterns occur ten or more times each, accounting for over half the total number. In order of frequency these patterns are:

	Pattern	No. of Occurrences		Pattern	No. of Occurrences
1.	III^{5}	80	12.	I^{6}	15
2.	III i^{5}	37	13.	O^{4}	15
3.	III^{6}	34	14.	IV^{2}	14
4.	II^{6}	32	15.	IV i^{4}	13
5.	II^{3}	29	16.	O^{7}	13
6.	II^{7}	29	17.	I^{7}	12
7.	IV^{4}	24	18.	IV^{5}	12
8.	IV^{7}	23	19.	III^{4}	11
9.	II^{4}	20	20.	III i^{6}	11
10.	II IV^{7}	18	21.	IV^{8}	11
11.	IV i^{7}	16	22.	II^{8}	10

In PR the following 12 patterns occur five or more times each:

	Pattern	Occurrences		Pattern	Occurrences
1.	III^{5}	35	7.	II^{4}	8
2.	II^{3}	13	8.	IV i^{4}	8
3.	IV^{4}	10	9.	III^{6}	7
4.	III i^{5}	9	10.	II^{7}	6
5.	II^{6}	9	11.	O^{4}	5
6.	IV^{7}	9	12.	I IV^{7}	5

Compared with all other important writers of blank verse, Milton is frugal in his indulgence in quick-paced lines. Naturally: his paramount concern is with paragraph-structure.

For example, in both *Alastor* and *Sohrab and Rustum* quick-paced lines are over 15 per cent of all lines; in *Hyperion* and *The Holy Grail* over 25 per cent. In Marlowe and Shakespeare the rate would be even higher. But in PL only 8 per cent, and in PR 12 per cent, of the lines are quick-paced.

APPENDIX II

CROSS-RHYTHMIC CONSTRUCTION IN PL AND PR

Over 4500 lines of PL are involved in E- and T-construction: roughly, 40 per cent. Space-limitations forbid giving analytic lists for more than two books of PL and one book of PR. Afterward I set down tables of frequency for all books. My basic texts have been those of H. C. Beeching (Oxford, 1900), F. A. Patterson (Columbia Ed., 1931), and Harris Fletcher's Facsimile Edition (Urbana, Ill., 1945-48). I have also had beside me a number of modernized texts, especially those of Masson, Verity, Wright, Merritt Y. Hughes, Douglas Bush, and J. H. Hanford.

For the reader's convenience, notes explanatory of certain constructions immediately follow them.

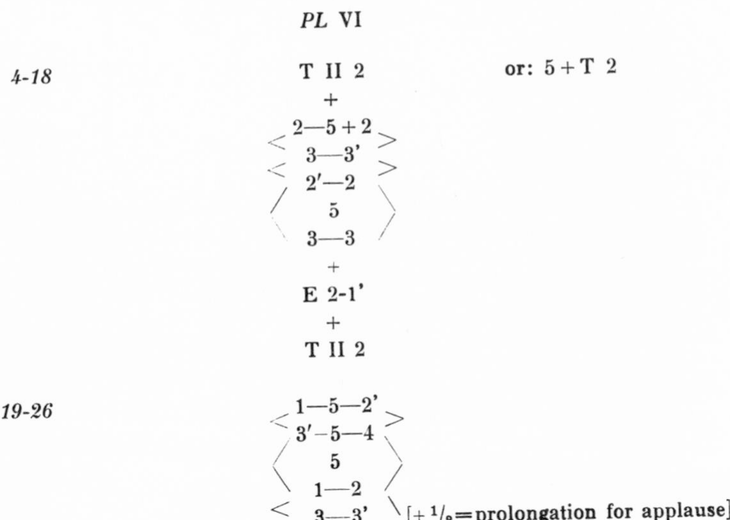

PL VI (cont.)

35-43 < 3—4 / 1—2 >
3—1' [reversing-unit]
< 4'+5—3 / 2—1 >
< 2—1 / 4 + 3 >
< 4 + 3 / 2—1' >

46-55 < 4—2 / 3—5 + 5—1' >
< 3—5 + 5—1' / 4'—2 >
\+
< 3—5 + 4 / 1—2 >
< 1—2 / 3—5 > :[4]: A

64-67 T II 2'

71-96 E 3-1' + T II 3 +
3—5—4
T 1
80 1'—5—5—2
< 3—5 + 5—3' > [+ $^1/_2$ = rest]
\+
T 2'
\+
88 2—5—1'
< 4'—2 / 3—1 >
4 + 3
\+
93 < 2—5—2 / 3—3' >

114-118 E 4-2 + E 4'-3

121 T 3

127 E 3-3

PL VI (cont.)

131-147 3—5—3' Abdiel to Satan
2'–5—2
\+
T III 3 (3—5+5—5—1' [+ 1/2=rest])
\+
139 4'—3'
2'—4
1—3'
5'
143 2—1
4—3
2—5—1

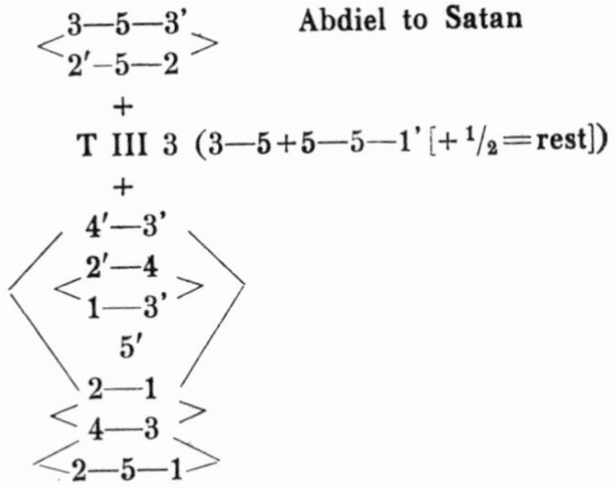

150-162 E 2-2 + 5' + 5 + T 2 + 5 + 5' + 5'
\+
2—2'
5
3—3

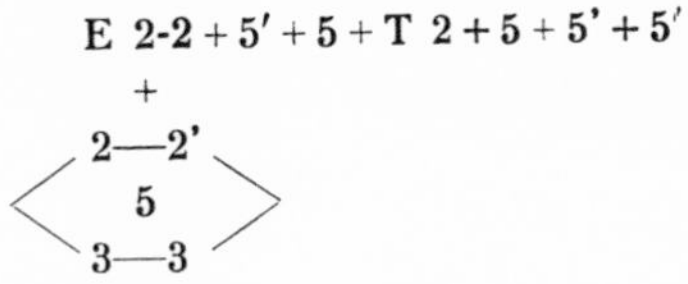

193-259 2—2 Michael vs. Satan
3—3
2—5—1
4—3
2—2
5'
200 3' + 5—1'
4'—2'
3'—1'
\+
204 4'—3
2—2'
5'
3—5—1'
4'—2' Note 1
210 3'—3
2—1'
212 4'–5—5 + 5—5—4
1—1'
218 4'—3

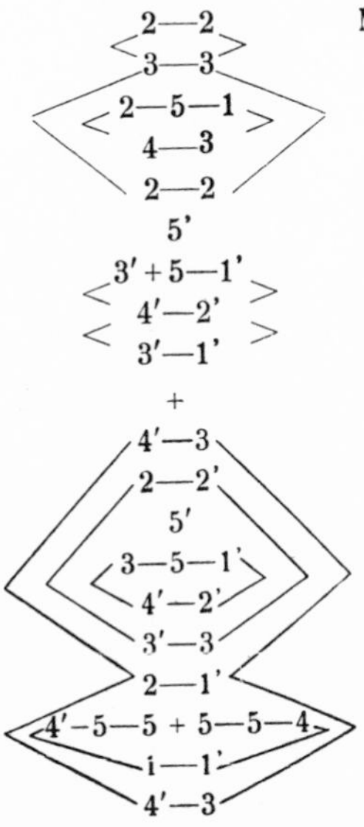

(cont. next page)

PL VI (cont.)

+

2—5—2

5

5'

3'–5—3'

T III 2'

229 2—5—2

+

231 3—1' [+ $1/2$ = rest] Note 2 [3—1' + $1/2$ = **5**]

+

232 4'—4

1—5—1'

4'—3 [+ 1 = rest] Note 3

+

236 2 + 5—2

T 3

3—3

2—2'

5'

3—3

2—2

245 5

3—3

+

247 2—1'

4'—4

250 1—5—5—5—1' Note 4

5''

4'—3

5

2—5—1

4—3

1 Integration within integration, like globular squadrons engaged within concentric spheres of execution. Observe that the outside Ecc, as befits the enveloping atmosphere of ruin, is the sinister descending series:

I 4'—3 / 2—1'

II 2—1' / 4'—3

PL VI (cont.)

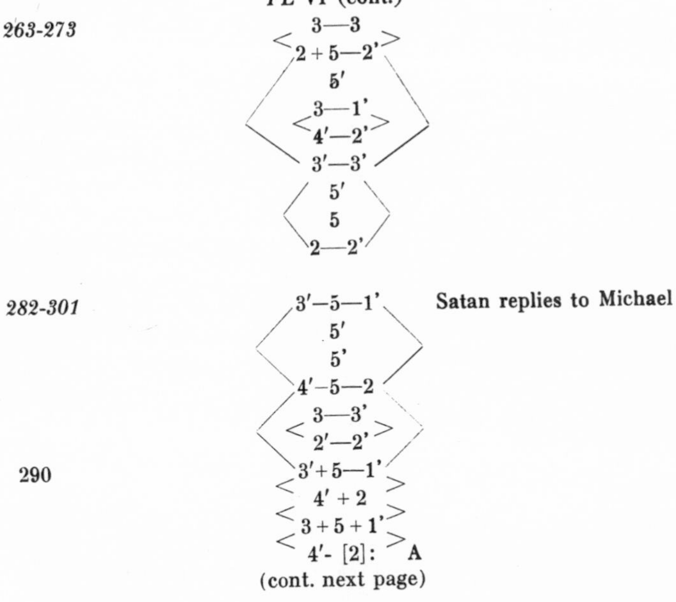

Between the overlaps of II the monstrous expansion of <4—4 / 1—1> parallels the monstrous canopy of missiles. Milton seems to reserve this particular pattern in expanded form for monstrous deeds and spectacles, as later in this paragraph at 248-253. At X, 531 ff. the description of Satan as he issues from Pandemonium in monstrous dragon-shape evokes an even longer expansion.

2 Here the rest at an impressive pause is long enough to augment an overlap-4' to a full 5. The metric foreshortening enables cross-rhythmic pattern to change in response to vicissitude of battle.

3 Again, at strong pause, the implied rest completes the chain. The very spelling of "Warr" (usual with Milton but not invariable) seems meant to prolong it.

4 Lines 249-258. Simultaneously, beneath the expansions of this chain there is a specific paralleling of rhythms and actions in the fable. The methodical blow-by-blow execution of Michael's sword is driven home by a series of four 5's which alternate with the members of a climactic series of units which increase from 3 to 8:

(249) 5 + 3: "at length . . . at once:"
(251) [5 + 4': "with huge . . . wide-wasting."]
(253) 5'' + 7': "Such destruction . . . tenfold adamant,"
(255) 5 + 8: "his ample . . . toil surceas'd."

PL VI (cont.)

—2 [paragraphs are linked]
5
< 3—5—3' / 2'–5—2 >

316-341
< 3—3 / 2—2' > Note 1 **Satan vs. Michael**
< 2—2' / 3'—3 >
5'
+
T 2'
+
322 2—4 Note 2
+
T 1
+
325 < 1—5—2 / 3—4 > Note 3
+
328 1—5—1' [reversing-unit]
+
330 < 4'—3 / 2—5—1 >
< 2—5—1 / 4 + 5 + 5—3 >
333 < 4 + 5 + 5—3 / 2—1 >
< 2—1 / 4—5—3 >
+
T 2

---

1 Lines 316 and 317 follow Wright's pointing, which is remarkably upheld by Fletcher's collation of copies. See Facsimile Edition.

2 This overlap-6 cannot be linked with any environing design. Its strange isolation seems meant to force change of pattern in the succeeding cross-rhythmic constructions. This in response to rapid action in the fable: not only change for its own sake, but to maneuver the next E-pattern into the symbolic sequence < 1—2 / 3—4 >. Perhaps, in addition, the independence of this 6-unit may be meant to profile the unparalleled quality of a sword tempered in God's armory.

3 The account of Satan's reverse of fortune when Michael's sword first causes him to feel pain contains in its sequence of rhythmic patterns a concealed sleight of numerical symbolism which is too carefully calculated to be ascribable to chance.

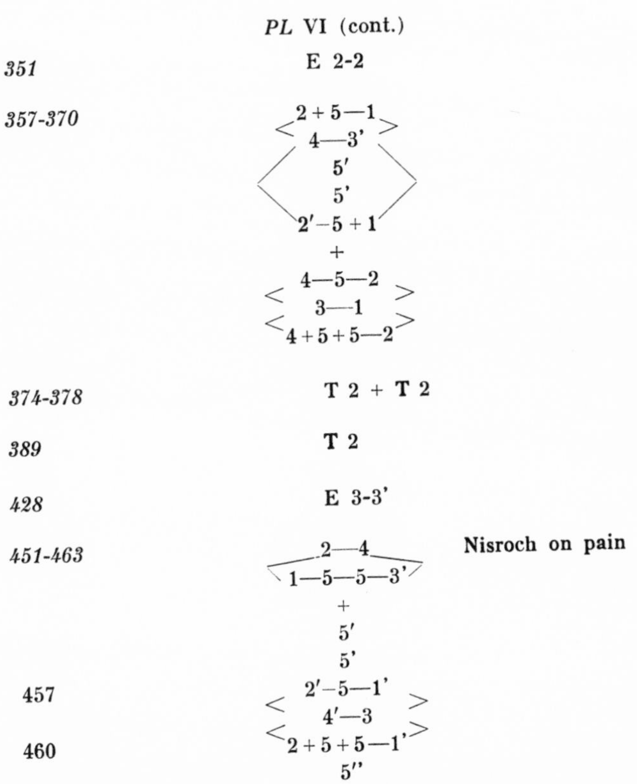

Suppose we want to turn $<\substack{1—2\\3—4}>$ completely round to $<\substack{4—3\\2—1}>$ as quickly as language in the metric frame permits. The most direct way would be to have an overlap 1—1 immediately succeed $<\substack{1—2\\3—4}>$, or — with greater chance of masking the operation — the overlap expanded to 1—5—1. Just so does Milton here reverse his pattern to symbolize Satan's reverse. Between $<\substack{1—5—2\\3—4}>$ (325-328) and $<\substack{4'—3\\2—5—1}>$ (330-333) the reversing-unit 1—5—1' (328-330) occurs in these words:

> so sore
> The griding sword with discontinuous wound
> Passed through him,

A similar reversing of symbolic pattern in response to context occurs at X, 509, where the change is effected — even more dramatically — by a simple mid-line **1'**. See analysis below.

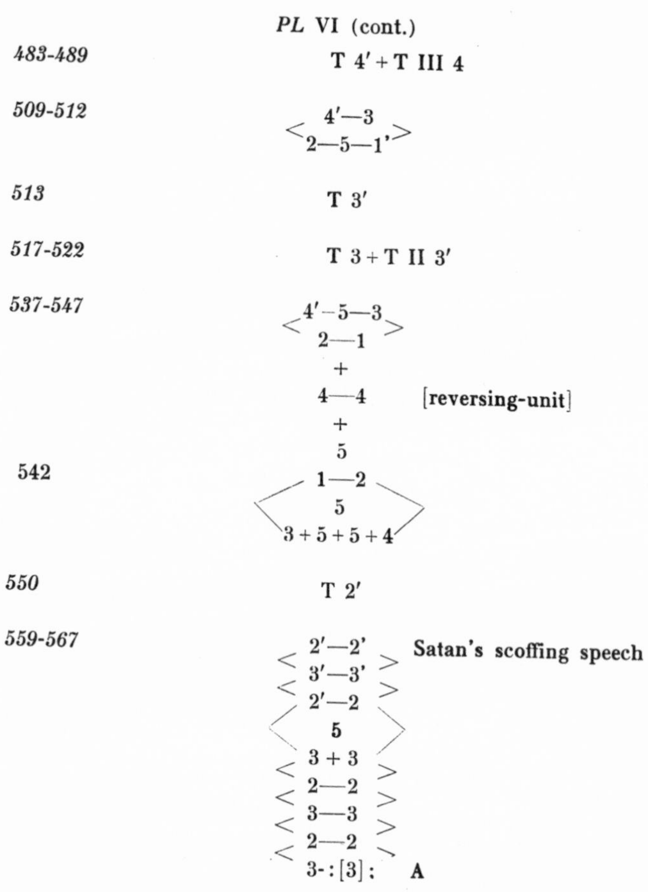

Note.

The regularized links in this chain accord with the ostensibly clear and intelligible military order with which Satan commands his squadrons to meet their foes "with open breast."

570-573 T II 4

576-580 T 2 + E 2-2

PL VI (cont.)

591-595 <4—5 + 3>
2—1'
< 4' + 3 >

602-606 4—3'
<2'–5—5—1'>

609-617 < 4 + 3' >
2'–5—1
+
2 [alteration-unit]
+
2—2'
< 3' + 1 >
4—2
3—5—3

629-636 < 4'—3 >
2—5—1'
< 4 + 3' >
+
2'—2'
< 3' + 3 >
<2—5- : [2] : A

657-660 E^{cc} 2-2

668 E 3-3

689 T 2'

700-708 2'—1'
< 4'—3 >
< 2—1' >
< 4'—3 >
2—5 + 5 + 5—1'

749 T 3

PL VI (cont.)

753-759

2—1'
< 4'—3 >
< 2—1' >
< 4'+5+3 >
< 2—1' >

773-778

2—1
< 4—5—3 >
< 2+5—1' >

792-799

2'—1'
< 4'—3 >
+
2—2'
< 3'—3' >
2'—4
< 1—3 >
2—2

818

E 2-4

856-866

2—5—4
< 1—5—3 >
+

861

2—1'
< 4'- 3 >
+
5'
+
2'—2
< 3—3 >
< 2—5-: [2]: A "the bottomless pit"

867-879

1—5—1'
< 4'–5+[9] > "Nine days they fell" — count 9
+ Note

(cont. next page)

Note.

A count of 9, being 5 + 4, will complete, very literally, the cross-rhythmic construction: < 1—5—1' / 4'–5—[5—4] >.

PL VI (cont.)

871 3—5—5—3'
2'–5 + 5—2
3 + 3
2—2
3–: [3] : **A**

882-891 T 2
+
2 + 5 + 5 + 5 + 2
3—3
2—5—1 [+ **1** = **rest**]

PL X

7 T 4′

12 T 3'

21-24 E^{cc} 3-4

27-31
2—2
T 3
3—3

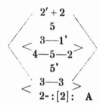

41-49 E 3′-3 + T II 3′ + 5 + E 3-1

72-79
2′ + 2
5
3—1'
4—5—2
5'
3—3
2- : [2] : A

97 E 3-3'

104-113

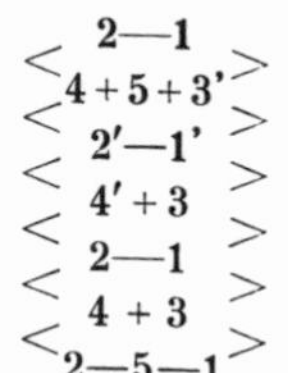

125-135 "in evil strait this day I stand"
4—2
3—3
2—2
3 + 1'
4′—2
5
3—1'

(cont. next page)

PL X (cont.)

\+

< 4′–5—4 / 1—1 >

148-156 (a) < 2′–5—5—4 / 1—5—3’ > Deity appraises the sexes

153 1 + 2’ + 2′ Note

153-156 (b) < 4—5 + 3 / 2—1’ > < 4′- : [3] : A

Note.

In this subtle overlapping of (a) and (b), not only is the unit 2’ ("not thy subjection") in line 153 common to both, but the concept it expresses determines that (b) be designed with the symbolic destruction-series.

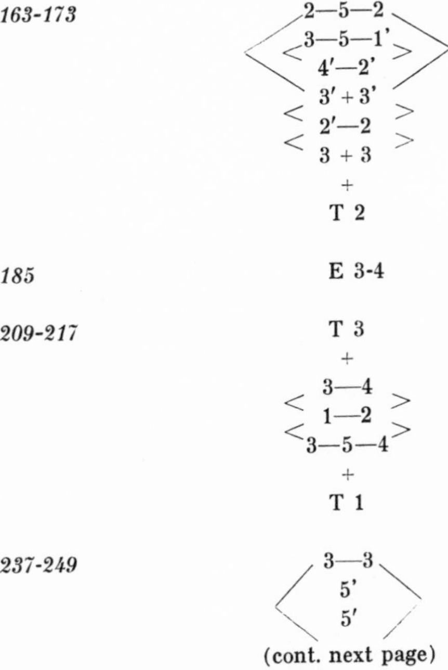

(cont. next page)

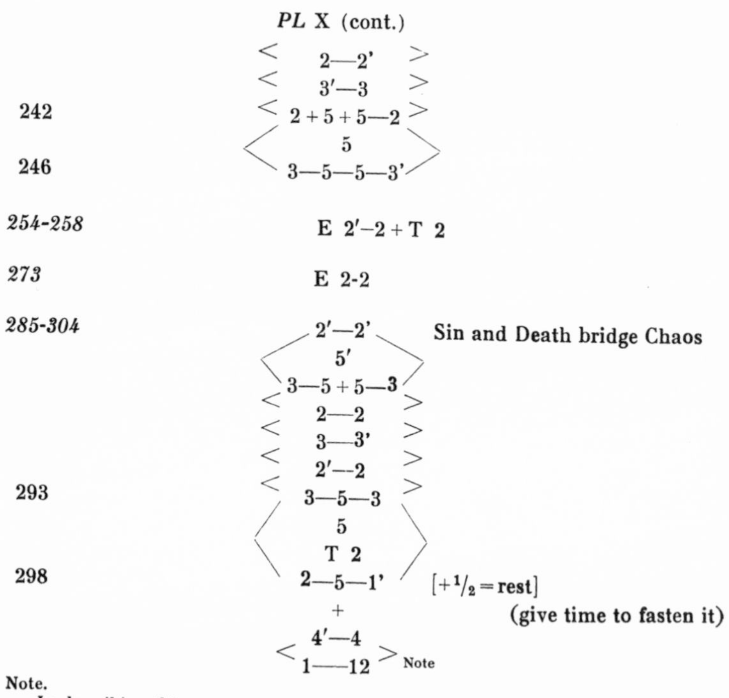

Note.

In describing this supernatural piece of engineering Milton chooses for his climactic cross-rhythmic construction that pattern in which the first over-lap is maximum: 4—-4, and the integrating overlap is minimum: 1—-1. To complete the latter the only word necessary would be "prodigious." But he deliberately thwarts this expected integration. He runs the minimal segment on and on and on to twelve times what is required.

Editors who insert a comma after "prodigious" are therefore ruining this rhythmic strategy.

Later in this Book, at line 566, another terminal unit 1 expands in obedience to context.

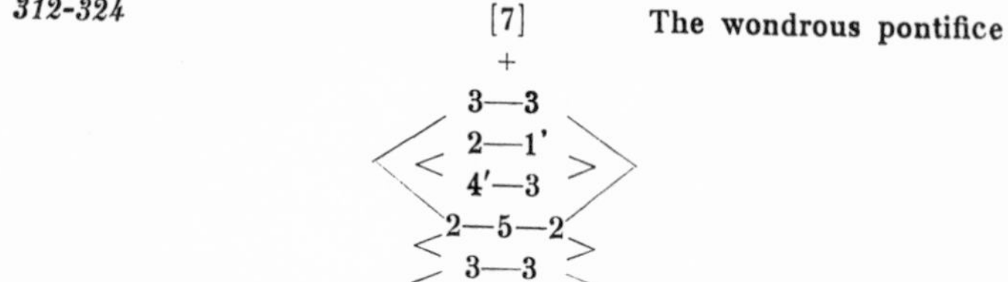

(cont. next page)

PL X (cont.)

2—2
T 3
3—3
+
[7]

333-349 2—2'
3'—3'
2'—2'
5'
3—3'
+
338 2'—1
5'
4'—3
2—1
342 4—5—3
+
2—4
1—5+3'
2'—4
1—3

376-380 E 4'–3 + T 4''

389-402 3'–5 + 3
2—2
3—3
2—2'
3'—3
2—2'
5'
397 3—5 + 3
2—5 + 2
3 + 3
2-:[2]: **A** "and lastly kill"

PL X (cont.)

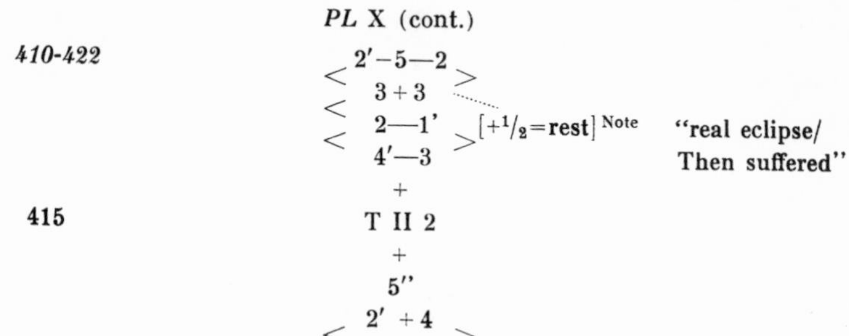

Note.

The overlap 2—1’ is a *vinculum anceps* before the dead stop, which supplies the beat to integrate with the preceding construction. At the same time in strict metre it integrates with the succeeding overlap, effecting a change of pattern. Cf. similar rhythmic maneuvers at II, 423 and XI, 751.

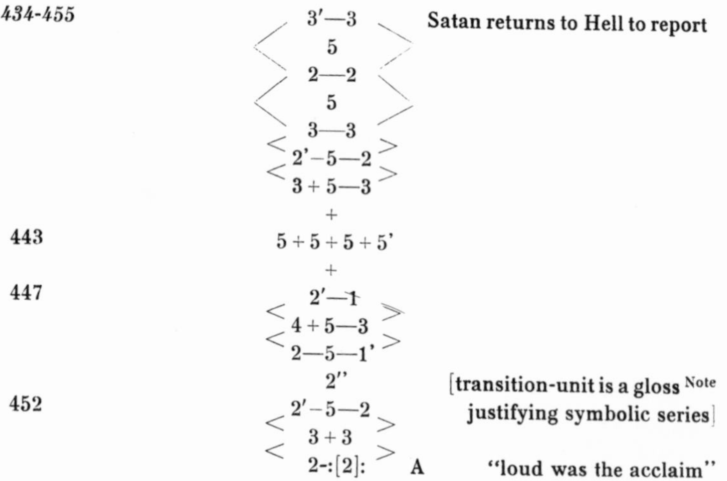

Note.

Satan’s outward glory as described in lines 447-451 may seem incompatible with the symbolic ruin-series in which its rhythms are loosely patterned. Aware of this, Milton no sooner completes the symbolic series than he glosses it with a brief quibbling paronomasia: all Satan’s glitter since his fall is “false glitter.” Hence the sinister series represents perfect hypocrisy. In this same book, at lines 21-25, there is a similar gloss, this time to justify a perfection series. In each case the gloss is detached from the E-construction.

PL X (cont.)

461-492 E 2-4 + T 2 + 5' + 5'
\+
467 < 2—2' >
< 3'—3 >
< 2—2 >
< 3—5—3' >
\+
472 < 2'–5—4 >
< 1—3' >
\+
5'
\+
475 < 2—5—5—2 >
< 3—3 >
< 5 >
< 2—2 >
< 3—3' >
< 5' >
484-485 < 2—1' > [+1/2=rest] *(vinculum anceps)*
< 4'–5—3' >
487 < 2'—1' >
< 4'–5—3 >
490 < 2—5—5—1 >
4-:[3]: **A**

498-503 < 3 + 5 + 5—3 >
< 2—2' >
< 3'–5–:[3]: > **A**

504-584 T 3 (begins with "a while he stood")
< 1'–5—2 > (,, ,, "expecting") Note 1
506 < 3—5—4 >
< 1—2 >
509 1' [reversing-unit] "he wondered"
< 2'—1' >
510 < 4' + 5 + 3 > Note 2
< 2'—1' >
513 < 4'–5 + 3 > [3 = 1' + 2'] Note 3

(cont. next page)

PL X (cont.)

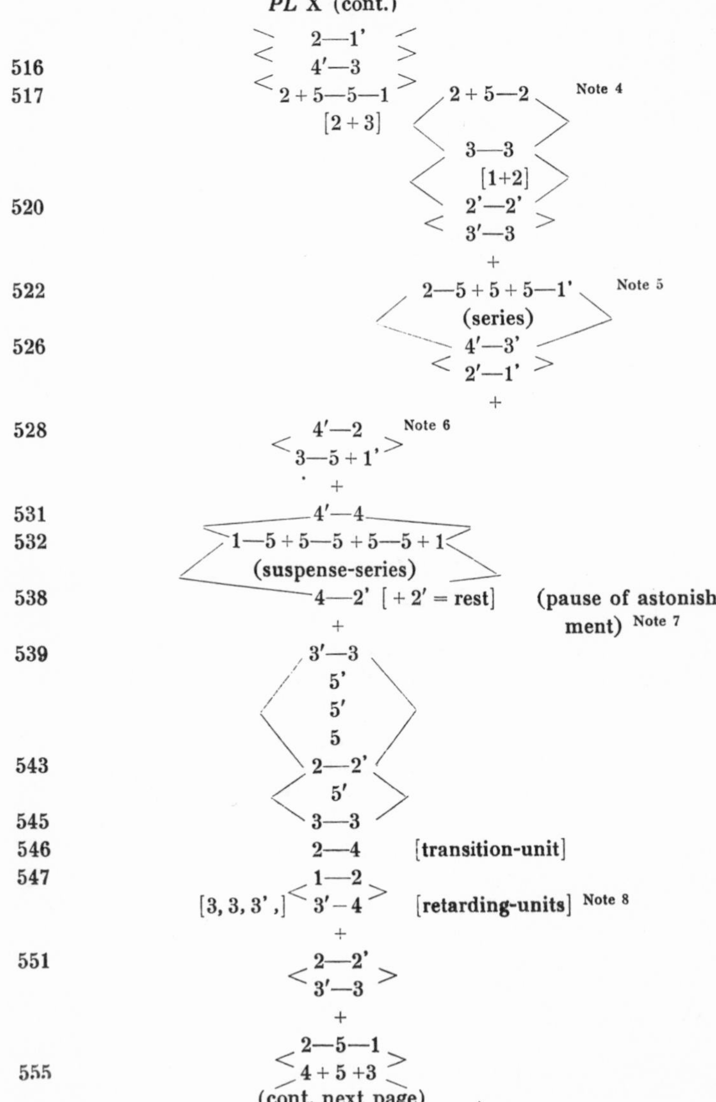
2—1'
516 4'—3
517 2 + 5—5—1
[2 + 3]
2 + 5—2
Note 4
3—3
[1+2]
520 2'—2'
3'—3
+
522 2—5 + 5 + 5—1'
Note 5
(series)
526 4'—3'
2'—1'
+
528 4'—2
Note 6
3—5 + 1'
+
531 4'—4
532 1—5 + 5—5 + 5—5 + 1
(suspense-series)
538 4—2' [+ 2' = rest]
(pause of astonishment) Note 7
+
539 3'—3
5'
5'
5
543 2—2'
5'
545 3—3
546 2—4
[transition-unit]
547 1—2
[3, 3, 3' ,] 3' – 4
[retarding-units] Note 8
+
551 2—2'
3'—3
+
2—5—1
555 4 + 5 +3
(cont. next page)

PL X (cont.)

557 > 2 + 5—1 <
< 4—5—3 >
559 < 2—5 + 5—1 >
561 < 4—3 >
564 < 2— Note 9

[completion of design frustrated by alteration of pattern]

< —2' >
566 < 3′—3' >
+
5″
568 T 2′
5'
5′
+
572 2—2'
< 3′—3' >
574 < 2′ + 5—5 + 2 >
< 3 -: [3]: > A
+
578 1' [transition-unit] (punct. Wright)
+
< 4′–5+3' > Note 10
580 < 2′—1' >
< 4′—3 >
< 2—5—1 >

---

1 Two cross-rhythmic constructions in simultaneous performance start in line 504. They overlap like allorhythmic voices in polyphonic music. The first words of a T-construction are: "a while he stood"; the last words are: "fill his ear" (506). The comma after "stood" is indispensable, for the word that follows, "expecting," begins the first expanded overlap of a <1—2 / 3—4>. Observe that since the T-construction is a rhythmically self-contained multiple of 5, and therefore static in its rhythmic environment, it parallels the standing, expectant posture of Satan.

As he thus stands, the second cross-rhythmic construction begins. It is of no haphazard pattern, but one symbolic of perfection — of the perfect storm of applause he is expecting. In other words, the T-construction is here the rhythmic medium for the physical, the E-construction for the psychical. And since the physical state is a necessary preparation and condition for emotional reactions, it is with nothing less than mathematical precision that the symbolic cross-rhythmic series emerges from the T-construction and overlaps it.

Now Satan's state of anticipation persists even after the hissing starts,

PL X (cont.)

even until he begins to wonder what's it's about, even till the perfection-series starts to develop into a chain, which indeed gets as far as the second 1—2. Then it stops. A single isolated foot, 1' — "he wondered" — interposes to cause reversal of pattern from exultation ($<\substack{1-2\\3-4}>$) to degradation ($<\substack{4-3\\2-1}>$). (Compare the similar maneuver at VI, 325-333.) Thus transformation of rhythmic design matches transformation of demons.

2 From "wondering at himself" (510) to "Alike" (520) the eleven lines depicting Satan's physical degradation comprise three successive descending series, each functionally symbolic. This is the second time that a triple sinister series has served as cryptic commentary on Satan's career. Back at lines 163-168, when God condemns the snake, the units of the series are in linear aggregate form: 12 + 9' + 6'' + 3′ = 3 × (4 + 3 + 2 +1) — obedient to the triple curse of Genesis. In the present paragraph there is still another triple cross-rhythmic series: at 553-568.

3 Observe that lines 515-516 contain an *ascending* symbolic series in *linear* form. Like the series at 492-493, it is concurrent with a negative cross-rhythmic series. The present linear series comes in the midmost of three sinister $<\substack{4-3\\2-1}>$'s, depicting Satan's degradation. In the first (at 510-513) Satan stands in wonder as he feels himself undergoing radical bodily change. In the second (at 513-516) he is incapable of upright form, and, despite all his struggling, drops down upon a serpentine belly, for "a greater power / Now ruled him." This greater power, the Dispenser of justice and retribution, is actually present in symbol at the moment Satan realizes his impotence.

> Reluctant, but in vain, a greater power 1', 2′, 3', 4′
> Now ruled him, punished in the shape he sinned.

By bracketing two subordinate rhythmic currents I have suggested how this linear series fits into the encompassing cross-rhythmic construction. Once these series are recognized, the punctuation of Edd. 1 and 2 becomes clear. After "in vain" a modernized text would put a semicolon. But Milton wants the numerical series symbolizing infinite affirmative power to advance with a minimum of interruption.

4 The earliest editions read:

(a)
> for now were all transform'd
> Alike, to serpents all as accessories
> To his bold riot: (519-521)

Fletcher, commenting in the Facsimile Edition, says of a certain "Copy 19":

"It contains corrections with a pen of the punctuation in line 520 as follows:

(b)
> Alike, to serpents all, as accessories

Whoever penned the change, first struck out the comma after 'Alike,' and inserted one after 'serpents,' then restored the comma after 'Alike,' struck out the insertion after 'serpents' and inserted a comma after 'all,' with the final result as in the above excerpt. There is one curious fact directly connected with this passage, though no editor to my knowledge has ever

PL X (cont.)

noticed it. In the 1667 text there is a space for punctuation [after 'all']. But I am inclined to think that some punctuation was originally set here in 1667, then Milton or someone for him intended to make some change. The only result of this intent was to make matters worse by removing the comma between 'all' and 'as' without other change. Whoever penned in the comma in Copy 19 probably came as close as anyone ever can come to understanding what Milton wanted here. There is also the possibility that the various penned corrections in this copy were performed in the printshop."

Now whoever authorized the two commas in version (b) knew exactly the cross-rhythmic management of lines 516-520. It could have been no one but Milton himself. He alone was aware of his thrice-uttered cross-rhythmic descending series. When he came to the final link in the chain his problem was to merge it into a non-sinister series.

His method is adroit. In expanding the final 2—1, he includes in the expansion a metric 5 that breaks into subordinate currents 2 + 3. And by beginning the next line with units 1 and 2 ("Alike, to serpents all,"), he makes it possible for "Alike" to be the terminal wing-segment of the expanded sinister link, and 1 + 2 to be the terminal segment in the first link of an emergent non-sinister E-chain. An examination of my analysis set beside the text will show that the two E-designs cannot be perceived as concurrent unless there is a pause not only after "Alike" to end the $\left\langle {4'\text{—}3 \atop 2+5\text{—}5\text{—}1} \right\rangle$, but also after "all" to end the $\left\langle {2+5\text{—}2 \atop 3\text{—}3} \right\rangle$.

It follows that Wright's punctuation of line 520, coinciding as it does with that of "Copy 19" of Ed. 1, as well as with Milton's demonstrable rhythmic intentions, must supersede that of the reprints.

There are similar instances elsewhere of one design flowing into another; e.g., at II, 817-822.

5 Observe the resumption of the sinister series as Milton gets to describing the infinite *variety* of monstrous shapes.

6 Between lines 526 and 538 Milton first includes the normally sinister $\left\langle {4\text{—}3 \atop 2\text{—}1} \right\rangle$, then alters it successively to the only other patterns that can start with 4 and end with 1, i.e., $\left\langle {4\text{—}2 \atop 3\text{—}1} \right\rangle$ and $\left\langle {4\text{—}4 \atop 1\text{—}1} \right\rangle$. The first of these, when expanded to $\left\langle {4'\text{—}2 \atop 3\text{—}5\text{—}1'} \right\rangle$, is the normally sinister form contorted out of shape and aptly reserved for the shadowy rhythmic mold in depicting Satan "Now dragon grown." The design $\left\langle {4'\text{—}4 \atop 1\text{—}1} \right\rangle$, with its monstrous expansion of the 1—1, is a yet more horrible distortion, a gross flattening out.

7 After the monstrous expansion, 1—5 + 5—5 + 5—5 + 1, mirroring the demons' colossal hopes of demonstrating in honor of their chief, the proper overlap to complete the integration would be 4—4. But this overlap fails to appear. The integration fails, even as those hopes of triumph fail. In place of 4—4 we get a suspended rhythm in 4—2', and the integration must be completed by an appropriate pause of astonishment at the sight of loathsome reptiles instead of splendid leaders.

But even as they pause they suffer change, parallel with which the rhythmic pattern changes. The truncation of 4—4 to 4—2' makes possible and necessary the pattern $\left\langle {3'\text{—}3 \atop 2\text{—}2} \right\rangle$, with intercalated overlap-5's, whose very regularity, with accompanying isopause, parallels the relentless and systematic administration of divine justice on the enemies of Light.

PL X (cont.)

8 From "There stood" (547) to "... in Paradise" (551) is an ironic adaptation of the cross-rhythmic perfection-series invented to accentuate the fiends' protracted expectation of fair fruit, that their penance may be the heavier. The rhythmic construction emerges from behind an unusual succession of five 3's, of which the first is the overlap 1—2. This gives the design a cross-rhythmic start. Conceivably we might complete a very loose $<\substack{1-2\\3-5-4}>$ down to "like that." But "like that / Which grew in Paradise" would then be left rhythmically isolated. The slightest study of these rhythms and of the context shows that this unusual cluster of 3's is deftly fitted into a cross-rhythmic E-construction — $<\substack{1-2\\3-4}>$ — whose anomalous feature is a *four-times-repeated third unit to delay integration.* Yet every added 3 makes it the more impossible to effect integration; and such indeed is to be forthwith the demons' impotence.

The presence of these three redundant 3's makes the number of beats in the complete construction 19. Thus Milton can shift to a different cross-rhythmic pattern, which becomes a chain of symbolic descending series suitable to the description of the demons' penance by plague and famine.

9 Again a sympathetic relationship between symbolic pattern and event in the fable. We have seen how the triple sinister series at 510-520 terminates by dovetailing into the beginning of a non-sinister pattern. The present sinister series (553-566) merges into a new rhythmic design in a way that recalls the pause of astonishment at 539. But though the contexts are not unlike, there is a remarkable difference in the rhythmic management. At 539 the demons expect to see before them an array of splendidly accoutred field-marshals: they see reptilian horrors. Here at 564-565 they climb trees that seem laden with true fruit of Paradise: they chew ashes.

At 539 the rhythm expected to complete the integration is drastically clipped from a 4 to a 2'. The pattern $<\substack{3-3\\2-2}>$ can therefore enter at once and guide the rhythms that follow. But here at 566 the rhythm expected to complete the integration is the nadir-unit of the sinister series, i.e., 1. Milton refuses to pause to demarcate it. So bitter and gritty with ash is the fruit, so ravenous the feeders. They cannot merely taste one sample, and have done with it all. They no sooner chew than they reject, but no sooner reject than their writhing jaws are at it again in perpetually frustrate hope of stanching hunger and thirst. From monsters so mad never expect restraint enough to complete a $<\substack{4-3\\2-1}>$ or any other regular construction.

What happens is that the normal 1 is augmented to 2'. The non-sinister pattern $<\substack{3-3\\2-2}>$ can therefore again appear, to be followed by a T and by overlap-5's, whose appreciable regularity again parallels the relentless administration of divine justice.

10 To clarify the much-disputed pointing of the last seven lines of this paragraph, one must recognize the functional presence of two successive symbolic series in cross-rhythmic form: $<\substack{4-3\\2-1}>$. "However" — the transition-word which effects a change of cross-rhythmic construction from the $<\substack{2-2\\3-3}>$-chain — seems to have been regarded by Milton as carrying with it so natural a pause as to dispense with any overt mark. An exactly parallel case is at *PR* IV, 321:

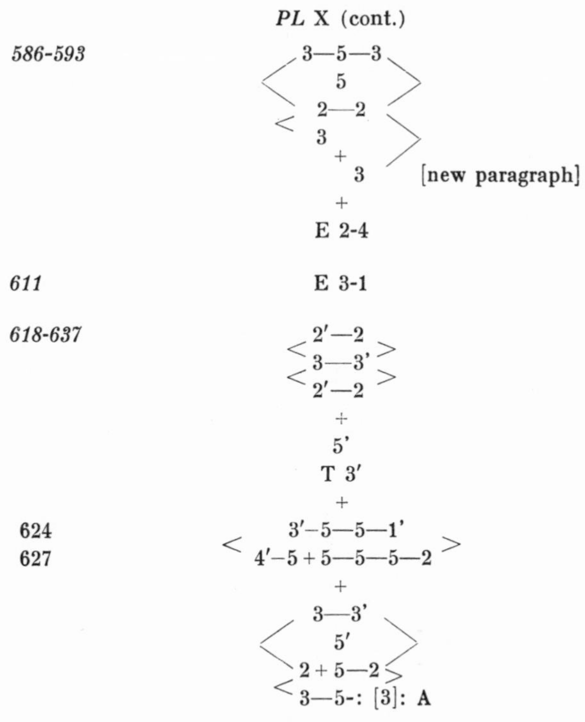

However many books
Wise men have said are wearisome.

The words that start the first descending series — "some tradition . . ." — are therefore clearly demarcated even without Wright's comma. The end-unit of the first series. i.e., "Ophion," precedes a pause so important to the sense that it should have a comma. Fletcher has noted other places where commas seem to have suffered misplacement. Almost certainly the mark that follows "Eurynome" should have followed "Ophion." Either that, or the compositor, who could make little sense of the passage anyway, dropped the comma in his confusion. A punctuation that perhaps comes closest to Milton's intended meaning is offered by Fletcher:

Ophion, with Eurynome the wide-
Encroaching (Eve perhaps), had first the rule
Of high Olympus, . . .

which not only makes the best sense but comports perfectly with a fluent 4—3 to start the second descending series. That Milton is striving for such fluency is remarkably evident in his unique end-line hyphenation (581), derived from Virgil's occasional device of synapheia.

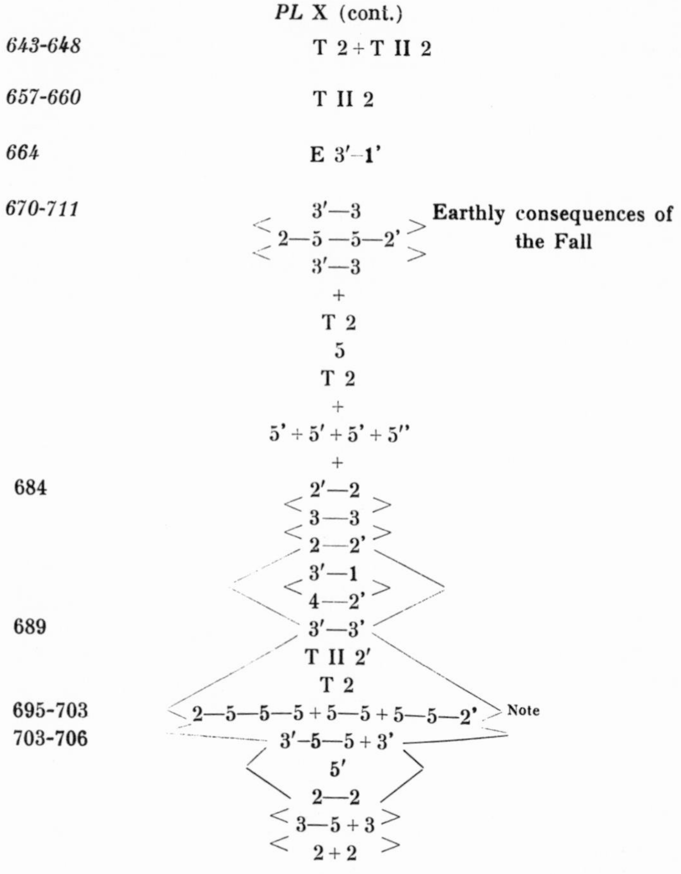

The inventory at I, 579-587 is patterned identically.

714 E 3′–3

723-730

3′—1
4—2
3—1'
4′—2'

(cont. next page)

PL X (cont.)

+
3′ + 3
5
2—2

760 E 2-2'

771-786 2′–5—2 “Why do I overlive?”
3 + 3
2—2
3—3'
2′—2
3—3
2—2
3—3
T 2
782 2′—2
3 + 3
2—2
3—3

796-802 3—5 + 3
2—2'
3′—3
5
2—2

809-817 2 + 2
5'
3′—3'
5′
+
T 2
+
E 2-2'

826 E 3′–1

PL X (cont.)

834-837
< 3—5 + 3' >
2′—2'

846-853
3 + 3
< 2—2 >
< 3 + 5—3' >
< 2′—2 >
< 5' >
3′—3'

867-895
3—5—1' "Out of my sight!"
< 4′–5—2 >
< 3'—1 >
< 4'—2 >
873 1″ Note
+
5′
5
5'
2′—2'
< 3′—3 >
< 2'—2 >
< 5 >
3 + 3
< 2 + 2 >
882 < 3 + 5—3' >
< 2—2' >
885 < 3′ + 5 + 5' -3 >
< 2 + 2 >
< 3—3 >
< 2—5—1' > [+ ½ = rest]
+
T II 4′

Note.

"Snare them" integrates with neither the chain before nor the rhythms following. It precedes a dead stop, after which comes a change from abusive exclamation to scornful reflection. It serves to alter chain-pattern: from E 3-1 to E 2-2, which is more manageable over many links.

PL X (cont.)

914-921

  2′–5—1’
< 4′—3 >
< 2—1 > [(2—1 + 2)] Note
917

+

918
< 2—2 >
  3—5—3

Note.
To affect transition out of the symbolic series, there is present in lines 917-918 an overlap-5: "thy suppliant / I beg, and clasp thy knees."

925-930

< 2—5 + 2’ >
< 3″–5 + 3 >
  2—2

937-940

< 3′ + 5—3 >
  2—2’

981-991

T 3
+
< 3—5—5—3’ >
< 2′–5—2 >
< 3 + 5 + 3 \
  2—5 -: [2]: A

1020-1028

  2—2
< 3—3 >
< 2—5—2 >
< 3—5—3 >
+
T 2

1033

E 2′–1

1042-1059

  3—3
< 2’—2 >
/ T 3 \
\ 3—5—3’ /
/ 5″ \
\ 5′ /

(cont. next page)

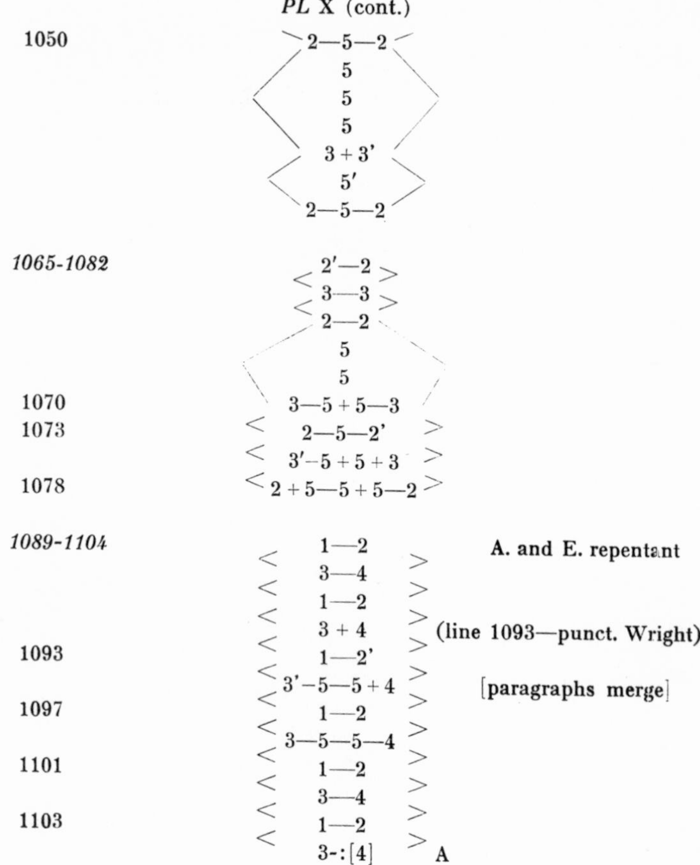
PL X (cont.)
1050 2—5—2
5
5
5
3 + 3'
5'
2—5—2
1065-1082 2'—2
3—3
2—2
5
5
1070 3—5 + 5—3
1073 2—5—2'
3'–5 + 5 + 3
1078 2 + 5—5 + 5—2
1089-1104 1—2 A. and E. repentant
3—4
1—2
3 + 4 (line 1093—punct. Wright)
1093 1—2'
3'–5—5 + 4 [paragraphs merge]
1097 1—2
3—5—5—4
1101 1—2
3—4
1103 1—2
3-:[4] A

PR III

23-27	2—4 < 1—5—5—3' >
61	E 3–1'
72-78	E 2–1' + 2'–5—2' < 3'–5—3 >
160-163	3'—1' < 4'—5—2 >
281	T 4'
299-306	T 3 + 3'—3' < 5' > 2—5—2 < 3—3 >
323	T 3
349-354	2'–5—2 < 3—5—5 + 3 >
359-368	2—5—5—2' < 3'—3 > < 2—2 > + 3—5—1' < 4—5—2' >
391	T 2
399	E 2'–2'
407-412	T II 2 + T 2
414	E 2-4
421	E 3-3'

TABLES OF FREQUENCY

Column (i) tells how many lines are involved; column (ii) percentage of frequency book by book. In (iii) the books are listed in order of frequency; in (iv) is rate of enjambement for each book.

	(i)	(ii)		(iii)	(iv)
	PL			*PL*	
I	403	50.5 per cent	X	54.4 p. c.	59.7 p. c.
II	496	47.	I	50.5	66.
III	201	27.	VI	49.2	59.3
IV	326	32.1	II	47.	64.4
V	405	44.8	XI	46.8	56.2
VI	447	49.2	XII	45.4	57.1
VII	284	44.3	V	44.8	60.8
VIII	214	32.7	VII	44.3	61.2
IX	430	36.1	IX	36.1	53.
X	601	54.4	VIII	32.7	50.
XI	422	46.8	IV	32.1	56.
XII	295	45.4	III	27.	52.2
	4524	42.8			
	PR			*PR*	
I	125	24.9	I	24.9	50.8
II	64	13.5	IV	16.5	42.4
III	67	15.1	III	15.1	44.4
IV	106	16.5	II	13.5	41.5
	362	17.4			

APPENDIX III

THE RHYTHMIC METHOD OF CONTRAPUNTAL MUSIC

The music of the Tudor period is now accessible to everyone. Edited collections are in every library. Thanks to Ernest Brennecke, I need not go for illustration beyond Milton's boyhood home if I choose a characteristic piece of his father's, an anthem, "O woe is me for thee, my brother Jonathan," which is for the first time scored in *John Milton the Elder and His Music* (pp. 171-189). The book is so generally circulated that it is unnecessary to quote the 19 pages of score.

The words, from 2nd Samuel 1 : 26, are in two sentences which form the two main sections. Each of these is subdivided, as if at any singer's will, into separate clauses and phrases, which may be sung once or more than once.

I {
a. O woe is me for thee,
b. my brother Jonathan.

II {
c. Thy love to me was wonderful,
d. passing the love of women,
e. and very kind hast thou been to me,
f. my brother Jonathan.

a and b of I intermesh melodically and rhythmically, just as do c, d, e, and f of II. Since any voice may sing once or more than once an entire phrase or only part of it, there are opportunities to apply separate rhythms to the following segments of the subdivisions:

a. woe is me for thee / O woe is me / woe is me / for thee
b. Jonathan

c. was wonderful

d. the love of women / of women

e. and very kind hast thou been unto me / hast thou been to me / to me / and very kind hast thou been / hast thou been unto me / and very kind / unto me

f. Jonathan

Twenty-two different clauses or phrases are therefore made available, and each one may have a different melody and rhythm.

The voices are five: Cantus — soprano (C); Quintus — extra soprano (Q); Altus (A); Tenor (T); and Bassus (B). If we include repetitions of clauses or phrases and add together the number of times all are actually sung, we find that

C	sings	23	phrases:	6 + 2 + 5 + 4 + 5 + 1 = 23
Q	"	33	"	9 + 3 + 6 + 7 + 4 + 4 = 33
A	"	35	"	10 + 3 + 6 + 6 + 5 + 5 = 35
T	"	35	"	13 + 2 + 3 + 6 + 4 + 7 = 35
B	"	18	"	7 + 1 + 0 + 2 + 3 + 5 = 18
				[a + b + c + d + e + f = 144]

Thus no singer and no significant clause or phrase in the text are neglected in this anthem of 51 measures. Observe that Q, A, and T are in close rivalry. C and B are less active. For the elder Milton, as an experienced vocalist, knows how to hold the top and bottom registers in reserve for special effects.

Examining the score further, we see that all five voices come together only twice: at the syllable *-than* which ends both I and II. At all other times they are singing as if independent, as if actuated only by individually felt emotion. When any two voices sing the same word or syllable simultaneously it is as if by inadvertence. When two voices sing the same phrase or fragment of phrase, i.e., when two rhythms momentarily merge, it is as if each, following its own emotional itinerary, suddenly finds its route coinciding with another's, and the meeting of voices, though never for longer than a phrase, seems to renew the fervor of each rival in a common cause. Thus C and A sing a brief duet of four beats, "Thy love to me was wonderful" (measures 21 and 22), whereupon Q displaces A and sings in duet with C for a half-measure, when Q goes his independent way, rhythmic as well as melodic, permitting A to continue the duet with C (measure 24). Later, C and T unite in duet at the words, "Passing the love of women" (measure 31), whereupon Q, A, and B sing the same words in rapid trio (measures 33 and 34). All the while the other voices maintain a free fugal counterpoint, each concerned with its own words, melody, and rhythm.

Only by close acquaintance with such a score can we imagine the effect of this polyphonic intricacy as sung by trained and earnest voices: their constant crossing of words in the text, of melodic themes, and of rhythms. Yet the composer has brought all these into perfect "concent." Melodic themes always bear harmonic relations with rival themes. As for the rhythms — our chief concern — they never, as Morris says, "degenerate into confusion," or, as Milton puts it in describing the polyphony of angel-anthems, they are "regular / Then most, when most irregular they seem." For a fundamental fact about them is this: just as the enjambed blank verse of PL is composed with reference to a stable metric frame whose norm is an ideal iambic entity of five beats, so the elder Milton's anthem, from start to finish, keeps time to a steady two- or four-beat measure. Mr. Brennecke has added the bar-lines to show this recurrent measure and assist our duller rhythmic perceptions.

We are for the moment ignoring the presence of symbolic series in Milton's verse. We are restricting contrapuntal analogues to Milton's free overlapping of his metric norm by irregular rhythmic lengths. Under this restriction we can assert that the rhythmic method employed in the elder Milton's anthem — of rival voices freely overlapping both the basic rhythmic measure and each other's individual rhythms — is more complicated than in any conceivable overlapping of rhythms in blank verse. For this very reason Milton wants to attain the maximum of expressive rhythmic complexity possible to a medium in which Marlowe and the earlier Shakespeare saw little opportunity for line-to-line complexity. Even if he had dared to try, Milton could not, merely by prosodic means, have interlaced rhythmic processes to the extent found in such a composition as "Woe is me for thee." He differentiates between the experience of a group of singers making music and the experience of a reader of verse. He knows that when five singers gather round a table, one of them is, and must be, something of a leader if the voices are to enter at the nick of time. He knows the availability of nervous arm, finger, head, or eyebrow to keep alive the beat of the basic measure.

But in highly enjambed blank verse he can trust only the texture of the verse itself to preserve his metric line. Hence his recurrent integral lines, his initial inversions, his penchant for strong flanking monosyllabic words, his indirect safeguarding of the norm with overlap-5's and E- and T-constructions.

To indicate what he did not dare to do in overrunning his rhythms in blank verse, I call attention to a startling fact. Only twice in the 51 measures of "O woe is me for thee" does the rhythm of any phrase sung by any voice exactly correspond with — exactly fill — the basic measure or any pair of measures. These two exceptional cases occur when C sings, "O woe is me for thee" at measures 9 and 10, and when A sings, "Thy love to me was wonderful," at measures 21 and 22. The fact is startling because with five voices there would be, as compared with a homophonic piece, five times the opportunity to make a complete rhythmic phrase and a full basic measure exactly tally. But the composer delights in avoiding it.

Had Milton essayed an equal freedom in blank verse, he would have thought little of enjambing a hundred lines continuously except for several lone integral end-stopped pentameters. But this he never dreamt of doing, knowing the limitations of the two arts. In his boldest rhythmic management of blank verse he is content with the anthemist's method much simplified. First, he makes rhythmic lengths overlap the metric base in unpredictable variety, though without obscuring it for more than a few lines at a time. Secondly, he makes audible rhythmic lengths of more than five beats overlap each other by means of cross-rhythmic displacement, this in direct emulation of the cross-rhythmic voices of madrigal and anthem.

Yet, as I have tried to show in most of my chapters, he does succeed in rivaling the most complex polyrhythmic content of any anthem. He does it — it is possible to do it — not by extending but by transcending prosody. He does it by inventing and applying a new organon of "depth"-expression, though the expression is clearly intelligible only to himself. He does it by investing sequences of rhythm — mathematically precise and directional progressions — with individualizing symbol. He sets these sequences in cross-rhythmic performance independent of all the overlapping rhythms of prosody, yet in "concent" with them. Hence the unique, inscrutable tensions of the resultant free-fugal play of rhythms in some of Milton's epic paragraphs.

No other craftsman in words ever felt the need of such complexity because none but Milton ever set his heart on rivaling the rhythmic devices of canonic music. And even if any poet should feel such a need, he would not be equipped to establish and maintain such a program.

APPENDIX IV

SYMBOLIC SERIES AND PUNCTUATION

1

If it is more than probable that in an undetermined number of paragraphs Milton has demarcated one or more numerical progressions, then certain punctuated pauses which editors reject as superfluous or illogical may be explainable as serving symbolic series. A good many such cases I have already pointed to in various chapters. Let us here examine two additional instances.

(i)

In the speech of the Father at PL III, 167-216, after "Deity" (187) in both Edd. 1 and 2 is a comma which many editors have discarded. The result is the elimination of at least three symbolic series: (a) PPP 3 ←—, (b) PPP 15 —→ ∞, and (c) PP 30 ←— ∞. Given $n = 50$,

(a) PPP 3: (3, 27, -7, -63) = *40, 3, 20, 7* [*7, 20, 3, 40*]
^ ↑ ^ ↑

PPP 3 ←— starts at "and deeper fall, . . ." (201—)
ends " ". . . shall not be slow;" (193)

(b) PPP 15: (15, -125, 125, -125, . . .) = *110, 15* ∞
↑

PPP 15 —→ ∞ starts at "so is my will: . . ." (184—)

(c) PP 30: (30, -100, 0, 0, . . .) = *70, 30* ∞ [*30, 70*]
↑ ^ ↑

PP 30 ←— ∞ starts where PPP 3 ←— starts
ends at " . . . the incensed Deity," (187)

Observe how retributive justice (PPP 3 ←—) is reinforced by the concept of the infinite in PP 30 ←— ∞, the two series starting at the same responsive point of pause.

(ii)

In the transformation-scene at PL X, 504-590 the demon-serpents feed on delusive fruit (572—):

Thus were they plagu'd
And worn with famine, long and ceaseless hiss,
Till their lost shape, permitted, etc.

Such is the punctuation of line 573 in both Edd. 1 and 2. For centuries, however, editors have been discontented. Following Newton's conjecture, some boldly drop comma after "famine" and place it after "long," unwilling to recognize that Milton is *not* tautological. His meaning is that each individual hiss is long, but the hisses are ceaselessly repeated.

But we can now defend the original punctuation with a different kind of evidence. Shift this comma, and two startlingly responsive symbolic series vanish. Each is appropriately retrograde: AP 1 ←— and PP 8 ←—.

AP 1 ←—: 4, 3, 2, 1. Starting at "Thus were . . ." (572—), we have 4', 3′, 2, 1'.

Given n = 87, PP 8: (8, 64, 77, -254) = *105, 8, 64, 77* [*77, 64, 8, 105*]
^ ↑ ^ ↑

PP 8 ←— starts at "long and ceaseless hiss, . . ." (573—)
ends " " . . . Us'd by the Tempter:" (552)

For Milton the symbolic meaning of 8, here and at other places, seems to derive from that Scriptural legend where the number is very prominent. There were eight survivors in the Ark. PP 8—→ = social life under God's providence, but PP 8←—, as here, = social life under the Adversary — a hellish life to which a descending series fitly responds.

2

Sometimes when Ed. 1 of PL differs in punctuation from Ed. 2, the presence of symbolic series may offer evidence of Milton's true intention. An instance is at PL XI, 142. The last word in the line, "descends," is also the last word on the page in Ed. 1 (see Facsimile Ed.). It is unpointed. It runs in a crowded way to the very margin, as if there were no more room for punctuation. The result is curious: though the rest of the passage seems over-punctuated, "some punctuation," as Fletcher says, "seems to be needed after 'descends.' "

In Ed. 2 a semicolon follows "descends." This doesn't mean that Milton must have dictated the correction. The printer could have set his type from a manuscript from which Ed. 1 had been set. And as evidence that there *was* punctuation in that manuscript after "descends," I submit the following fact: without such punctuation a most responsive numerical series vanishes.

Adam finds it hard to believe, yet he must from his own experience believe, in the miraculous efficacy of prayer. To think that God Almighty should concern himself with "one short sigh of human breath," and that such a sigh should be "up-borne / Even to the seat of God!"

Now the number 9, here and at other places, seems to carry the Dantean meaning of miracle. (Observe, by the way, a passage in Book IX where this attribution is almost explicit. Eve is astounded when she hears a serpent articulate human speech. She wants to hear more:

> Redouble then this miracle, and say,
> How cam'st thou speakable of mute, (562-563)

— 9 beats.)

If ever the number of miracle is called for it is in this paragraph at PL XI, 141-161, in which Adam marvels at the miraculous power of prayer. Given $n = 21$,

PP 9: (9, -24, -6, 51) = *6, 15, 9, 21*
↑ ^

PP 9 ⟶ starts at "hard to belief may seem; . . ." (146—)
ends " " . . . placable and mild," (151)

Significantly, only the ascending series is present. Editors sometimes drop comma after "admit" (141), and the progression vanishes.

3

In preparing Ed. 2 of PL it is unlikely that Milton had all the paragraphs read back to him. There was no need of it. With few exceptions, the paragraphs of Ed. 2 are meant to reproduce those of Ed. 1. Only on this hypothesis can we explain the otherwise mysterious retention of *Fowle* for *soul* at PL VII, 451, and the short line followed by the long line at PL XI, 989-990.

Moreover, if Milton did have any of the proof-sheets of Ed. 2 read back to him, he did not require the reader to describe the punctuation, mark by mark. For, in the case of paragraphs in which he had scribed symbolic series, he himself no longer knew exactly what they were. He would have no way of redetermining them except by re-scribing them. He knew they were duly demarcated in Ed. 1; he had faith in the efficacy of their presence; he wished merely that the punctuation of Ed. 2 be that of Ed. 1. And for almost all the paragraphs such a check could be made by any literate printshop drudge who worked with anxious loyalty to serve an exacting author.

In general, then, the punctuation of Ed. 1 is to be preferred to that of Ed. 2.

NOTES

Chapter I

Note 1 (p. 19)

Helen Darbishire's excellent text of PL (Oxford, 1952) was not available to me during the course of the present investigation. But the use of it would not have caused me to alter any of my pages. Its departures from the reprints are mostly by way of normalizing Milton's spelling. A rapid survey shows that Miss Darbishire drops very few points of pause as given in Ed. 1 — hardly seven in all. She even retains — commendably I think — the seemingly superfluous comma after "found" at XI, 137. As for the pauses she adds to Ed. 1, they are also very few. Six follow Ed. 2, three follow Bentley, and several are her own emendations, which she justifies as needed to clarify the meaning, or as accordant with syntactical pointing elsewhere in the poem.

Here and there, however, without warrant of the earliest editions, she breaks a paragraph in two, her assumption being that printers "neglected it" (*Intro.* p. xxiii). By the same reasoning one could justify dozens of other re-paragraphings, including assuredly the break-up of that long passage at I, 331-621. Miss Darbishire's own indentations occur seven times: at II,845, III, 694, IV, 834, V, 853, VII, 110, VIII, 338, and IX, 553. These, and her three or four clarifying commas, although they make her text, to an infinitesimal extent, arbitrary, do not lessen its great value as a supplement both to Beeching and to Fletcher's facsimiles.

Note 2 (p. 24)

Already in *Comus* we find —1i (90, 229), but neither —1i nor —½i seems present to any appreciable extent before Milton. In drama I have found occurrences at Chapman's *Bussy D'Ambois* II.i.130 and Beaumont and Fletcher's *Maid's Tragedy*, III.ii.66 and V.iii.63. How indeed can so conscious a device be more than accidental in verse-dialogue where the steady encroachment of feminine endings on facile enjambement robs it of all its effect? An example in Milton himself (at PL X, 236) demonstrates how the tang and power of —1i vanish after a feminine ending.

Could Milton have found either precedent or analogy in Latin writers? Ovid's *Metamorphoses* begins with a declaration that ends with a heavy stop after the first foot of the second line:

> In nova fert animus mutatas dicere formas
> Corpora;

The Miltonic shock of inversion of an expected normal foot is of course not present, being impossible in hexameter. But the beginning of Ovid's second line is exceptional: the ending of a first foot with a diaeresis so strong that it dispossesses any caesural pause in the rest of the line. The concept of "bodies" is what he wants to stress. A similar diaeresis does not occur in the next hundred hexameters.

Turn to Virgil. In the *Aeneid* the frequency of a strong dramatic pause after an initial dactyl which ends an enjambed period occurs with almost the same frequency as Milton's —1i. Indeed at times Virgil's very word seems to be in Milton's mind. At *Aeneid* II, 77 ff. Sinon, immortal type of treachery, is telling why he learned to hate Greeks: they had done to death his friend Palamedes: "If haply there has come to your ears the glory of his fame"—

> Fando aliquod si forte tuas pervenit ad auris
> Belidae nomen Palamedis et incluta fama
> Gloria,

which singularly recalls "Glories" of PL I, 573 as applicable to the pride of Milton's prototype of all Sinons. I would not urge any echo here except that this is Virgil's only employment of "Gloria" in the position analogous to —1i.

At *Aeneid* X, 99 the word of emphasis is "Murmura." Up in Olympus Venus and Juno have just had a verbal combat quite as implacable as that of Gabriel and Satan at the close of PL IV. Only the dread will of Jupiter ends the contention. But after Juno's special plea, her sympathizers, who are as hostile to Aeneas as Satan is to Adam, agree with every word she says—

> ceu flamina prima
> Cum deprensa fremunt silvis et caeca volutant
> Murmura,

which Milton may be unconsciously echoing in the last line of PL IV:

> [the Fiend] fled
> Murmuring, and with him fled the shades of night.

I would not urge a parallel here except that in *Epitaphium Damonis,* 130 Milton transcribes Virgil's word in the same line-position.

Virgil's initial word is not always a dactyl. At *Aeneid* X, 777 and XI, 201 the pause is actually a feminine caesura in the first foot (cf. *Ecl.* IX, 36, X, 59, and *Georg.* III, 444). Between this sort of arresting pause and Milton's —1i it is hard to conceive a closer analogue in two different tongues.

Virgil has still another and rarer means of expressive emphasis. When he can find a monosyllabic substantive to fit thought or image at a particularly solemn or dramatic moment, he may end his line with it. The result in Latin is a most peculiar caesural effect just where caesura is never expected, and where any pause is ordinarily intolerable. The last foot becomes a spondee whose second syllable is so heavy that the ear may be inclined to let the line end with a pause after the spondee's first syllable. Some such drastic effect as this may have been part of Milton's purpose in his use of —½i. There are but half a dozen instances of Virgil's device in the *Aeneid,* but they are justly celebrated. I need only cite the words of prophecy at *Aeneid* III, 390:

> Litoreis ingens inventa sub ilicibus sus,

and the tremendous blow the bull gets at V, 481:

> Sternitur, exanimisque tremens procumbit humi bos,

or night falling heavy as lead at II, 250:

> Vertitur interea caelum, et ruit, oceano nox,

in which the anomalously placed "nox" probably produced the same effect on the Roman ear as Milton's "Day" produces on us at PL III, 42.

Note 3 (p. 25)
Here I must acknowledge many kind favors received from my friend John F. Carabella, at present organist and choir-master at St. Mary's, Albany, and formerly director of music at Monte Cassino. From his lifelong familiarity with 16th- and 17th-century polyphonic masters, he helped to establish for me the ideals of instrumental polyphony which confirmed in my mind Milton's own definition of fugue.

Chapter II

Note 1 (p. 46)
A fine example of precision when Milton even counts the syllables before responsive pauses is at PL X, 306-311, where the bridge that Sin and Death build over Chaos is likened to that built by the ancient Persian invader. Many editors add a comma at the natural pause after "Susa," but though the comma is absent from Edd. 1 and 2 the following analysis would have no basis if Milton had not consciously counted syllables to produce a very definite response of rhythm to theme.

So, if great things to small may be compar'd,
Xerxes, the liberty of Greece to yoke,
From Susa his Memnonian palace high
Came to the sea, and over Hellespont
Bridging his way, Europe with Asia join'd,
And scourg'd with many a stroke th' indignant waves.

Pontoon by pontoon, with accretions of plank by plank, that bridge grows and advances, even as the sentence telling it grows syllable by syllable, and the places of pause advance farther and farther across the verse. We have but to remove the chief subordinate modifiers, and the skeletal proposition that remains — "So . . . Xerxes . . . From Susa . . . Came to the sea . . . Europe with Asia join'd, / And scourg'd with many a stroke the indignant waves" — reveals in its successive elements a progressive increase in number of syllables: 1 + 2 + 3 + 4 + 6 + 10. Arrival at 10, number of completeness, marks the spanning of that difficult strait.

Note 2 (p. 48)
A notorious passage in *The Winter's Tale* is involved in cross-rhythmic experimentation. Prefixed to Act IV is a Prologue spoken by Time. Its length is 32 lines, exactly that of each of the prologues to *Henry VIII* and *The Two Noble Kinsmen*. It exhibits an intimate alliance of (i) continuous loose-couplet rhyming, (ii) free indulgence in both weak endings and feminine endings, (iii) high rate of enjambement, and (iv) continuous cross-rhythmic construction. Certainly to Milton an unholy alliance, a prosodic nightmare — even as it has been to Shakespearean scholars since 1765. The rhythms are wrought into a chain whose links are so little diversified as to display perfectly what not to do if art is to conceal art.

	lines
3 × 5	1-3
+	
2	4
+	

(cont. next page)

	lines
3—3'	4-5
2'—5—2	5-7
3—5—3'	7-9
2'—2	9-10
3—3	10-11
5	
5'	
5"	
2'—2	14-15
3'+5—2	15-17
T 2	17-19
2+5—2'	19-21
3'—3	21-22
2—2'	22-23
3'—3	23-24
2—2'	24-25
3'—3	25-26
5	26-27
T 2	27-29
+	
2	29
+	
3×5	30-32

One result of so persistent a chain is that only five out of thirty-two lines are integral — half the average for PL. Though the experimenter may be depending on his rhymes and feminine endings to keep his basic line demarcated, it's unlikely he cares for demarcation at all. His rhyme soon becomes an irritating drag against free overlapping. The rhythmic product is banausic because the medium of expression is being flogged to do too many things at once: rhyme continuously, enjamb continuously, offer hospitality to both light and feminine endings, and deploy overlaps into successive E- and T-constructions. The joint maintenance of all these operations for thirty lines is a stunt. Shakespeare may be amusing himself — if it be Shakespeare. He is deliberately cobbling a style of "stumbling emptiness," as Kittredge describes it, to fit a toothless ancient. "If the speech were better, it would not be so good." (*Complete Works of Shakespeare,* p. 432)

Chapter IV

Note 1 (p. 66)

Most editors tamper with the pointing of PL X, 515-516. Bentley drops comma after "Reluctant," and changes comma to colon after "in vain." (Many editors change it to semicolon.) Darbishire repeats Bentley's colon. Logical enough; but symbol here overrides logic. By retarding this linear symbolic series Bentley devitalizes it. For, once we perceive its presence, and how it fills exactly two metric lines ($1 + 2 + 3 + 4 = 10$), we realize that Milton is pressing God's "greater power" hard up against Satan's vain "reluctance." Maximum rhythmic speed is essential.

Note 2 (p. 83)
See George Sarton: *A History of Science: Ancient Science through the Golden Age of Greece,* Harvard, 1952, p. 211.

Note 3 (p. 89)
Some editors drop comma after "conspicuous" (258), thus eliminating AP 15 ⟶.

Note 4 (p. 91)
I am indebted to Mr. Willam H. Scheide, Director of the Bach Aria Group of New York, for this valuable information concerning recent German research into Bach's employment of numerical symbol. One of the latest critical estimates is in Hermann Keller's *Die Klavierwerke Bachs,* Leipzig, 1950, p. 129. Keller accepts as sound the researches of Friedrich Smend: J. S. Bach: Kirchenkantaten, 6 Hefte, 1947—, Berlin-Dahlem.

Chapter V

Note 1 (p. 96)
The geometry studied by Phillips — Peter Ryff's *Questiones Geometricae* — was also published in Frankfurt. All the diagrams and pictures in it, though differently distributed to accord with a differently arranged text, are identical with those in Schonerus' edition of Ramus. The same woodcut blocks, the same publisher's colophon are used by Schonerus and Ryff. The very last woodcut pays a quaint tribute to Ramus. Over an archway of heavy stone masonry is blazoned P. RAMUS, and on the ground beneath are four geometricians standing at four different points of vantage, each very diligently manipulating a cross-staff to get angular readings in the hope of taking the measure of great Ramus's memorial. Ryff's book appeared in 1600.

These and other old books of mathematics were made available to me through the courtesy of librarians at the Library Company of Philadelphia and at Columbia University.

Chapter VI

Note 1 (p. 130)
Every interlock creates a sequence of bilateral symmetry. Girdling interlocks, especially those composed of repeated ∞-series, create rotational symmetry. Consorts of interlocks create ornamental symmetry, which is a "discontinuous grouping of congruent mappings of the plane," or "a manifold of invariant lattices" in which may occur a variable element. I quote from the current authority, Hermann Weyl: *Symmetry,* Princeton, 1952, pp. 83 f.

Note 2 (page 132)
In his well-informed book, *The Italian Element in Milton's Verse* (Oxford, 1954), Frank Templeton Prince shows (p. 53 f.) how the aging Tasso tried to make the verse of *Le Sette Giornate del Mondo Creato* conform to certain theorizings of his *Discorsi.* Tasso would have each metric line end in a word with double consonants before the last syllable, to achieve — so he imagines — "magnificence." The effect, however, must inevitably retard line-endings almost as sharply as do the demarcations caused by repeated feminine endings of Italian hendecasyllabics.

Thus Tasso's prosodic ideal in *Mondo Creato* is as remote from the characteristic rhythmic method of PL as are Trissino's monotonous *versi sciolti.* For the structure of Milton's epic paragraph is founded on freedom, a far more drastic sort of freedom than mere freedom from rhyme. It is the freedom to draw out the sense "variously . . . from one verse into another." And the English language, with its capacity for absolutely unimpeded enjambement, offers incomparable opportunities for such freedom, as Italian does not. "Italian prosody is based upon rhyme, even when rhyme disappears, as in *versi sciolti*" (*The Italian Element*, p. 165). What Tasso does, then, is to carry over into his rhymeless pentameters the end-stopping spirit of rhyme. This inherent tendency, abetted by feminine endings and terminal double consonants, results in a wearisome predominance of what I have called "integral lines." The *Mondo Creato*, even if it were an animate work of art instead of a tedious verse-paraphrase, could have contributed nothing to the contrapuntal triumphs of Milton's epic style.